KU-452-627

WATERFORD CITY AND COUNTY
WITHDRAWN
LIBRARIES

1517

Martin Luther and the Invention of the Reformation

PETER MARSHALL

OXFORD
UNIVERSITY PRESS

OXFORD
UNIVERSITY PRESS

Great Clarendon Street, Oxford, OX2 6DP,
United Kingdom

Oxford University Press is a department of the University of Oxford. It furthers the University's objective of excellence in research, scholarship, and education by publishing worldwide. Oxford is a registered trade mark of Oxford University Press in the UK and in certain other countries

First Edition published in 2017

Impression: 1

Published in the United States of America by Oxford University Press
198 Madison Avenue, New York, NY 10016, United States of America

British Library Cataloguing in Publication Data
Data available

Library of Congress Control Number: 2016963351

ISBN 978–0–19–968201–0

Printed in Great Britain by
Clays Ltd, St Ives plc

1517

For Bernard Capp

Acknowledgements

A number of institutions and individuals have helped in the writing of this book, which was made possible by a timely grant of research leave from the University of Warwick and some welcome financial assistance from the Social Sciences and Humanities Research Council of Canada. Among various scholarly supporters, I am particularly indebted to Scott Dixon, who not only offered me an advance viewing of his seminal forthcoming article on the Ninety-five Theses, but read my entire manuscript with great care and kindness, and saved me from several blunders. David Whitford similarly brought the skills and sensibilities of a seasoned Luther expert to drafts of the early chapters, and reassured me I was not chasing my own tail. I am also grateful to Tal Howard, for allowing me access before publication to his important book on *Remembering the Reformation*, and to Barry Stephenson for answering my queries about Wittenberg and directing me to some rich visual sources. Some of the material in this book was first aired at a conference at St Patrick's College, Maynooth, in the spring of 2015: I am indebted to Declan Marmion and Salvador Ryan for the invitation to that event, and to other participants, particularly David Bagchi, for lively and encouraging discussion. I must also thank Angela McShane for alerting me to the existence of the splendid Luther beaker in the Victoria and Albert Museum, and Charlotte Methuen and Christoph Mick for assistance with the translation of some tricky German passages. At OUP, Matthew Cotton has been an outstanding editor, ever cheerful, patient, and supportive, and I am equally grateful to Luciana O'Flaherty and Kizzy Taylor-Richelieu for steering me smoothly through the final stages of the manuscript's preparation and submission. My loved ones—Ali, Bella, Maria, and Kit—have, as always, helped me in innumerable ways, not least by providing much-needed IT support. The dedication, to a Warwick colleague, represents an inadequate recompense for many years of warm friendship and wise counsel.

Peter Marshall
Leamington Spa
October 2016

Contents

List of Figures

Prologue: Postings

Document

It is one of the greatest remembered moments in western history. With one action, lasting no more than a few minutes, a solitary monk sets in motion a chain of events which will change forever the religious, political, and cultural development of Europe, and of the wider world beyond. It is the moment, many people have thought, when the middle ages come suddenly to an end, and modernity commences. A moment which asserts the rights of individual conscience against unquestioned ancient authority; of public probity against corruption and venality; of reasoned faith against superstition and fear. The date is 31 October 1517. The place is Wittenberg, an unprepossessing town on the River Elbe in north-eastern Germany. The monk is Martin Luther, a thirty-three-year-old member of the Eremitical Order of Augustinian friars. The action is the nailing to the doors of the *Schlosskirche*, the church attached to Wittenberg Castle, of a single-sheet document. The document is a list of ninety-five theses—assertions or propositions—against papal teaching on indulgences. The result is a revolution.

Everyone, more or less, has heard of the Ninety-five Theses. They constitute one of the most famous written works of the last millennium. If a text can be 'iconic', then the Ninety-five Theses surely meets the criteria. Anthologies of 'Great Documents of Western Civilization', 'Milestone Documents in World History' or '100 Documents That Changed the World' regularly reprint them, alongside such works as Magna Carta, the American Declaration of Independence, The Communist Manifesto, and the Charter of the United Nations. A British daily newspaper recently ranked them, together with the 1833 Act abolishing slavery in the British Empire, the 1919 Treaty of Versailles, Mao's Little Red Book of 1964, and Watson and Crick's 1953 detailing of the molecular structure of DNA, as one of '10 Documents that Changed the World'.[1]

The allegedly world-changing character of the Ninety-five Theses has ensured a place of honour in the mental library of European culture. Martin Luther wrote and published a great deal between 1517 and his death in 1546, but only those who have made some specialist study of his life and career can without difficulty recall the titles of any other of his works. For many people, the Ninety-five Theses are synonymous with Martin Luther, and Luther is synonymous with the Reformation, and everything which that word has come to represent in our understanding of the past. Admittedly, detailed knowledge of what the Ninety-five Theses actually say may be at something of a premium. Their numerical quantity certainly militates against easy rote learning of their contents. The compilers of a book of 101 'Great Cultural Lists', beginning with the Seven Wonders of the World, have admitted that 'because we wanted to include only lists that could plausibly be memorized, we reluctantly excluded Luther's ninety-five theses'.[2]

But, in other ways, the sheer number of the Theses serves to reinforce their potency as a cultural point of reference. How could indulgences have been reputable or defensible when it was possible to think of so many—ninety-five!—good arguments against them? Ninety-five was in 1517 an entirely arbitrary number, without any previous mathematical or symbolic associations (and, as we shall see, it was not entirely clear to everyone in 1517 that the assorted Theses did add up to ninety-five). Yet, in modern times, the number has assumed a totemic significance for the definitive articulation of a compelling case. If 'Ten Commandments' still represents the ultimate framing mechanism for any programme or manifesto, Ninety-five Theses arguably runs a close second.

It is perhaps unsurprising if in religious circles in particular the Ninety-five Theses retain a specific meaning and resonance. Within the last few years, an assortment of conservative Protestant authors and organizations in South Africa, the United States, New Zealand, and Germany have solemnly produced *95 Theses for Reformation Today*, *95 Theses for the Twenty-first Century Church*, *95 Theses for a New Millennium*, *95 Thesen für 2017*. Not to be outdone, more liberal Protestant authors offer in contrast *95 Theses which Dispute the Church's Conviction against Women*, *9.5 Theses for a New Reformation* (on the treatment of LGBT people), or *Mainlining Christianity: 95 Theses for the 21st Century*. A front-cover slogan of the latter book exhorts: 'Moderate and liberal Christians, Unite! Reclaim Jesus from the evangelical Christian right!'[3]

More remarkable is the extent to which the production of '95 Theses' has established itself as a genre of protest and persuasion across a wide range of areas in social and cultural life, particularly in the United States. A sampling of the titles of some twenty-first century books and pamphlets takes us from the realms of serious scholarship—the political scientist Anne Norton's *95 Theses on Politics, Culture and Method*—via a variety of earnest single-issue campaigns (*A Case For Homeschooling: 95 Theses Against the School System*; *95 Theses Project: Let's Save Our Constitution*; *ProGenesis: Ninety-Five Theses Against Evolution*), and on to the charming quirkiness of *The 95 Theses of Kay's Beauty Shop* and the erotic promise of *Theses on 95 Sexdecillion Indulgences: With Flirts and Spices*.[4]

There is clearly something satisfyingly appealing to people in the prescriptive certainty of ninety-five arguments, proposals, or instructions. An immensely influential American business text of the early twenty-first century was *The Cluetrain Manifesto*, which presented Ninety-five Theses for the conduct of marketing operations in the Internet age. While not referencing Martin Luther explicitly (an indication in itself of the instant recognizability of the Ninety-five Theses), the authors' use of the tag-line 'the end of business as usual', to herald the potential and challenges of new information technology, somehow manages to evoke the comparable technological leap of Luther's own age, the invention of printing with moveable type.

At times, the referencing of the Ninety-five Theses in contemporary culture seems to have become almost completely detached from their point of historical origin. Luther himself would surely be bemused by the American sports bloggers offering readers '95 Theses On The NBA [National Basketball Association] Lockout' and '95 Theses for keeping your faith in the Knicks' [New York Knickerbockers'] rebuild'. And it is hard to know what he might have made of a 2014 report in *The Los Angeles Times* that a club in San Diego was supplying its DJs with a list of rules amounting to 'a provocative 95 Theses for modern EDM [electronic dance music] venues.'

As a lifelong sufferer from a range of painful ailments, Luther might have approved of the medical campaigners avidly promoting '95 Theses for a New Health Ecosystem', though he would surely have frowned on the New York financial investment company offering clients '95 Theses for Managing Your Wealth'. In fairness, the firm in question prefixes its advice-leaflet with an explanation of how the original Theses were a protest against the selling of indulgences: 'essentially, "get out of jail" documents, which purportedly absolved the purchasers from divine punishment for their sins. In Luther's view, remission of sin was obtainable for free, through confession and God's grace, and therefore selling it was an act of corruption.' It is a far from risible summary, and serves to illustrate the mnemonic threads that can powerfully attach the past to the present. In 2013, Kieran Long, a British architectural journalist, television presenter, and curator at the Victoria and Albert Museum in London, offered to the heritage sector '95 Theses for Contemporary Curation'. It was, he conceded, a 'gentle joke' at a time when the 'V & A' had recently appointed a German director. But with admirable historical awareness, Long also suggested the format was highly appropriate for the self-inspection of 'an institution at a crisis point in its public role'.[5]

In fact, none of these examples really captures the spirit of Luther's Ninety-five Theses in the cultural imagination of the modern world. For the Ninety-five Theses are, almost uniquely among the foundational texts of western culture, supremely bound up with the circumstances of their declaration to the world. They represent, in the words of a late-twentieth-century briefing paper for American high school teachers, a pre-eminent example of 'Taking a Stand in History'. Mention of the Ninety-five Theses evokes not so much the contents of a written treatise, as the timing of an event and the undertaking of an achievement: the posting of the Theses on the church door in Wittenberg. At the end of a year of tumultuous change, a policy advisor to the US government wondered whether 'in symbolic importance, future historians may compare the night of November 9–10, 1989, when the Berlin Wall was opened, with October 31, 1517–when Martin Luther posted his Ninety-five Theses on the door of the Castle Church'.[6]

The town of Wittenberg itself is a location which, since 1995, has been designated a UNESCO World Heritage Site: it has 'outstanding significance for the political, cultural, and spiritual life of the western world that extends far beyond the German borders'. For it was here, the UNESCO Evaluation Report noted, that 'Luther launched the Reformation by nailing his 95 Propositions to the north door of the Castle Church'.

It is hard to think of many other texts (especially theological ones) so closely associated with a particular time and place. As it is usually portrayed, the posting of the Theses represents a moment of decisive historical rupture, one commemorated in countless timelines, calendars, and chronologies, in print and on the Internet. As an example, we can cite the entry for 31 October in the 'this-day-in-history' section of the website of 'History' (formerly, 'The History Channel'), the commercially successful US cable and satellite TV channel devoted to historically themed output: 'On this day in 1517, the priest and scholar Martin Luther approaches the door of the Castle Church in Wittenberg, Germany, and nails a piece of paper to it containing the 95 revolutionary opinions that would begin the Protestant Reformation.'

Not just popular media outlets and UNESCO consultants, but professional scholars too, remain wedded to the notion that the great movement of change which came to be known as the Reformation had its origin in one place at a single identifiable moment. The philosopher A. C. Grayling, to take but one example, writes of 'the Reformation, which began on 31 October 1517 when Luther nailed his ninety-five theses to the church door of Wittenberg'. Similar assertions could easily be culled from the pages of countless books and scholarly articles. A recent study of the role played by religion in contemporary attitudes towards European political integration ranks the posting of the Ninety-five Theses above the French Revolution, and on a par with the Conversion of Constantine, in the immensity of its impact on the Church.[7]

Luther's deed thus belongs to a select company of 'turning-points' in history that manage to be both momentous and memorable. For the English, perhaps the most unforgettable historical date is represented by the victory of Duke William at Hastings on 14 October 1066; for the French, it must be the revolutionary Storming of the Bastille on 14 July 1789; for Americans, the signing of the Declaration of Independence on 4 July 1776, or the firing of the guns on Fort

Sumter on 12 April 1861; for the world as a whole, the dropping of an atomic bomb on the Japanese city of Hiroshima on 6 August 1945.

The posting of the Ninety-five Theses nonetheless sits somewhat incongruously in this catalogue of wars and political revolutions. The Reformation, as historians now usually understand it, certainly involved periodic outbreaks of violence, and in various respects it had a pronounced revolutionary character. But the Reformation was ultimately a broad phenomenon of social and cultural change. Conceptually, it seems to belong in the company, not so much of short, dramatic, political upheavals, as of protracted periods like the Renaissance, the 'Scientific Revolution', the Enlightenment, or the Industrial Revolution—processes of transformation which are not readily associated with any single initiatory moment. If Luther's posting of the Theses is identified, and remembered, as such a moment, it must surely be for good reason.

Re-enactments

The image of the lone friar, hammering his propositions to the church door, exercises an understandable appeal. It is a gesture that seems at once assertively public and honourably private, challenging yet peaceful, a call to arms, and a call to calm reflection. It is a powerful and resonant symbolic gesture. For this reason, it is one which in modern times has inspired numerous imitators, eager to draw on the rich reserves of moral capital which the Theses-posting has accrued over the centuries.

Among such re-enactments, and the men (usually it is men) who have performed them, pride of place belongs to a Protestant pastor bearing Luther's own name. On 10 July 1966, civil rights protestors gathered in their tens of thousands in Chicago, to attend a rally and to hear an oration by Dr Martin Luther King Jr. After the rally, the crowd marched on City Hall, to present to Mayor Richard Daley their demands for social and racial justice. The mayor was absent, the building locked up, but King had come prepared. 'In a magnificent symbolic gesture that rang down the centuries from his namesake', King's widow Coretta later recalled, 'he nailed his demands to the closed door of the City Hall, as Martin Luther had nailed his Ninety-Five Theses to the door at Wittenberg.'

Martin Luther's Wittenberg protest resonated strongly with King, and with his philosophy of peaceful civil disobedience. He mentioned it again in his very last sermon, now referred to as 'I've been to the Mountaintop' or 'I see the Promised Land', which was preached in Memphis on 3 April 1968, the day before his assassination. The theme was that God was at work and that 'something is happening in our world'. King declared that if he were offered the chance to live in any period of history and witness its great events, he would still choose the latter years of the twentieth century. The half dozen or so seminal moments he would reluctantly move along past represents a revealing selection. 'I would even go by the way that the man for whom I'm named had his habitat. And I would watch Martin Luther as he tacked his ninety-five theses on the door at the church in Wittenberg.'[8]

Martin Luther King's tenancy of the German reformer's name undoubtedly lent moral authority to the appropriation of Luther's gesture. But King has scarcely been the only figure in recent American history to stage a re-enactment of the Theses-posting for immediate political impact. The exploit was equally amenable, in the years following King's assassination, to the purposes of a more confrontational style of civil rights campaigning. In 1969, the radical African-American activist James Forman drew up his 'Black Manifesto', which demanded $500 million dollars in reparations from churches and synagogues for historic collusion in the oppressions of slavery. The claim was underpinned by a highly publicized campaign to disrupt church services, and by Forman's own action, on 6 May 1969, of nailing a copy of the Manifesto to the doors of the New York City headquarters of the Lutheran Church of America—a hardly coincidental choice of denomination to target in this way.[9]

The 1960s were an era of demonstrative politics, but the imitation of Martin Luther's Reformation-starting act retained its appeal into the ensuing decades, especially among the spiritually minded. In 1981, proposals were advanced for closer union between the Church of England and the Methodist, United Reform, and Moravian churches. It provoked a group of uncompromising ministers and lay people to affix to the West Door of Canterbury Cathedral '95 Theses in Vindication of Freechurchmanship, against Episcopacy and Sacerdotalism'. That same year, in Denver, Colorado, a Pentecostalist pastor was reported to have nailed to the doors of hundreds of churches in the city a set of ninety-five theses denouncing the doctrine of the Trinity as 'the most diabolical religious hoax and scandal in history'. Luther, who expended much energy fighting against the 'schwärmer' (radicals, fanatics) who rejected such ancient and core doctrines of Christianity, would have been truly appalled by this.[10]

More widely publicized was the religious protest mounted in 2005 by Matthew Fox, a popular spiritual writer and one-time Dominican friar turned Episcopalian priest and 'creation theologian'. Fox was dismayed by the election of the (allegedly) deeply conservative Cardinal Ratzinger as Pope Benedict XVI, an event immediately preceding an invitation to a speaking engagement in Germany. Rather than just give the scheduled lecture, Fox woke in the night with the idea of drawing up theses for a 'new Reformation', and he determined to post them on the very door where Luther had placed his. This involved tricky negotiations with the local civic authorities in Wittenberg, but eventually Fox was allowed to post his theses on a wooden frame set against the actual 'Thesenportal' or Theses-Door. He found it a profoundly spiritual and archetypal action: 'the sound of the nails entering the wooden frame was not unlike the sound of nails being driven into a cross'.

In 2010, Fox attached an Italian translation of the same theses to the door of the Basilica of St Maria Maggiore in Rome, titular church of Cardinal Bernard Law, the American prelate widely held to be responsible for covering up evidence of clerical child sex abuse in the archdiocese of Boston. It is safe to assume that Luther would have approved of Fox's strident denunciations of clerical corruption and papal power, though he might have found himself mystified by some of the other theses, such as that 'Ecojustice is a necessity for planetary survival'; 'Dancing... is a very ancient and appropriate form in which to pray'; or 'The prejudice of rationalism and left-brain located in the head must be balanced by attention to the lower chakras as equal places for wisdom and truth and Spirit to act.'[11]

Theses-posting is an activity adaptable to a variety of modern spiritual concerns. A group calling itself 'Mormon Reformation' has over the last few years sought every 31 October to circulate a set of ninety-five theses protesting against doctrinal conservatism and alleged 'thought control' in the Church of Jesus Christ of Latter Day Saints. The action harnesses the power of modern social media, with posting—an interestingly relocated word—of the theses across blogs, email, and Internet discussion boards. But sympathizers are also encouraged to affix (tape, rather than nail) paper copies of the theses to the doors of LDS church buildings. It is perhaps no great surprise that those doing so 'have reported a general sense of satisfaction and, indeed, a closer identification with that great 16th century Reformer than just virtual cyber posting seems to provide.'[12]

Modern theses-posting is not confined to the religious or spiritual sphere. In 2004, an environmental activist calling for a more inspiring approach to politics posted a set of 'Theses on the Failure of the Democrats' to the door of the Democratic National Committee in Washington DC. Nor is it a uniquely American phenomenon. In 2009, creationists in the Netherlands attached a translation of a Swiss set of '95 Theses against Evolution' to the entrance of the Free University in Amsterdam. The condition of the UK National Health Service in the run-up to the 2010 general election was, in the view of a contributor to the *British Medical Journal*, something which 'begs for a Martin Luther to nail his 95 Theses to the door.'

In 2012, a hardy group of Irish protestors against fiscal austerity measures, and the bailing out of bank bondholders in the wake of the 2008 financial crash, took their grievances to what they called 'one of the new churches of European society – in fact to its very cathedral', the headquarters of the European Central Bank in Frankfurt, and fixed them to the door. The emblematic action was the culmination of a couple of years of regular demonstrations in the villages of Ballyhea and Charleville in County Cork. Interestingly, this heartland of protest is a conservative and Catholic area, where the scheduling of the marches was dictated by mass times and the fixtures for traditional Gaelic sports: the symbolic potential of Luther's grand gesture of protest is evidently no longer the preserve of Protestants alone. Indeed, a recent book canvassing opinion on ways of making the Catholic Church more attractive to young people in Ireland summarized the propositions as 'A New 95 Theses'.[13]

Yet, without any doubt, it is in Germany itself that recreations of the event of 31 October 1517 have most commonly been undertaken as a resonant form of social or religious protest. The episode even has a specific name in German, to which the compound English translation theses-posting does not really do justice. It is the *Thesenanschlag*. The word *Anschlag*, sounding almost stereotypically Germanic to untutored Anglo-American ears, is a complex, multi-layered one. It can signify a poster, notice, or bulletin, as well as the act of striking home or affixing. Other recognized meanings include 'impact', 'attack', and even 'assassination'. It has an ardent, emphatic character that no English equivalent quite captures. Equipped with its definite article, *Der Thesenanschlag* denotes unambiguously a single, particular, historical event, and a categorically German one.

The last few years have seen something of a rash of *Thesenanschläge*, the confluence of a current vogue for performance-theatre as a form of political action, and of a heightened awareness of the historical event itself stimulated by the forthcoming five-hundredth anniversary of the 'start of the Reformation'. In Germany, the entire ten years, 2008–17, has been designated a 'Reformation decade', with commemorative events of various kinds scheduled across the country.

Setting aside simple 'heritage' or educational re-enactments of Luther's original deed—itself a popular pastime—modern *Thesenanschläge* generally seek to make their point with a deadly playful seriousness. The context is sometimes religious, or at the least ecclesiastical. In 2014, for example, a group of atheists and secularists affixed a list of theses to the door of St Paul's Cathedral in Münster, in protest against the giving of public subsidies for the biennial Church gathering known as the *Katholikentag* or Catholic Day (for good measure, they added an 11th Commandment: 'Thou shalt pay for thine own Kirchentag').

Concerned members, as well as hostile critics, of the Catholic Church in Germany have also been drawn to the format. In May 2011, members of the *Bund Der Deutschen Katholischen Jugend* (Federation of German Catholic Youth), holding their annual meeting in Altenberg, decided to undertake their own version of the event. They pinned to scaffolding in the grounds of the cathedral posters advocating a greater role for women in community leadership, as well as a reassessment of Church teaching on sexual morality. The German Catholic Bishops' Conference considered it all distinctly unhelpful: 'a *Thesenanschlag* is the very opposite of a dialogue'.[14]

Within a couple of years, however, one of the more conservative members of the German episcopate was to find himself on the sharp end of just such an *Anschlag*. Franz-Peter Tebartz-van Elst, bishop of Limburg in the Archdiocese of Cologne, became notorious internationally, as evidence emerged of lavish personal spending and an extravagant refurbishment of his official residence—the English-language media christened him 'the Bishop of Bling'. On 31 October 2013, in the week after Tebartz-van Elst was suspended from office by Pope Francis, a paper appeared on the door of Limburg Cathedral: 'Hello, Herr Bishop of Limburg! We already had the theme of money and misdemeanour in October 1517, with quite an effect. Forgotten? Here they are to read again.' Not new theses, but Luther's original ninety-five seemed on this occasion the appropriate material to post.[15]

Contemporary German theses-posters by no means limit themselves to ecclesiastical issues. To coincide with the 2009 UN Climate Change Conference in Copenhagen, young environmental activists in Bamberg, rigged out for the occasion in monastic habits, posted on the doors of St Martin's Church and the Town Hall a set of thoroughly secular theses concerning greenhouse gases, renewable energy, and global warming. Anti-capitalist protestors in Leipzig, declaring that 'protection of the banks is the modern indulgence-trade', fixed their '21st-Century Theses' to the door of Deutsche Bank on 31 October 2011. The following year, campaigners for a fixed minimum wage used the occasion of 'Reformation Day' to launch a publicity drive, festooning job centres in Berlin and elsewhere, as well as churches and other buildings, with a set of ten theses in support of the initiative, easily downloadable from a campaign website. Meanwhile, Thuringian tenant farmers, angry about practices of land allocation, were nailing their statements of grievance to the door of the Michaelis Church in Erfurt, the town where Luther became a monk and studied at the university. Here, indeed, the intended target was the Evangelical (Lutheran) Church in Central Germany, a significant landowner in the region.[16]

Unsurprisingly perhaps, the idea of a *Thesenanschlag* has appealed particularly to German student protestors, drawn to its subversive theatricality and potential for generating publicity. In June 2009, student leaders at the Technical University of Dresden, concerned about tuition charges and changing numbers of students and teaching staff, organized a posting of demands on the door of the City Hall. Their press release stated that 'the reference to Luther was deliberately chosen, as we too face a rigid and inflexible system'. This followed a similar action, on the campus itself, at the Technical University of Chemnitz, where the issues of concern were study conditions and teaching quality. Curiously, the Chemnitz document comprised only ninety-three theses, but by the time an anonymous 'author's collective' published them in the newspaper *Der Freitag* another two grievances had been identified. In 2015, at the Martin-Luther-Universität in Halle, left-wing students demanding diversity in education used hammer and nails to plant their statement on the door of the university administration building. In offering her support to the students, a regional politician from the Green Party pointed out the almost too obvious: 'the Martin-Luther-University is the perfect place for this action.'[17]

In Germany, the cultural copyright to Theses-posting does not belong wholly to the political Left. In 2015, largescale protests against immigration were organized by the populist right-wing movement known by the acronym 'Pegida' (Patriotic Europeans against the Islamization of the West). These culminated in both Dresden and Leipzig with the fixing to the doors of prominent churches of a list of Ten Theses, beginning with a demand for respect for 'our culture'. 'We immediately took it down' said the pastor of the Dresden Lutheran *Kreuzkirche.*[18] Luther's legacy, even when it is being acknowledged and celebrated, still lends itself to diverse interpretations.

Martin Luther's action of 31 October 1517, in nailing his Ninety-five Theses to the door of the Wittenberg Castle Church, holds a treasured, perhaps unique, place in the historical consciousness of modern people, particularly, but not exclusively, in Germany and the United States. It marks a remembered turning-point of civilization. It also represents a pre-eminent example of how the struggles of the past can help people to think about analogous situations in the present, as well as a vehicle for affirming dissident positions of various kinds, and for taking a stand against some supposedly delinquent and unresponsive authority. It is a deeply familiar image, a pattern in the wallpaper of modern western cultural identity. It is one of the treasured moments of history that has helped to make us who we are.

Imagination

And yet there is a problem. The *Thesenanschlag* is an event which most likely never took place at all. Or if it did, it may have occurred at a time other than on 31 October, or in more than one location, and it may not have involved Luther directly at all. Even if it did, in some fashion, 'happen', it certainly didn't mean at the time what most people, over most of the last 500 years, have taken it to mean.

This is not a new revelation. It is now over fifty years since Erwin Iserloh, a German Catholic historian and theologian, first suggested that the historical evidence argues strongly against any *Thesenanschlag* taking place on 31 October 1517. His assertions prompted a lively row among scholars in the 1960s (revisited in Chapter 5) and the evidence for and against a theses-posting on the Eve of All Saints 1517 has been regularly picked over and picked apart ever since. I review the evidence, for and against, in the first two chapters of this book.

Even in advance of the findings of that review it can, categorically, be stated that the *Thesenanschlag* is a myth. That is not the same as to say it is a lie or a deception, and even less to imply that it is something peripheral or unimportant. Studies of Luther and the Reformation quite often suggest that in the end it does not really matter very much whether the Theses-posting of popular imagining took place or not. One eminent authority on Luther describes the issue as 'largely irrelevant'; another calls it a 'comic-opera debate'. Surveying the documentary evidence, two leading scholars have recently declared that 'most historians agree that the question of the posting of the Theses, measured by its importance for the history of Western Christianity, carried little weight'.[19]

This book will attempt to show why the question does matter, and why examining the genesis and evolution of what may be modern history's pre-eminent example of 'false memory syndrome' is indeed a worthwhile exercise. What follows can best be described as a cultural history of an imagined event. My hope is that it is one which can shed considerable light on how societies construct their understandings of the past, on how those understandings develop and change over time, and on how scholarly and popular views of history co-exist with each other, as well as combine, collude, and occasionally clash.

Questions of authenticity or 'historicity' surrounding the posting of the Ninety-five Theses have been in the public domain for quite a long time now. Popular histories, websites, heritage materials, and tourist brochures do in fact quite often recognize that the 'legend' may not fully align with the 'facts'.[20] Yet it is striking that all the examples cited in this opening prologue of people lauding, evoking, or imitating the *Thesenanschlag* are drawn from the period during which scepticism about its historical basis was becoming widespread in academic circles. It is noteworthy too that numerous books and articles, even of a scholarly variety, still take for granted both the fact and the significance of a theses-posting in October 1517. The stubborn intractability of the traditional image, the rootedness of a public or collective memory of the event, is a powerful pointer to its cultural and historical importance.

All human cultures rely on myths. They are not simply fallacies or misconceptions about the nature of some otherwise readily explicable 'reality', but powerful and meaningful narratives, which give shape to deeply engrained values, beliefs, and ideals. They are, quite simply, 'the stories which a group, a society, or a culture lives by'.[21] For historians, the debunking of myths may be superficially satisfying, but a more important task is to explore and seek to understand them. That task is arguably never more necessary than now, as we arrive at the 'five-hundredth anniversary' of the European Reformation. It is an occasion being marked with huge waves of publicity and festivity in Germany, and which is being widely recognized elsewhere as a significant moment for assessment and reflection. The questions of what we are commemorating, and why, will no doubt be much discussed. But the argument of this book is that important aspects of our understanding of the Reformation can be brought into sharper focus by looking at the larger picture through the small aperture of what happened, and of what has been thought to have happened, in Wittenberg on 31 October 1517.

'History' and 'memory' are sometimes conceived of as opposing, or at least alternative, forms of relationship to the past, with the objective rigour of the former acting as a counterweight to the uncritical pieties of the latter.[22] In reality, the two have always been thoroughly enmeshed and implicated with each other. Pierre Nora, a French historian and public intellectual, has made famous (in scholarly circles at least) the concept of *lieux de mémoire*, 'sites of memory'. These are defined as significant entities—whether places, events, anniversaries, artefacts, texts, rituals, or practices—which form a symbolic element of the remembered heritage of a community, and which constitute one of the key means by which 'hopelessly forgetful modern societies, propelled by change, organize the past.' They also share with each other the characteristics of being artificial, constructed or fabricated, rather than representing a form of memory preserved spontaneously or organically in the culture of a people.[23]

Luther's posting of the Ninety-five Theses, to the door of the Castle Church in Wittenberg, in October 1517—an 'entity' bringing together an individual, an action, a document, a place, and a date—undoubtedly meets the criteria for a 'site of memory'; several times over, indeed. But at the same time it represents more than just a 'case-study' in how a particular moment from the remembered past is memorialized, or mythologized, in the present. For over the past few centuries, the *Thesenanschlag* has meant different things, at different times, and to different groups of people, in different national and cultural settings. It is an exemplar, and perhaps an exemplar par excellence, of memory itself as a fluid historical phenomenon, of what the historian Peter Burke has called 'the social history of remembering'.[24]

As the anniversary moment of 2017 dawns, it is important to bear in mind that our contemporary commemorations of the start of the Reformation are not—cannot be—a completely unmediated look back to the events of the sixteenth century. They are themselves a product of history: the outcome of a long-evolving historical memory, of inherited patterns of invention and reinvention, of selective remembering and forgetting about the past.

Anniversaries and centenaries are valuable—and enjoyable—educational and social occasions. They help connect the generality of people to an awareness of the historical past, and to connect sometimes closeted and self-absorbed professional historians to the interests and concerns of actual people. They can serve as important expressions of cultural identity, and, especially in diverse and fragmented modern societies, they can offer a rare opportunity for articulating shared values or beliefs.

Yet they are not without challenges and hazards. In politically or culturally divided territories—such as Northern Ireland, Israel/Palestine, or parts of the Balkans—historical commemorations can all too readily serve overtly partisan ends. Different sections of the community will choose to commemorate different historical events. Where current social and political conditions are, by contrast, relatively calm and harmonious, commemoration can easily slip into celebration, and celebration can become complacent or self-congratulatory. There is a risk that the renewal of historical memory becomes little more than an exercise in ritually performed heritage, reminding us of who we are by telling us what we already know.

Martin Luther is a founding figure of the modern West, an inspiration to millions, and for Germans at least, a potent symbol of national identity. Yet he was a truly divisive figure in his own time, and has remained so for much of the intervening centuries. As a remembered historical episode, Luther's posting of the Ninety-five Theses is a singular, almost pre-eminent, expression of modernness, westernness and Germanness—and indeed also of divisiveness. In this book I attempt to relate a story that has never before been told in full, exploring how a 'non-event' ended up becoming a defining episode of European history. I will show that to retrace the tracks of the *Thesenanschlag* is to follow a fascinating trail through the changing meanings of Luther and the Reformation, along the fractures and fault-lines of the modern historical imagination.

1
1517: Theses

Wittenberg

'Luther, burning with eagerness of piety, issued Propositions concerning Indulgences, which are recorded in the first volume of his works, and these he publicly affixed to the church next to the castle in Wittenberg, on the eve of the Feast of All Saints in the year 1517.'[1]

It seems, on the face of it, a solid and reliable documentary basis for a defining episode in modern European history. The recorder of the event, moreover, was no merely casual chronicler. The account was written by Luther's closest ally and collaborator in the emergent Reformation movement. Philip Melanchthon was a Rhinelander, a product of the prestigious universities of Heidelberg and Tübingen, and a brilliant scholar. He was a dozen and more years younger than Martin Luther and proved the almost perfect disciple and foil. Where Luther was rash and abrasively charismatic, Melanchthon was cautious and conciliatory. Luther fired out challenging ideas in sometimes erratic fashion; Melanchthon ordered and arranged them. Melanchthon, rather than Luther himself, has arguably the better claim to be the founder of 'Lutheranism', as a distinct and organized religious system. It was he who in 1530 served as principal drafter of the 'Confession of Augsburg', a declaration of the core beliefs of the new 'evangelicals'. It was presented to the Diet, or gathering of the imperial estates, meeting in the city that year. The document became and remained the principal statement of faith of the Lutheran churches in a religiously divided Germany.

Melanchthon was also among the first and most important custodians of Luther's memory. His account of Luther posting his complaint against indulgences on the (presumably door of the) Castle Church in Wittenberg appeared near the start of a 9,000-word memoir of his friend. It can claim to be the first proper biography of the great reformer. Melanchthon's *Life* was composed to serve as the preface to the second volume of Luther's collected Latin works, issued shortly after the reformer's death in 1546. Two years later, it was published again in Heidelberg as a free-standing 'History of the Life and Acts of Luther'. Melanchthon regretted that Luther himself died before being able to write a full version of his own life, though Luther used the preface to the first (1545) volume of his Latin writings to give an account of his actions leading up to and following the composition of the Ninety-five Theses. In addition, fragments of reminiscence and autobiography pepper his sermons and other published works.[2] None of these writings, and none of Luther's thousands of letters, makes any mention of the church door, or the act of posting propositions upon them.

The Ninety-five Theses themselves are one of history's least likely bestsellers. Luther confessed in 1518—to the pope, no less—that 'I cannot believe everyone understood them. They are theses, after all, not teachings, not dogmas – phrased rather obscurely and paradoxically'. Yet the work made him a celebrity. In early 1517, Luther was, if not exactly nobody, then certainly not much of a somebody, little known outside of his own order of Augustinian Friars. The author of the Ninety-five Theses was a professor of theology at a not particularly prestigious university, well away from the great European centres of culture and commerce. His only published works were the preface to an incomplete edition of a fourteenth-century mystical tract known as the *Theologica Germanica*, and a commentary on the Seven Penitential Psalms. A document drawn up in 1515, most likely to drum up recruitment to three, somewhat second-tier, universities in eastern Germany—Leipzig, Frankfurt-an-der-Oder, and Wittenberg—listed the noteworthy achievements of 101 professors associated with the institutions. Martin Luther was not even on the list. Yet in 1518, when he wrote to Pope Leo X, Luther was on his way to becoming the most famous priest in Germany.[3]

Wittenberg in 1517 was a small and unsophisticated, yet prosperous and expanding, community of about two thousand inhabitants, its wealth based on its proximity to regional centres of mining, the industry in which Luther's father had made his career. The university had been founded only recently, in 1502, at the command of the local ruler, Frederick 'the Wise'. Frederick was Elector of Saxony, overlord of one of the more significant of the myriad of small states making up the Holy Roman Empire. Covering most of central Europe between eastern France and the modern-day border of Poland, the Empire was a patchwork-quilt of towns and territories, held together only by the fact that most of their inhabitants spoke German, by their common Catholic faith, and by their nominal allegiance to the Emperor, who was chosen by seven Electors—a mixture of secular and ecclesiastical princes.

Luther's Augustinian monastery was at one end of the main street around which Wittenberg's buildings clustered. At the other was the Elector's imposing castle, and its adjacent church, which served as a princely chapel and as a site of burial for the electoral princes of Saxony. It was also the place of worship and main building of assembly for the new university. The church, too, was a recent creation, work on it beginning after an older chapel was pulled down in 1496–7. Construction was only just coming to an end in 1508, when Luther transferred from the Augustinian house at Erfurt to that of Wittenberg, and took up his position at the university.

An illustration of 1509 by the Wittenberg court painter Lucas Cranach (see Fig. 1.1) depicts the recently completed church, with wooden walkways across ground still damp and dug-over from the construction work. In the centre, flanked by statues, the artist depicted the main entrance to the church, the portal which, though no one yet knew it, was to become the most famous door in western history.[4]

In 1509, the Castle Church of All Saints was famous for something else entirely. Frederick the Wise possessed, and preserved there, an extraordinary quantity of relics. Cranach produced exquisite illustrations of them, along with that of the church's exterior, for a book cataloguing the collection and promoting pilgrimage to the site. In 1508, there were reckoned to be at least 5,005 relics of saints in the collection, housed in precious reliquaries of gold, silver, and jewelled inlay. By 1520, it had grown to 19,013 items, and included such rarities as a thorn from the crown of Christ, a portion of the milk of the Virgin Mary, and the complete body of one of the Holy Innocents slain by Herod.

Relics were conduits of sacred power. They inspired reflection on the exemplary lives of the holy saints who left bones or other physical attributes behind them on earth. More importantly, the saints in

Fig. 1.1. The Castle Church in Wittenberg, by Lucas Cranach (1509).

heaven were expected to listen more intently to prayers made in proximity to their remains, and even petition God to perform miracles in response to such prayers. The act of journeying to view relics—pilgrimage—was itself a good work, a source of God's grace. In Wittenberg, as in numerous other places in medieval Europe, it was also one with explicit prospect of reward. People visiting the Castle Church, and praying before the relics there (as well as those contributing towards the church's rebuilding work) received the spiritual benefits of specified indulgences.

Frederick was as avid an acquirer of indulgences as he was of relics, an accumulation of pious collectibles going hand-in-hand. Even before its lavish rebuilding at the end of the fifteenth century, Frederick was receiving from the papacy special grants of indulgence to attach to his chapel. Indeed, it was the money pouring into the foundation of All Saints from spiritual tourists visiting the relics and seeking the associated blessings that supplied most of the funds for the establishment of the university in 1502. Luther's career was one built on indulgences and relics, years before it was to be profoundly and permanently altered by them.[5]

In 1503, the layers of indulgence enveloping the church of All Saints and its relics were significantly enhanced. The French Cardinal Raymond Peraudi, legate, or authorized deputy, of the pope, visited Wittenberg that year to inaugurate the new church and bestow further blessings on it. Peraudi was a skilled and seasoned preacher of indulgences, or 'pardons'. He was now on his third tour promoting them in Germany and across northern Europe, with the principal aim of raising money for a papal crusade against the Turks. Peraudi's visits to German towns were spectacular and well-orchestrated affairs, combining ringing of church bells, ceremonial processions, declarations of amnesty to offenders, open-air masses, and powerful sermons. It all contributed to an atmosphere of heightened devotion which encouraged participants to come forward and receive the proffered indulgences in exchange for the expected donation.

In early sixteenth-century Wittenberg, however, the indulgences were not just one-off opportunities, linked to the visit of a high-profile preacher. They were organically attached to the treasures of the locality. The mere act of visiting the *Schlosskirche* on the Feast of All Saints, on that of St John the Baptist, or on one of several other specified days, guaranteed one hundred days of 'remission'. Persons praying in front of the Holy Thorn, or other exhibited relics, and performing additional named acts of devotion, earned further days of indulgence. The amounts obtainable were cumulative. In 1513, anyone with the stamina to perform all of the devotions stipulated by the indulgences attached to Frederick's relics could in theory earn nearly 42,000 years of remission; by 1518, the achievable target had risen to a precisely calculated 1,909,202 years and 270 days.[6]

Indulgences

For most people nowadays, this is a head-spinningly alien and even alienating world. What did these figures and aggregations mean; for or from what were people seeking 'remission'; and what indeed were indulgences, and how were they supposed to work?

There is no doubt that indulgences enjoy a bad reputation in modern society, even—or especially—among modern Christians. They are widely thought to exemplify the corruption and venality of the late medieval Church and papacy, and widespread detestation of them was undoubtedly a principal 'cause' of the Reformation. Like most caricatures, this one has some truth to it, but the reality is both more complicated and more interesting.

Indulgences were a part—not the central part, but a far from insignificant one—of a sophisticated system of spiritual exchanges, designed to overcome an inescapable fact about the human condition. That fact was the propensity to sinfulness which, left to itself, made it impossible for human beings to be friends with God, or, after their deaths, to enjoy the right to dwell with Him eternally in heaven: in other words, to be saved.

Salvation is the desired aim, end, and outcome of the Christian life. This was never more obviously so than in the later middle ages, when rates of mortality made death and bereavement a facet of everyday experience, and served to focus everyone's minds on the life after this one. The principal road-block to salvation was 'original sin', a primordial defect intrinsic to humanity, the baleful inheritance of Adam and Eve's disobedience in the Garden of Eden. God's decision to become a member of the human race in the person of Jesus of Nazareth, and to 'atone' for the collective sins of the world by dying painfully on the Cross, restored the potential for friendship and made salvation possible. But there was still a great deal to do in order for the result to be achieved in the case of any individual Christian.

The process involved a combination of solitary effort and reliance on collective support. The support was offered by the community of believers which Jesus himself established during his time on earth: the Church. It was through the Church, and its life-giving rituals known as sacraments, that God's favour—his grace—was channelled to people eager to receive it. Such grace was received in marriage, and—the alternative path that Luther chose—in ordination to the priesthood. It was renewed regularly by participation in the eucharist, also known as the mass: a re-enactment of Christ's Last Supper with his disciples, in which the priest played the part of Jesus, and bread and wine were believed to become, in a fundamentally real way, the body and blood of the Saviour.

Before any of these came the sacrament of baptism, performed as soon as possible after the birth of an infant. Baptism made a person a Christian. In both a symbolic and literal sense, it washed away the stain of original sin. But as experience all too clearly taught, the inclination to sin remained, in both children and the adults they became. The more serious sins were 'mortal' ones: unless remedial action was taken, they killed the soul's prospects of salvation and consigned it to the infernal custody of the devil.

Yet remedy was ever at hand: the flipside of sin was the offer of forgiveness. There was a sacrament for that too: penance. It offered God's forgiveness of both mortal and less serious ('venial') sins in return for feelings of penitence and an honest attempt at a full confession of those sins to a priest, acting here as God's representative. Theologians argued over whether for the sacrament to take effect people needed to feel genuine sorrow for their sins ('contrition') or just a desire to want to feel sorry ('attrition')—the second interpretation placed more emphasis on the sacramental power of the priest. But either way, 'absolution' wiped the slate clean, and even the most heinous criminal or murderer, if they confessed sorrowfully after the deed, could then die and be assured of a place in heaven.

There was a catch—or rather, as theologians saw it, a perfectly logical and reasonable corollary. God was infinitely merciful: hence the offer of forgiveness for all manner of sins. But he was also infinitely just, and bad behaviour had consequences. Confession and absolution removed the guilt of sins, but not the need to make some kind of restitution for them. God's justice required penalty, punishment, 'satisfaction'—just as the modern victim of a serious crime might be willing to forgive the culprit but still expect them to be sentenced and 'do time'. It was part of the ritual of confession, just before absolution was conferred, for the priest to assign penances. Typically these involved reciting prayers, periods of fasting, or acts of alms-giving; occasionally, undertaking a pilgrimage or some other work of ostentatious devotion. But such penances, and even a lifetime's tally of worthy deeds and intentions, might scarcely cover the tariff. The typical, averagely good Christian of the later middle ages died with spiritual debts still to pay.

The problem was not insoluble. Centuries earlier, Christian theology had managed to escape from being backed into the corner of teaching that only the extraordinarily virtuous achieved salvation, while the majority were condemned to eternal damnation. The name of that escape-route was purgatory, a third place in the afterlife alongside heaven and hell. Purgatory had somewhat shaky foundations in scripture, and it was a doctrine that emerged and evolved over the course of the early middle ages. But it fulfilled a vital salvific function and served to democratize the afterlife. The unpaid debts, the 'temporal punishment' still due for sins, could be paid off there, allowing cleansed souls to proceed in due course to heaven.

It was not an entirely cheerful prospect. Purgatory was a place of punishment, and the consensus of theologians, preachers, and the occasional spiritual visionary was that the penalties endured there by souls were extremely unpleasant. In all likelihood, the experience involved purgation by some kind of spiritual fire, differing from the fire of hell only in its temporary nature. Temporary was a relative term. The nature of 'time' in a world beyond this one was understandably perplexing, if not downright impenetrable. Theologians insisted it could be measured only in terms of units of equivalence to periods of earthly penance. But the imaginations of ordinary people latched onto the idea that the likely sentences in purgatory would be handed out in tens, hundreds, thousands—perhaps tens of thousands—of years.

This bleak prospect was an incentive to action: there were ways to reduce the length of the purgatorial stay. At the centre of these was one of the Church's most compelling and attractive ideas. The ancient statement of faith known as the Apostles' Creed confirmed that all faithful Christians, living and dead, formed a 'communion of saints'—their fates were linked, and good deeds could be performed by one Christian for the benefit of another. Through prayers, alms-giving, and works of charity, the living could assist the dead and help speed their passage through purgatory. The most powerful work or 'suffrage' that could be performed on their behalf was the mass itself, as every mass was a re-enactment in the contemporary world of Christ's historic sacrifice on Calvary. Across Europe, the dead—or rather, the soon-to-be dead—urged the living to remember them. In their wills, people gave gifts to churches, or to the poor, in return for prayers, and they left funds for sequences of requiem masses to be said for their souls; sometimes for a period of months or years, sometimes 'for as long as the world shall stand'.[7]

Here, by a long and circuitous route, indulgences enter the picture. Briefly stated, an indulgence was a certificate granting remission of some or all of the temporal punishment due for sins—they did not 'forgive' sins, though, in the way they were spoken about, that crucial distinction was occasionally fudged and blurred. Nor were they ever straightforwardly 'sold', though sight of that fact too was sometimes lost.[8]

Their origins lie in the great, doomed enterprise of medieval western Christianity: the crusades to retake the Holy Places from the occupying forces of Islam. Soldiers of Christ risking death in foreign lands (including Muslim-held Spain) were promised remission of penalties as an incentive to take up the cause. Thereafter, indulgences were offered for undertaking a wide variety of other 'good works', and, increasingly, for supporting such good works vicariously by making a monetary contribution towards them.

The question of where this remission 'came from' was answered by pointing to the communion of saints. Some members of that communion—holy men and women earning the right to be called Saints with a capital 'S', as well as Jesus himself—passed from this world, not in deficit, but with a superabundance of merits. Those surplus tokens of satisfaction remained within the compass of the Church. By the thirteenth century, the view had emerged that they comprised a 'Treasury of Merit', whose riches could be drawn upon by the competent authorities. The popes, as heads of the visible Church on earth, were quick to assert that they were custodians of the keys to this treasury—a claim grounded in Christ's pledge to St Peter and his successors that 'I will give to you the keys of the kingdom of heaven, and whatever you shall bind on earth shall be bound in heaven, and whatever you shall loose on earth shall be loosed in heaven' (Matt. 16:19). Only the pope could grant a complete, or 'plenary' remission of *poena* (penalties), removing all the punishment due for sins. Other authorities were delegated to remit lesser amounts; bishops could usually grant forty days of indulgence on their own account.

In light of what was to happen in 1517, it is important to stress that most indulgences were not dispensed outwards from Rome in imperious, high-to-low fashion. As with Elector Frederick's initiative in Wittenberg, but usually on a much smaller scale, they originated with local communities, with people petitioning Rome to grant an indulgence in support of their particular causes and concerns. The aim might be to add lustre to pilgrimage sites, but was often in aid of the building or rebuilding of churches, or even to assist with what might look to us like 'community projects', such as the construction of roads and bridges. It seems likely that people quite often purchased indulgences, not out of a neurotic concern with the condition of their souls, but in order to support such worthwhile causes, much as we might take a sticker from a charity-collector today.

In the main, indulgences were ancillary, not foundational, to the late medieval 'industry' of penance and purgatory, whose main focus continued to be on the provision of post-mortem prayers and masses. They were certainly not ever supposed to be some kind of golden ticket, guaranteeing swift entry to heaven with minimal effort or anxiety. To receive the benefits, it was necessary to have been to confession and received absolution, and to remain still in a 'state of grace'. The grants' insistence that requisite prayers or good works must be performed 'devoutly' was a reminder that indulgences did not work automatically. People making sensible plans for navigating their way through the afterlife rarely relied on indulgences alone.

Still, powerful and genuine longings for spiritual assurance, a desire to assist meritorious causes, and the potential for raising considerable quantities of ready cash, all combined to make indulgences a growth area of late medieval religion. Their scope expanded significantly in the years immediately preceding Luther's birth. Medieval theologians had long debated the question of whether indulgences could be granted to the already dead. One view was that souls in purgatory were not under the jurisdiction of any bishop, so grants of remission could not be applied to them. Another, put forward by the thirteenth-century Franciscan theologian, Bonaventure, was that indulgences could benefit the dead as well as the living, but in a different way: they were not an act of jurisdiction but an act of intercession on behalf of the dead—albeit a particularly powerful one. However, Bonaventure's great contemporary, Thomas Aquinas, and other members of the Dominican order, maintained indulgences could be applied to the dead in the same way as to the living.[9] Rivalries between religious orders would play a far from insignificant role in the events of 1517.

In 1476, heavily influenced by the arguments of Raymond Peraudi, Pope Sixtus IV issued the bull *Salvator Noster*. It ruled definitively that indulgences did benefit souls already in purgatory, and could be acquired on their behalf, though they were effectual *per modum suffragii*—that is, by way of suffrage or intercession. The immediate occasion for the 1476 indulgence was a conventional one—the repair of a church; in this case the cathedral of Saintes in south-west France. But a deal was also being cut with the newly appointed dean of the cathedral, none other than Peraudi himself. Some of the money raised from this plenary indulgence would go towards the perennial papal objective of a crusade against the Turks. The phrasing of the indulgence embedded in the text of Pope Sixtus's bull is suggestive of the expressive, emotional terms in which indulgences were preached. It was addressed to 'parents, friends or other faithful Christians', in the hope that they would be 'moved by pity for those souls exposed to the fire of purgatory, for expiation of penalties which are theirs according to divine justice'.[10]

Tetzel

The controversy over indulgences exploding in Germany in 1517 was a reaction to a compound of elements prefigured in the bull of 1476. It involved a declaration of remission to Christians (which could be applied to the accounts of deceased relatives in purgatory) in return for supporting the good work of rebuilding a church, as well as a campaign of selling made possible by a quiet arrangement between Rome and the authorities on the ground.

The circumstances in 1517 were familiar, but also exceptional, for the church in question was the pope's own: the great Roman basilica of St Peter's, which Julius II began to rebuild in elegant Renaissance style in 1506. The following year, Julius declared a plenary indulgence in support of the project, and this was reissued by his successor Leo X in 1513 and again in 1515, as the building work progressed.

The second renewal was intimately and fatefully connected to the ecclesiastical affairs of Germany. In 1514, Germany's most important archbishopric, Mainz—one of three which made its holder an Elector with a voice in choosing a new emperor—fell vacant. Albrecht, the twenty-four-year-old second son of the Elector of Brandenburg was eager to obtain the see. Rome was eager to oblige the high German nobility, but the expense for the young nobleman was steep. In addition to the usual fees associated with the appointment, Albrecht needed a costly dispensation to exercise episcopal office below the minimum age stipulated by canon law. He needed another one to hold Mainz alongside the archbishopric of Magdeburg, which he had also recently acquired: a total eye-watering sum of 24,000 ducats. Without the cash reserves in hand, Albrecht borrowed heavily from the wealthy banking family of Augsburg, the Fuggers.

The indulgence, or so it seemed to Pope Leo, was a win-win solution for all the leading players. Albrecht would permit the papal indulgence to be preached throughout his territories. Half the money would go to the pope and the construction of St Peter's; with the other half, Albrecht would pay off his loan to the Fuggers. It was, as virtually every commentator since has concluded, a pretty disreputable financial arrangement.[11] Luther, like most ordinary priests and lay people at the time, knew nothing about it. His reservations were about aspects of the theology of indulgences itself, and about the ways it was being interpreted and presented by those charged with preaching the indulgence in Germany.

To promote the indulgence, Albrecht turned to the Dominican Order, and in particular to Johan Tetzel, a native Saxon and graduate of the University of Leipzig, with an established reputation as a successful and charismatic indulgence preacher. It was a tough commission. Successive issues of plenary indulgences in Germany, stretching back to the campaigns of Peraudi, meant the market for them was almost saturated. Moreover, Elector Frederick, fearing competition for his own indulgenced relic-collection, forbad the indulgence from being sold in electoral Saxony.

In preparation for the campaign, Albrecht's court theologians drew up an *Instructio Summaria* (Summary Instruction) with guidelines to preachers on how to present it most effectively. This confirmed that the new issue superseded and invalidated all previous grants of indulgence for the next eight years—a source of understandable annoyance to people who had bought earlier ones in literal good faith. Generally, the *Instructio* took a maximalist line on the indulgence's power and efficacy. Most notoriously, it suggested that people buying the indulgence on behalf of the dead had no need to make confession or exhibit contrition, as its effectiveness depended on 'the love in which the deceased died, and the contributions of the living'.

This was at best questionable theology, and in preaching the indulgence with the customary pomp and theatricality, Tetzel pushed the boundaries still further. It is likely that he did use some form of the crass and already clichéd slogan that 'as soon as the coin in the coffer rings, at once the soul to heaven springs.' He may also have taught, though he later denied saying it, that the indulgence was so powerful it would obtain full remission even for someone who had violated the Mother of God.[12] This was, perhaps, technically within the bounds of orthodoxy—if one could imagine such a hypothetical sin being properly confessed and absolved. But it was undoubtedly provocative and distasteful to serious-minded pastors and theologians.

Martin Luther was just such a serious-minded pastor and theologian. Born in Eisleben in Saxony in 1483, he was brought up in nearby Mansfeld, where his father ran a successful mining business. Hans Luder (the form of the name used by the family) wanted his son to become a lawyer, and the young Luther's decision to enter the Church was an act of rebellion as well as of piety. It was also, he later claimed, the immediate fulfilment of a vow—taken to St Anne, mother of the Virgin Mary, during a ferocious summer thunderstorm: if he survived, he would devote his life to the service of God. In July 1505, abandoning the study of the law, Luther sought admission to the monastery of Augustinian friars in Erfurt, a house of the Observant, or strictly reformed, branch of the order.

Luther was ordained to the priesthood in 1507, and the following year was summoned by his mentor, Johann von Staupitz, Vicar General of the Observant Augustinians in Germany, to the monastery in Wittenberg and a post in the University, where Staupitz was dean of the theological faculty. Luther was a scrupulously devout young priest, filled, as he later remembered it, with an overpowering sense of his own unworthiness and gnawing doubts about his salvation. At the same time he was building a reputation as a scholar, and succeeded Staupitz as professor of biblical studies in 1512. But, other than in the technical sense, he was not a 'cloistered' academic, cut off from contact with ordinary people. In 1514, Luther was appointed preacher at Wittenberg's city church of St Mary's; with the position came a powerful sense that souls were entrusted to his care.

As an Augustinian, Luther was also inclined to be suspicious of friars, like Tetzel, from the rival Dominican Order. Luther was on the other side of the argument in 1513–14, when the Dominicans of Cologne tried to bring heresy charges against the scholar Johan Reuchlin because of his interest in Hebrew books. It seemed to many a contest between the forces of old-fashioned, obscurantist, 'scholastic' theology, and the new wave of 'humanist' learning sweeping through European intellectual life. Humanists believed Christian life could be enriched and renewed by serious engagement with ancient texts, and by returning *ad fontes* (to the sources)—which of course also meant a greater emphasis on scripture itself. Whether or not Luther was ever really a humanist (this is debated), his lectures from 1513 onwards showed ever greater concern with the Bible in its literal sense.

He was also wrestling with deep questions of faith and repentance, and struggling to understand how Christians achieved 'righteousness' or became 'justified' in the eyes of God. It would later become crystal clear to him that human effort played no part in this process; that righteousness was 'imputed' to, not achieved by, humans on account of Christ's sacrifice on the Cross; that justification came 'by faith alone'. Some scholars have dated this 'break-through' to as early as 1514, though Luther himself later wrote that the pieces only finally fell into place for him in 1519. Others have doubted there was any single moment of conversion and enlightenment. Wherever the truth lies, it is unhelpful to think of Luther at the time of the indulgence controversy as some kind of 'Protestant-in-waiting'. Early sixteenth-century Catholicism was culturally as well as theologically a broad and often fractious Church. Luther's emphases on human sinfulness, on the need for humility before God, and on the unforced character of God's mercy, were characteristic of trends in contemporary piety. Nor was it unusual for preachers, friars in particular, to issue condemnations of institutional corruption and make calls for moral reform. Luther may not have been a 'typical' late medieval Catholic, but he was a late medieval Catholic nonetheless.[13]

Tetzel's preaching campaign got underway in January 1517. He was banned from preaching in Wittenberg, or entering Saxon territory, but Elector Frederick's subjects could easily travel to towns just beyond the border—to Eisleben, Halle, Zerbst, and Jütterbog—where Tetzel was plying his trade. In due course, Luther would have seen the certificates they brought back with them, and, as preacher and pastor at the city church of St Mary, he would have heard their confessions and learned to his dismay what they thought indulgences meant.

Even before this, in response to the start of Tetzel's campaign, Luther was expressing public reservations. In a sermon very likely preached at the Castle Church on the eve or day of the anniversary of its dedication (17 January 1517)—itself, ironically, an occasion for acquiring an indulgence—Luther preached a sermon which, he recalled years later, 'earned Duke Frederick's disfavour'. In it, he drew a clear distinction between external penance and 'the interior and only true penance of the heart'. Luther did not deny that indulgences were useful, or that the pope's intentions in issuing them were good, but their proper function was simply to remit externally imposed ecclesiastical penalties, and he worried that 'frequently they work against interior penitence'.

Over the coming months, as reports of Tetzel's activities multiplied, and a copy of the Mainz *Instructio* came into his hands, Luther increasingly reflected on what indulgences were and how they should be explained to the people. He included a few swipes against excessive reliance on them in a series of sermons on the Lord's Prayer, preached during Lent 1517. And, either over the summer or in the autumn, he composed a short tract to clarify his own thinking on the issue.

In this text, Luther elaborated the idea that indulgences, in this life or in purgatory, were solely concerned with remission by the Church of temporal punishments, penalties which the Church itself had imposed. It was indeed 'most useful to grant and to gain these indulgences', but principally as a way of clearing the ground for individual spiritual growth. Luther strongly denied that indulgences infused God's grace into the soul of a recipient, bringing about any increase of charity or any lessening of the inclination to sin ('concupiscence'). Nor did they provide guarantees of any kind that a soul was ready to enter heaven. Such readiness was the result, not of any plenary indulgence, but of a progression in charity, inner virtue, and detachment from worldly things, whether achieved in the present life or in purgatory. Luther's main objection to indulgences, as they were currently being preached, was that they encouraged a false sense of certainty and security. What was more, rather than serving as a way to teach people the meaning of salvation, they had become blatantly commercialized, 'a shocking exercise of greed'.[14]

Even before he began writing this tract, Luther may have been contemplating the idea of a formal academic disputation on indulgences, to raise awareness of the abuses of the trade and clarify the key theological matters at issue. So it was to that end that he drew up a list of theses or propositions concerning indulgences—not, or not necessarily all, as affirmations of his own fixed beliefs, but as challenging assertions designed to stimulate argument and, so it was hoped, to produce collective enlightenment.

This was a standard way of doing things in late medieval universities. Debates or disputations, which in Wittenberg generally took place on Fridays, supplemented and enlivened the often dull diet of undergraduate lectures. Students defended theses at their promotion to higher degrees, and professors could propose them on topics of their choosing. Luther presided over a controversial disputation in September 1516, at which his student Bartholomäus Bernardi defended theses (heavily based on Luther's own lectures) attacking the methods of scholastic theology, and the idea that humans could do anything on their own account to deserve God's favour. On this occasion, Luther suggested to his university colleague Andreas von Karlstadt that he compare the works of scholastic doctors with those of the great father of the Church, St Augustine, whose theology heavily emphasized the unmerited nature of God's grace. In April 1517, Karlstadt composed a set of strongly Augustinian and anti-scholastic theses which were due to be debated over several days by Saxon theologians chosen by Elector Frederick. This disputation may not in the end have taken place, but Luther sent copies of Karlstadt's theses to various friends and acquaintances. He also drew up his own set of Ninety-seven Theses against Scholastic Theology, which were debated at the conferral of a degree upon his student Franz Günther on 4 September 1517. These theses were deeply provocative, suggesting that the study of Aristotle—lynchpin of the scholastic curriculum—was actually harmful to Christian theology.[15]

The number of theses, ninety-seven, was about par for the course in debates initiated by professors, though there were a full 151 on the list drawn up by Karlstadt. On 28 April 1517, Karlstadt wrote to Georg Spalatin, chaplain and chancellor to the Elector Frederick, to say that he had publicly posted them up ('publice affixi') two days earlier. It was normal to advertise a forthcoming disputation in this way. Karlstadt did not explicitly say so, though it is perhaps safe to assume, that his theses were posted on the door of the Castle Church.[16]

Penitence

No manuscript of the Ninety-five Theses, which Luther composed fairly shortly after he compiled the Ninety-seven, survives in the form in which he originally wrote them. The earliest printed versions are prefixed with the announcement of a formal disputation:

> Out of love and zeal for bringing the truth to light, what is written below will be debated in Wittenberg with the Reverend Father Martin Luther, Master of Arts and Sacred Theology, and regularly appointed lecturer on these subjects at that place, presiding. Therefore, he requests that those who cannot be present to discuss orally with us will in their absence do so by letter.[17]

It seems virtually certain that no such disputation ever took place, for there is no record or mention of it. But the Theses were certainly produced in the form of controversial discussion points for a university debate—of the more rambunctious and rhetorical style taking place at Wittenberg over the course of the preceding year.

They began with a categorical and emphatic assertion: 'Our Lord and Master Jesus Christ, in saying "Do penance" [*poenitentiam agite*], wanted the entire life of the faithful to be one of penitence.' The second thesis added to this that Christ's words (in Matthew's Gospel 4:17) 'cannot be understood as referring to sacramental penance, that is confession and satisfaction as administered by the clergy'.

To many subsequent readers down the centuries, this has sounded like a clarion call to insurrection, a declaration of theological revolt against the authority of the pope and the sacramental teaching of the Catholic Church. The impression is misleading. In questioning a conventional reading of the Latin Vulgate Bible's *poenitentiam agite*, Luther was showing himself to be an acolyte of the great humanist scholar, Desiderius Erasmus, whose edition of the original Greek text of the New Testament, accompanied by his own new Latin translation and explanatory notes, was hot off the press in 1516. It may be significant that it was in a letter forwarding the Theses, written on 31 October 1517, that Hans Luder's son first gave his name as Martin 'Luther'. He derived the new spelling from 'Eleutherius', a Greek word meaning freed or liberated, the form he used to sign more than two dozen letters over the course of the following year. 'Classicizing' one's identity like this was a humanist affectation: Melanchthon was a literal Greek translation of the solidly Germanic surname Schwartzerdt ('black earth').

Erasmus argued that the Greek verb *metanoeite* (used likewise by John the Baptist in Matt. 3:2) actually meant 'repent' or 'be changed in your heart'—it had nothing to do with 'the prescribed penalties by which one atones for sins'.[18] The change of interpretation was certainly significant, and represented a powerful cry for moral renewal and the reordering of Christian priorities: an authentic inner spirituality over and against the mere externals of worship and conduct. Yet neither Erasmus nor Luther was advocating the abandonment of confession or denying its sacramental character.

The Ninety-five Theses were, without doubt, intended as an excoriating critique of current teaching and practices around indulgences. A number were direct responses to the reported preaching—the 'daydreams' (no. 70)—of Tetzel and his fellow commissaries; the 'human opinions' of those claiming that 'as soon as a coin thrown into the money chest clinks, a soul flies out of purgatory' (27); the 'insanity' of teaching a papal indulgence could absolve a person violating the Virgin Mary (75); the 'blasphemies' of suggesting St Peter himself could not grant greater graces than those currently on offer (77); or that the cross, emblazoned with the papal crest, and set up in churches where indulgences were preached, 'is of equal worth to the cross of Christ' (79).

Such extravagances made it difficult to answer what Luther called 'the truly sharp questions of the laity' (81), though whether these were concerns he had actually heard ordinary people uttering is debatable. Why, for example, 'does the pope not empty purgatory for the sake of the holiest love and the direst need of souls as a matter of the highest justice, given that he redeems countless souls for filthy lucre to build the basilica as a completely trivial matter?' (82). And again, given his vast wealth, why does the pope not simply construct the Basilica of St Peter 'with his own money rather than the money of the poor faithful?' (86). If the pope is seeking the salvation of souls rather than money, 'why does he now suspend the documents and indulgences previously granted . . . ?' (89).

These were indeed sharp questions, and Luther articulated them to underline the dire consequences when papal claims about indulgences exceeded their acceptable bounds and undermined efforts to persuade people of the need for genuine repentance. The more theologically substantive of the theses reiterated points made by Luther in his earlier sermons and his indulgence treatise. The pope had no power to remit guilt, and could only lift penalties which he himself or other ecclesiastical authorities had imposed on the living (5–16, 20–1, 33–4, 61, 76). Papal jurisdiction did not extend to purgatory (22). Several of the theses worried away at the connection between remission and contrition, arguing that people were deceived to think that declarations of plenary remission could be effectual for anyone other than the truly contrite, while at the same time noting that, by definition, the truly contrite had no need of them (23–4, 30–1, 35–6, 39–40, 87). Of all the theses, Luther's prophetic denunciation of abuses was perhaps most neatly summed up in number 32: 'those who believe that they can be secure in their salvation through indulgence letters will be eternally damned along with their teachers'.

Yet, despite their vehemence of expression, there is little in the Ninety-five Theses to justify seeing in them the manifesto of a new movement, or the declaration of any kind of break with the existing order. While sharply critical of recent papal teaching on indulgences,

Luther was in no sense repudiating the authority of Rome, and he was not merely being sarcastic when he complained that one of the problems with unbridled preaching of indulgences was that it 'makes it difficult even for unlearned men to defend the reverence due the pope from slander' (81).

Luther's intention was to limit the scope of indulgences, not abolish them entirely. He conceded (69) that 'bishops and parish priests are bound to admit commissaries of the apostolic indulgences with all reverence'—a stricture that evidently didn't apply to Electors of Saxony! Luther did not even deny that indulgences might have some efficacy for those already dead, though the pope's claim to be able to grant remission to souls in purgatory was 'not by "the power of the keys", which he does not possess here, but "by way of intercession"'. This, in fact, was the majoritarian late medieval view of how indulgences could be applied to the situation of the dead; even Sixtus IV's expansionist bull of 1476, as we have seen, claimed that in purgatory indulgences worked *per modum suffragii*.

Later Protestants would reject purgatory itself as a fiction and a fraud, an unscriptural accretion to the deposit of Christian faith. Yet at the end of 1517, Luther took the existence of purgatory for granted. More than that, it occupied an important place in his thinking as a site of purification and spiritual growth (15–19).

Another subsequent Protestant (and Lutheran) preoccupation—the denigration of good works—was likewise absent from the Ninety-five Theses. One of Luther's objections to papal plenary indulgences was that people might 'mistakenly think they are to be preferred to other good works of love' (41). Giving to the poor, and similar works of mercy, were certainly ways in which 'a person is made better' (44, 42–3, 45–6). Strong emphasis on a sense of assurance of salvation—the bedrock of later Protestant spirituality—is likewise in short supply. In denouncing the false assurance of indulgences, Luther played up the spiritual value of insecurity, stressing that 'no one is secure in the genuineness of one's own contrition' (30). He even speculated that the souls in purgatory might be uncertain of their own eventual salvation (19). This was to go against the considerable (scholastic) authority of St Thomas Aquinas, though other late medieval luminaries, including the great visionary saint, Bridget of Sweden, did believe that certainty of salvation was withheld from them.[19] Luther even wondered whether all the holy souls in purgatory would actually want to be fast-tracked out of it (29).

Such abstruse speculations are another reminder that the Ninety-five Theses were propositions for discussion and debate, not a fully worked-out platform or polished dissertation. It is uncertain how fully Luther endorsed all the theses he was putting forward, and one at least—that the pope's power over purgatory 'corresponds to the power that any bishop or local priest has in particular in his diocese or parish' (25)—he surely did not believe to be true. The document contains some aphoristically paired sets of contrary propositions: 'Let the one who speaks against the truth of the Apostolic indulgences be anathema and cursed' (71), 'but let the one who guards against the arbitrary and unbridled words used by declaimers of indulgences be blessed' (72). And it draws near conclusion with a set of rousing yet paradoxical slogans: 'away with all those prophets who say to Christ's people, "Peace, peace", and there is no peace!' (92); 'May it go well for all of those prophets who say to Christ's people, "Cross, cross", and there is no cross!' (93).

The historian David Bagchi has shown that at least fifty-nine of the Ninety-five Theses correspond closely to comments made by Luther in his earlier writings. Martin Luther would indeed develop a revolutionary new theology, but the Ninety-five Theses wasn't yet it. Critical doubts about indulgences were a fairly widespread phenomenon in late medieval Europe, and many of Luther's objections stood in both a longer and more recent tradition of concern about abuses of the system. Anxieties that indulgences might work against an understanding of the necessity for true repentance were expressed by such pillars of fifteenth-century orthodoxy as the French theologian Jean Gerson, the Netherlander Dionysius Rickel (known as Dionysius the Carthusian), and the Scot John Major. Tetzel's 1509 indulgence campaign in the diocese of Strasburg had been roundly condemned by the renowned preacher Johann Geiler von Keysersberg, for paying inadequate attention to the importance of contrition. The recent papal practice of suspending earlier plenary indulgences when a new one was promulgated had already been attacked in a set of grievances presented to the Emperor Maximillian by the German Estates in 1510.[20]

Humanists generally showed little enthusiasm for indulgences. They were concerned, like Luther (Theses 53–4), that they should not be allowed to usurp the preaching of the Gospel. In his satirical *Praise of Folly* (1509), Erasmus wondered what there was to say about those who 'enjoy deluding themselves with imaginary pardons for their sins? They measure the length of their time in purgatory as if by water-clock, counting centuries, years, months, days and hours as though there were a mathematical table to calculate them accurately'. The reference to 'imaginary pardons' perhaps allowed Erasmus to claim it was only fake indulgences (of which remarkable numbers circulated in late medieval Europe) that he condemned. Yet elsewhere Erasmus took broad swipes at the folly of pinning hopes of salvation 'on a piece of parchment instead of on a moral life'.[21]

Especially after the appearance of his New Testament in 1516, Erasmus's theological probity was suspect in some quarters; nowhere more so than in the ultra-orthodox Sorbonne, the Theology Faculty of the University of Paris. Yet in a ruling of early 1518, the Paris Faculty denounced as 'false, scandalous, detrimental to suffrages for the dead' the proposition that souls fly immediately to heaven the moment the coin drops into the indulgence coffer. In a cautious judgement, at odds with inflated papal claims, the Sorbonne declared, 'it must be left to God, who decides as he pleases whether the treasury of the Church is applied to the said souls.' The Paris theologians even sent a circular letter to all the French bishops, to warn them against false preaching as well as the shortcomings of the recent papal bull itself—prompting King Francis I, who had recently signed an agreement with the pope over the governance of the French Church, to step in and close down the debate.

Even some figures close to Rome and the Dominicans expressed reservations about teaching on indulgences. Tommaso de Vio, known from his place of birth (Gaeta) as Cajetan, was an Italian Cardinal, papal diplomat, and Master General of the Dominican Order, no less. In early December 1517, he completed a *Tractatus de indulgentiis* (treatise on indulgences) for the benefit of Cardinal Giulio de Medici (later to be Pope Clement VII). Cajetan would soon be up to his ears in Luther's case, but it is unlikely that at this stage he knew anything about the Wittenberg friar or his Ninety-five Theses. Nonetheless, some of Cajetan's conclusions—expressed in a considerably more measured way—mirrored Luther's own.

Cajetan was concerned that indulgences were sometimes granted 'indiscreetly', without sufficient emphasis on the penitence of the purchaser. He insisted that for souls in purgatory they operated only *per modum suffragii*, and—exactly like Luther—he took the minimalist view that indulgences could only remit penalties imposed by the Church, not the wider satisfaction required by God's justice.[22] Cajetan did not proceed from this to raise explicit doubts about the Treasury of Merits, as Luther did (56–66), nor to declare that 'the true treasure of the Church is the most holy gospel of the glory and grace of God' (62). But one could hardly ask for a more persuasive witness to the fact that, in the early sixteenth century, criticism of indulgences was fairly conventional among thoughtful Catholic theologians. Or that—despite their sharp tone—Luther's critiques remained within the bounds of what could reasonably be considered orthodoxy.

There was nothing about the Ninety-five Theses that made a schism in the Western Church inevitable, or even likely. How, then, did it happen? In the first instance, that involves examining what actually took place after Luther laid down his pen on the last words of Thesis Ninety-five: 'the false security of peace'.

Halloween

The date 31 October 1517 is pivotal here—though not because there is any contemporary evidence that on that day Luther marched to the *Schlosskirche* and defiantly nailed his Ninety-five Theses to its door. Rather, it is because, in a letter dated 'the Eve of All Saints Day', Luther wrote respectfully to Albrecht, Archbishop of Mainz, who was also, as Archbishop of Magdeburg, the most senior churchman of the province in which Wittenberg lay. Luther's original letter survives in the royal archives in Sweden. There was at least one other letter, which does not survive, which we know that Luther wrote, probably on the same day or just after, to the bishop of Brandenburg, Jerome Schulz, his immediate ecclesiastical superior.

The forms of Luther's address to Albrecht were appropriate to the disparity of rank between them. He begged forgiveness 'that I, the dregs of humanity, have the temerity even to dare to conceive of a letter to Your Sublime Highness'. Luther also confessed that he had long put off writing, and did so now 'motivated completely by the duty of my loyalty, which I know I owe to you, Reverend Father in Christ'.

Still, the letter did not pull many punches. Luther remorselessly itemized the faults of indulgence preachers, misleading the people 'under your most distinguished name and title': the coin springing in the box, the insult to the honour of the Mother of God, the erroneous teaching 'that through these indulgences a person is freed from every penalty and guilt'. Much of the blame lay with the 'Summary Instruction', which taught that contrition was unnecessary to purchase remission for souls in purgatory, and that the St Peter's indulgence would supply 'that inestimable gift of God by which a human being is reconciled to God and all the penalties of purgatory are blotted out'. Luther was tactful enough to say—and perhaps he really believed—that, though the booklet was published under Albrecht's name, he was sure this was 'without the consent or knowledge of your Reverend Father'. He therefore begged the Archbishop to withdraw the Instruction, and to 'impose upon the preachers of indulgences another form of preaching'.

There was, too, the hint of a threat. If the indulgence preachers were not checked, 'perhaps someone may arise who by publishing pamphlets may refute those preachers and that booklet—to the greatest disgrace of Your Most Illustrious Highness'. Was Luther thinking of himself for such a role? The eventuality was, he protested, 'something that I indeed would strongly hate to have happen', and unless we think we are hearing here the cynical tones of the Mafia-enforcer, we should probably take him at his word.

Along with his letter, Luther supplied Albrecht with a copy of his treatise on indulgences: we know this as Albrecht later forwarded it to the Theology Faculty of the University of Mainz. He also sent the Ninety-five Theses, adding in a postscript—almost, it seems, as an afterthought—that he would be grateful if the Archbishop 'could examine my disputation theses, so that he may understand how dubious a thing this opinion about indulgences is, an opinion that those preachers disseminate with such complete certainty.'[23]

The critical point to consider here is whether, at the time he wrote to Albrecht of Mainz, Luther had already announced the public disputation on indulgences; whether, as it were, he came to his writing-desk hotfoot from the door of the Castle Church. The wording of Luther's postscript gives no clear-cut indication as to whether these were the theses for a disputation already set in motion, or for one envisaged for some future date. As we shall see, there are good reasons for thinking the latter is more likely.

The letter does at least seem to supply a terminal date for the writing of the theses—yet even this is not quite certain. Erwin Iserloh hypothesized that, having composed the letter on 31 October 1517, Luther left it lying on his desk for a few days before sending it off, time he used to draw up in haste his list of theses. This would account for Luther's reference to his theses appearing in the letter as an appendix, below the inscribed date. It also helps to make sense of a curious later reminiscence, recorded by one of the guests at Luther's dining table in February 1538. Luther recalled that on the day after All Saints 1517 he travelled to the nearby village of Kemberg, in the company of his university colleague Hieronymus Schurff. It was on this occasion that Luther announced to his friend that he intended 'to write against the blatant errors on indulgences'. 'What', replied Schurff, 'Do you want to write against the pope?'—adding, presciently, 'they won't put up with it'.[24]

The issue of when precisely the Ninety-five Theses were composed is tied up with the question of the format they were in when Luther sent them to Albrecht of Mainz, either on, or soon after, 31 October 1517. Some scholars suppose that Luther arranged for them to be printed in Wittenberg, and that it was in this form that they were mailed to Albrecht and—supposedly—nailed to the door of the *Schlosskirche.* If this were so, Luther clearly already intended a wide public circulation of his critiques at the time he wrote to the Archbishop, making his deferential protestations that he was content for the moment to leave matters in Albrecht's hands seem more than a little disingenuous.

There was a (single) printer in Wittenberg, Johan Rhau-Grunenberg. He operated out of premises in the basement of the Augustinian monastery, and was well known to Luther. We know that disputation theses in this period sometimes were published, and a printed copy survives (discovered in the early 1980s) of Luther's Ninety-seven Theses against Scholastic Theology, produced by Rhau-Grunenberg. No copy of a Wittenberg printing of the Ninety-five is extant, however, and there is no documentary evidence for its production—though stylistic similarities between the single-sheet broadsheet form in which the Ninety-seven were published, and editions of the Ninety-five printed later in Nuremberg and Basel, have been used to argue that there must have been an original Wittenberg text, on which the others were based.[25]

Perhaps. Yet the possibility of a printed Wittenberg edition of the Ninety-five Theses does not necessarily equate to such an edition being ready at the end of October, or to its being the form in which Luther sent the Theses to Albrecht, and fairly soon afterwards to other correspondents. It has recently been suggested that 'it strains credulity that he should have arranged for the Theses to be copied out laboriously by hand so many times to send them to his various friends.'[26] But the Theses were a relatively short document, and, despite printing presses having been around in Germany for nearly seventy years, Luther lived in a deeply scribal culture. Literate people (monks especially) were quite used to making multiple handwritten copies of important documents.

Disputation

The next fixed and certain date in any attempt to establish a timeline of events is 11 November 1517. On that day Luther sent a copy of the Ninety-five Theses, his new 'paradoxa' as he called them, to an old friend, Johannes Lang, prior of the Augustinian monastery in Erfurt, where Luther himself had once been part of the community. He had previously sent Lang a copy of his Ninety-seven Theses on scholasticism, and it seems to be in reference to these that Luther remarked how 'all men are saying everywhere about me that I am all too rash and proud in passing judgement'. The impression from the letter is that Luther assumed his new theses would be unknown to his Augustinian brethren in Erfurt—unlikely if they had been posted with any panache in Wittenberg twelve days earlier.

Luther requested that Lang and the theologians of the order would tell him honestly what they thought about his conclusions, and 'indicate to me the faults of error, if there are any'. But he was not promising the false modesty of waiting to 'make use of their advice and decision before I will publish'. The verb Luther used here, *edere*, covers a range of modern English meanings: to publish, publicize, give out, put forth. It seems highly improbable that Luther would use the word here in its future tense if he had already arranged for the Theses to be printed, and seems at the very least unlikely if he had already posted them publicly in Wittenberg.[27]

Very probably it was now, in mid-November, that Luther began the process referred to in the heading to the printed editions of the Ninety-five Theses, and started to solicit written submissions by letter from 'those who cannot be present to discuss orally with us'. It would certainly make sense if the Theses were advertised publicly in Wittenberg around the same time.[28] So, conceivably, there may have been a *Thesenanschlag*, on or around 11 November 1517; but if so, no one in the sixteenth century ever made reference to the event.

Luther, it would seem, had waited. He alerted the relevant ecclesiastical authorities to what he saw as a notorious scandal in the preaching of indulgences, and hoped they could be trusted to do something about it. The problem is that he did not wait very long: less than a fortnight after writing to Archbishop Albrecht on 31 October 1517 (assuming the letter was actually posted on that day). Luther certainly wanted and perhaps expected a swift response. Most likely, he sent the treatise and theses to Halle, seat of the Archbishops of Magdeburg, lying little more than a day's ride to the south-west of Wittenberg.

It was here, at the Moritzburg Castle, rather than in his Rhineland archdiocese of Mainz, that Albrecht chose principally to reside. But in early November 1517, and unbeknownst to Luther, Albrecht was hundreds of miles away, at Aschaffenburg in Bavaria. For whatever reason, Luther's packet was not opened until 17 November 1517, by diocesan officials in Calbe, halfway between Halle and Magdeburg. They sent it on to the Archbishop in Bavaria. Albrecht had seen the letter by 1 December 1517, when, perfectly sensibly, he forwarded Luther's materials to the Theology Faculty of the University of Mainz, requesting their opinion. Ten days later, he wrote again, pressing the theologians for an answer, and around the same time Albrecht sent Luther's letter, treatise, and theses to the pope in Rome. The ruling from Mainz arrived on 17 December 1517. It was brief and fairly non-committal, but judged that Luther had diverged from the teaching of the Church in placing restrictions on the pope's power to distribute indulgences. The Mainz theologians seemingly assumed that the theses had already, quite properly, been 'disputed publicly and in scholarly fashion' at Wittenberg.[29]

By the standards of large, bureaucratic organizations, it was not a particularly slow or inadequate response. But Luther did not have the cool head of an administrator, and he was itching to start telling the world what he thought. Nonetheless, in his own mind, he had acted entirely properly, even with commendable restraint. Letters by Luther, written over the course of the succeeding year, do not provide an exact timeline of events, but they at least allow us to reconstruct a sequence of causes and justifications in Luther's own perceptions of the unfolding crisis.

The most important was a letter to the pope himself. Leo X was a cultured scion of the Medici family, who, when he first heard about the indulgence stirs in Germany, was inclined lightly to dismiss them as some 'quarrel among friars'. Luther wrote to him in May 1518, to defend himself from slanderous reports 'that I have endeavoured to threaten the authority and power of the keys and of the Supreme Pontiff'. Luther reiterated his complaints about the iniquities of the indulgence preachers, and described how he found himself 'burning, as I confess, with the zeal of Christ' to confute them. But he knew it was not his place to take a lead. 'For that reason I privately warned a few prelates of the Church'. He elicited a mixed response: 'I was accepted by some and ridiculed by others'. It was only later, when he felt he could do nothing else to check the preachers who were bringing ecclesiastical power into disrepute, that 'I decided to give at least some little evidence against them; that is, to call their teachings into question and debate. So I published a disputation list and invited only the more learned men to see if perhaps some might wish to debate with me.' Luther was, he reminded His Holiness, 'a teacher of theology by your apostolic authority', someone who possessed 'the right to hold disputation in public assembly according to the custom of all universities'.[30]

The impression of an initially very restricted circulation of the Theses is reinforced in a letter of early 1518 to Spalatin, apologizing for not having informed him or the Elector about them sooner: 'I did not want my theses to fall into the hands of our illustrious prince or anyone from his court before those . . . who believe they are branded in them, so they do not come to believe that they were published [again, that ambiguous word] by me either by the orders or favour of the prince against the bishop of Magdeburg.' Luther wrote to

Frederick himself later in the year, expressing dismay at reports that he had acted from the start on the Elector's instructions:

> In actual fact, not even any of my intimate friends was aware of this disputation [i.e. disputation document] except the Most Reverend Lord Archbishop of Magdeburg and Lord Jerome, Bishop of Brandenburg . . . I humbly and reverently warned these men by private letters, before I should publish the disputation, that they should watch over Christ's sheep against these wolves.[31]

All this chimes, more or less, with what Luther wrote to Bishop Jerome Schulz of Brandenburg himself, on 13 February 1518. Luther had not at first wanted to get involved in a controversy over indulgences, but found himself persuaded by the arguments of those who condemned the preachers. Still, 'it seemed the best plan neither to agree nor disagree with either party, but to hold discussion on such an important matter, until the Holy Church might determine what opinion was to be held.' To this end, 'I announced a disputation, inviting and requesting all men publicly, but as you know, all the most learned men privately, to make known their opinion in writing.'

No disputation, however, took place: 'I summoned all into the arena but no one came forward'. The curiousness of this non-happening has not always been sufficiently remarked. If a time and place for a disputation was advertised in the usual way, either on 31 October 1517, or a few weeks later in November, it stretches credulity to believe that literally no one turned up for it.[32] Luther may have meant that on the day only his supporters materialized, and so the event was a damp squib, though this is a strained construction on his words, and such an occurrence could surely have readily been portrayed as a triumph. It is noteworthy that the announcement of the disputation prefixed to the (printed) Theses themselves does not specify any date or venue. The possibility cannot be excluded that, touching as they did on issues of politics and authority, as well as theology, the theses were never actually intended for a 'normal' academic disputation; rather that, in a more free-floating way, Luther was advocating public debate and discussion, either in person or by written exchange of views.[33]

Whatever the truth of this, a clear impression from Luther's letters of 1518 is that at some point he believed he had lost control of the prospects for an orderly 'disputation' of his theses. To Pope Leo in May he confessed that 'it is a mystery to me that fate spread only these my theses beyond the others . . . so that they spread to almost the whole world'. Around the same time, Luther told the Erfurt professor Jodocus Trutfetter that he was 'not pleased with their wide dissemination'. On 5 March 1518, Luther informed a friend in Nuremberg, the humanist Christoph Scheurl, that 'it was not my plan or desire to bring them out among the people, but to exchange views on them with a few men who lived in our neighbourhood'. Luther was in fact apologizing to Scheurl for not having sent him the Theses earlier, in itself an indication of his seriousness about maintaining a tightly restricted circulation. Yet now, 'far beyond my expectation, they are printed so often and distributed that this production is causing me regrets'.[34]

In short, rather than remaining within narrow and self-contained scholarly channels, the Theses had got out and caught the public imagination—or at least the imagination of the humanist-leaning, sophisticated town-dwellers who could read Latin. Whatever the complexity or opacity of the theological issues, the impression that an Italian pope was putting one over on honest Germans struck a chord with grievances and prejudices of long standing. Christoph Scheurl arranged for the printing of the Ninety-five Theses in Nuremberg. He was also instrumental in the production of a German translation, though no copy of this vernacular version survives and it may well have remained in manuscript.

Scheurl himself, in an unpublished chronicle compiled a few years later, recalled that at this time Luther's Theses were 'frequently copied out and sent here and there throughout Germany as the latest news'. He also reported that Luther allowed his Theses to be printed in response to the opposition they generated—statements which are difficult to reconcile with any printing of the Theses in Wittenberg, prior to any supposed posting on 31 October 1517.[35]

In addition to the Nuremberg printing, two more editions of the Ninety-five Theses were produced, in Leipzig and Basel, and it is possible there may have been others, now lost. Purchasers of these editions may indeed have been confused about the number of theses Luther had written. The Nuremberg broadsheet divided them into four batches, renumbering from the start of each section; the Leipzig printing made a series of errors in numbering, and gave the impression there were eighty-seven (see Fig. 1.2). Only the Basel edition, in booklet form, itemized them consecutively through from 1 to 95. In the cities, the Theses passed from hand to hand, and through networks of humanist communication travelled further afield. In March 1518, Erasmus thought it worthwhile to send a copy of 'the conclusions on papal pardons' to his good friend, Thomas More, in faraway England. Years later, Luther recalled with wonderment that his Theses against Tetzel 'went throughout the whole of Germany in a fortnight'. This may well be so, but, contrary to what is often assumed, that feverish fortnight could not have been in the first half of November: it was probably just before, or more likely just after, Christmas of 1517.[36]

Luther's recognition that his Theses were 'obscure' and 'paradoxical'; that he had not set them out 'clearly'; that they were being received everywhere 'not as something for discussion, but as assertions', impelled him to declare himself with greater clarity. In the early spring of 1518, he began work on a set of *Resolutiones*, explanations, of the Ninety-five Theses. At the same time Luther composed a short tract in German, a 'Sermon on Indulgences and Grace', which aimed to set out in simple and comprehensible terms his understanding of penance and the need for repentance. This work, rather than the Ninety-five Theses themselves, was the real bestseller, going through at least twenty-four separate printings between 1518 and 1520. There was no retreat from the position of extreme scepticism about the value or efficacy of papal pardons. Luther declared his desire to be 'that no one buy an indulgence'. Yet he did not deny that indulgences numbered among 'the things that are permitted and allowed', and cautioned that 'one should not hinder someone from buying them'. Luther himself doubted whether they could actually rescue souls from purgatory, but some authorities asserted so, 'and the Church has not yet decided the matter'.[37]

In 1518, then, Luther was still placing himself firmly within the parameters of acceptable Catholic opinion and debate, and he went to some effort to avoid giving the impression he was deliberately escalating a confrontation. He told Scheurl in March that he had not yet published his Resolutions because he was waiting for formal permission from his superior, Jerome Schulz: 'my worthy and gracious Lord

Amore et studio elucidande veritatis: hec subscripta disputabūtur Wittenberge. Presidente R. P. Martino Luther: Artiū et S. Theologie Magistro: eiusdemq ibidem lectore Ordinario. Quare petit: vt qui non possunt verbis presentes nobiscū disceptare: agant id literis absentes. In noie dñi nostri hiesu chri. Amē.

M.D.xvij.

Fig. 1.2. The Ninety-five Theses: a broadsheet printed at Nuremberg.

Bishop of Brandenburg, whose judgment I consulted in this matter, has been very busy and is delaying me a long time'. In the end, episcopal permission was given, and the set of explanations was published in May, with dedications to Johann von Staupitz and to Pope Leo X.[38]

By conventional reckonings, the Reformation was now already well underway, though no one at the time, including Luther himself, can have cast the matter in those terms. How did Luther, in a relatively short period of time, go from respectful address to the pope, even dedicating important works to him, to completely rejecting the pope's authority and naming him as the Antichrist, the principle of evil incarnate? It did not happen in 1517, the year the Reformation is supposed to have begun, nor even in 1518, and it was not inevitable that it would happen at all.

2
1517: Responses

Escalation

It was Luther's opponents who pushed him down a road of radicalization. From the outset they focused on the question of papal authority, with the German Dominicans playing a leading role in fomenting charges against him. In January 1518, at a chapter of the Saxon province of the order in Frankfurt-an-der-Oder—a university disputation which did take place—Tetzel defended 106 Theses attacking the Ninety-five, written for him by the theologian Konrad Koch (Wimpina). In April, Tetzel published a treatise in German attacking as heretical Luther's 'Sermon on Indulgences and Grace', and he defended a further fifty anti-Luther theses at the award of his doctorate the same month. Printed copies of Wimpina's theses had already in March been shipped to Wittenberg, where a group of students seized the consignment, and committed it to the flames in the market square—this minor outrage, carried out by Luther's enthusiastic youthful supporters, was the first book-burning of the Reformation era.

Rome, meanwhile, was proceeding cautiously. In February 1518 Pope Leo wrote to the Vicar General of the Augustinians, asking him to silence the German friar who was spreading 'novelties' among the people, but the Augustinians were given four months to sort the matter out internally. With attacks on Luther looking like a matter of Dominican vindictiveness, the Augustinian authorities did little to rein him in. Luther attended a general chapter of the German Augustinians at Heidelberg in April 1518, but he used the occasion of a disputation there to defend theses denigrating the power of human free will; what he called a 'theology of glory'. In its place, Luther advocated a 'theology of the cross', of utter dependence on God's unmerited grace. The claims advanced in these—today largely forgotten—theses were considerably more profound and radical than anything in the Ninety-five.

In the meantime, the pope delegated the task of examining the Ninety-five Theses for possible heresy to another Dominican, Sylvester Mazzolini of Priero (Prierias). The judgement of Prierias, published in June 1518, was unreservedly hostile: 'whoever says regarding indulgences that the Roman church cannot do what it *de facto* does, is a heretic.' Prierias also bluntly asserted that the authority of the popes was greater than that of scripture. It was a response, a modern Catholic authority has conceded, not 'showing Roman theology at the top of its form'.[1]

The Emperor Maximilian now forced the pace of the process, writing to Leo in August 1518 to accuse Luther of obstinate heresy. In consequence, Luther was summoned to meet with the papal legate Cardinal Cajetan, at the Diet of Augsburg in early October. Cajetan, though a Dominican, was no partisan inquisitor baying for Luther's blood. He refrained from directly accusing him of heresy, and his notes on the interviews expressed some sympathy with Luther's original criticisms of indulgences. But Cajetan detected various errors in Luther's theology and made abundantly clear to Luther there was nothing for him to do but recant them. Fearing that a safe-conduct arranged by Elector Frederick might be rescinded, Luther secretly left Augsburg—disillusioned, angry, and unrepentant. Before doing so, he arranged for his appeal to Pope Leo against Cajetan's ruling to be posted to the door of Augsburg Cathedral. In Rome, in November, Leo issued a bull confirming that indulgences drew upon the Treasury of Merits.[2]

In January 1519, Germany witnessed an event of infinitely greater significance than the stubborn insubordination of a Saxon friar. The death of Maximilian I created a vacancy for the Holy Roman Emperor. The pope was not alone in hoping that Maximilian's successor would not turn out to be his grandson, Charles of Habsburg, already quite mighty enough as ruler of the Netherlands and King of Spain. In the event, the Electors did choose Charles, his largesse towards them lubricated by huge loans from the Fugger Bank. But for several critical months, the official process against Luther stalled, while both he and his German critics continued to publish and preach.

The most formidable of those critics was a theologian at the University of Ingolstadt, Johann Eck, whose attack on the Ninety-five

Theses provoked Karlstadt to compose and publish an impressive 406 theses in their defence. The sequel was a public disputation at Leipzig in June–July 1519, at which Eck rather got the better of both Karlstadt and Luther. After Augsburg, Luther had appealed against the pope to a General Council of the Church—a familiar if provocative gambit in the theological politics of the later middle ages. But at Leipzig, Eck manoeuvred Luther into conceding that General Councils as well as popes could err. The point at issue was the treatment of the fifteenth-century Bohemian reformer, Jan Hus, condemned to death by the Council of Constance in 1415. Luther was pressed into declaring agreement with Hus's teaching that communion should be given to the laity in two kinds, wine as well as bread. It was a seminal moment: if popes and councils were fallible, then only scripture remained as the source of trustworthy authority for the Christian.[3]

Precarious bridges between Luther and the institutional Church were burned in 1520, for all that in a portrait by Cranach of that year he still looks every inch the traditional Catholic friar (see Fig. 2.1). Luther published three pamphlets which made the critiques of papal authority and traditional doctrine found in the Ninety-five Theses seem mild and inconsequential. One called for the German nobility to step forward and reform the Church, denying there was any difference between priests and laypeople but that of function and office. Another reduced the number of sacraments from seven to three, claiming the others were simply invented by the church of the pope. The third, 'Concerning Christian Liberty', disallowed any value to good works and placed unambiguously before the public Luther's hard-thought-out doctrine of justification by faith alone.

While Luther was producing these revolutionary manifestos, Rome had come to its definitive judgement. Pope Leo's bull of June 1520, *Exsurge Domine* ('Arise, O Lord') promulgated a list of Luther's errors and threatened him with excommunication if he did not recant. Luther's response was literally inflammatory. On 20 December 1520, outside Wittenberg's Elster Gate, Luther threw the bull onto a bonfire, along with copies of the decretals (cumulative body of papal rulings) and the canon law which regulated the life of the medieval Church. A large body of students had been summoned by an announcement of the impending event, which Melanchthon placed on the door of Wittenberg's parish church. The burning of the instruments of the

Fig. 2.1. The friar Martin Luther: a 1520 portrait by Lucas Cranach.

pope's authority was a moment of symbolic rupture. Luther wrote shortly afterwards to Staupitz to say that he had undertaken the act 'at first with trembling and praying; but now I am more pleased with this than with any other action of my life'. He shortly afterwards published a defiant 'Assertion of All the Articles Condemned by the Last Bull of Antichrist'. Not surprisingly, in January 1521, the pope confirmed Luther's excommunication.[4]

The next act in an increasingly intense drama was directed by the new emperor. Charles V was firm in the faith of his fathers, and unsympathetic towards Luther's calls for a complete overhaul of the Christian life. But he was responsive to the Elector Frederick's plea that Luther should not be condemned without a hearing, and was willing to offer him a guarantee of safe conduct to attend the imperial diet at Worms. Luther arrived there in April 1521, and was called upon to disown a list of works he had written or edited. In front of the emperor and the assembled notables of Germany, Luther declined to do so. His Latin speech, according to the official record, concluded with a ringing statement:

> Unless I am convinced by the testimony of scripture or plain reason (for I believe neither in pope nor councils alone, since it is agreed that they have often erred and contradicted themselves), I am bound by the scriptures I have quoted, and my conscience is captive to the Word of God. I neither can nor will revoke anything, for it is neither safe nor honest to act against one's conscience.

Soon afterwards, accounts printed by Luther's supporters in Wittenberg, and possibly drawing on his own testimony, added to the speech several further phrases in German: 'I can do no other, here I stand, God help me. Amen.' It is possible that Luther never said these famous words, though the contemporary evidence for his doing so is considerably stronger than for his posting of the Theses. Either way, the words he used, and the imposing context in which he said them, were impressive and memorable.[5]

The consequence was an imperial condemnation, the Edict of Worms, drafted by the papal legate at the diet, Girolamo Aleander. It castigated Luther as 'a demon in the appearance of a man', demanded Luther's capture and deliverance, and declared forfeit the property of anyone supporting him. Yet those supporters, whose numbers were swelling across Germany, included the Elector Frederick, whose agents arranged the 'kidnapping' of Luther on his way back from the diet, and his safe bestowal in the Elector's hill-top castle of the Wartburg. Here, Luther employed his enforced leisure time writing sermons and translating the New Testament into clear and idiomatic German.[6]

Luther returned to Wittenberg in 1522. After Frederick—despite everything, a deep-dyed conservative in religion—was succeeded by his brother John 'the Constant' in 1525, Luther began to oversee the creation of a new territorial Church in Saxony, now decisively separated from the Church in communion with Rome. Other towns and territories followed the same path, and the religious landscape of Germany fractured.

Without planning or intending it, the once obscure Augustinian friar had become the prophet and pattern of profoundly new ways of being Christian. 'Lutheran', the derisive label attached to his supporters by Catholic opponents, would in time become a potent badge of pride and identity. Luther continued to write and to preach, and to lead by practical example. His marriage in 1525 to the ex-nun Katharina von Bora was intended to signal that there was no fundamental distinction between layperson and priest, and that the 'good work' of celibacy was in no way superior to the raising of a family and enjoyment of sexual relations. For many of his followers, as for Luther himself, his insistence on the Christian's total dependence on God's redeeming grace, and that all human actions were intrinsically sinful, was a paradoxically liberating message.

At the same time, Luther strongly upheld the claims of political authority, and condemned in vehement terms the German peasants who rose in rebellion against oppressive landlords in 1524–5, claiming 'the gospel' as their justification for doing so. Revolutions in the understanding of salvation, and dramatic restrictions on the social and political power of the clergy, were not to be accompanied by any overturning of the hierarchical order of society. It was on these terms that the new evangelical faith sold itself to numerous German princes, and to the rulers of the Scandinavian kingdoms.

Through to his death in 1546, Luther was read, regarded, and revered. His Bible translation, catechisms, liturgy, and hymns were the meat and marrow of a new corpus of German religious culture.

Even so, from an early date Luther ceased to be the 'leader' of the anti-papal movement in any practical sense. Other reformers, with theological agendas sometimes diverging dramatically from Luther's own, took the initiative in shaking off the shackles of Rome, across Germany and beyond. The influential leader of reform in the Swiss city of Zürich, Ulrich Zwingli, later insisted that 'I began to preach the gospel of Christ in 1516, long before anyone in our region had ever heard of Luther.' Yet this in itself was an acknowledgement of Luther's widely recognized place of primacy. He was seen, by both admirers and detractors, as the founding father of something which was not yet routinely called 'the Reformation', but which was already regarded as the opening of a new chapter in the story of the Church, and of God's revelation of himself through history and time.[7]

Recollections

How, then, did the posting of the Ninety-five Theses to the door of the Castle Church in Wittenberg come to seem the initiating and defining moment in this ever-evolving process? It is more than a little curious. There were, in Luther's activity of these years, numerous pronouncements of considerably more theological weight and novelty than the Theses, as well as several episodes of quite evidently greater drama and resonance than their posting: the confrontation with Cajetan in Augsburg, the disputation at Leipzig, the burning of the pope's bull, the appearance before the emperor at Worms. There is also the further, and far from trifling, consideration that these were all episodes which we know to have really taken place.

As we have seen, there is no strictly contemporary evidence that the Theses were ever posted to the door of the Castle Church. Luther himself, in repeated insistences that he raised the matter privately with the responsible bishops, and only 'went public' in consequence of their failure to act, is the strongest witness against the likelihood of any posting on 31 October 1517, the day he wrote to Archbishop Albrecht. It is possible the Theses were fixed to the church door later, in mid- or late November. But if so, Luther never mentioned it: in reams of correspondence, in voluminous theological and pastoral writings, or in the anecdotes and reminiscences recorded by eager students and acolytes.

Some years later, in 1538, a renegade Wittenberg student called Simon Lemnius produced a volume of satirical Latin verses lampooning local dignitaries, which he dedicated, with brazen tactlessness, to Archbishop Albrecht of Mainz. Copies of the work were discovered being sold outside the entrance to the Castle Church, provoking a pulpit tirade from Luther against the dishonour brought on the town and university, and against a book-dedication which 'made a saint of the devil'. But there was no suggestion that a site of particular significance in the campaign against Albrecht and indulgences had been in this way profaned.[8] If a Theses-posting at the Castle Church happened at all, it cannot have seemed to Luther an occasion worthy of recollection and notice.

Such an omission was not because Martin Luther lived solely in the moment, uninterested in the twists and turns of his life, or the providential pathways that led him to defy the pope, and become the figurehead for a rediscovery—as he saw it—of the pristine Gospel of Christ. On the contrary, the later Luther spoke and wrote avidly, if sporadically, about the course of his earlier career, and reflected deeply on the significance of his past actions. Luther was intensely concerned with the origins of the movement he had summoned into being, and quite capable of waxing nostalgic about places of personal significance. In 1532, for example, he expressed concern that repair work on Wittenberg's town defences might end up destroying the study where 'indeed I stormed the papacy'.[9] Luther himself, in fact, was the earliest historian of the Reformation. And in his mind, without any doubt, the date 31 October 1517 was lacquered with profound significance.

The clearest indication of this is a letter Luther wrote on 1 November 1527 to Nicholas von Amsdorf, one of his earliest disciples and oldest friends, by then pastor of the reformed church at Magdeburg. Luther informed Amsdorf that he and another old comrade, Justus Jonas, were drinking a memorial toast together at Wittenberg, 'on the day of All Saints, in the tenth year after the indulgences had been trampled underfoot'. At that time, the vigil of a major feast was considered part of the day itself, so it is likely that Luther was here thinking of the letters he wrote, and probably despatched, along with the Theses, to the bishops on 31 October 1517. Another possibility, and a perhaps more plausible one, is that the Ninety-five Theses were themselves completed on that day.[10]

Luther's later reminiscences could occasionally be fuzzy. In the 'Table Talk', the collections of notes taken by guests and students generously and loquaciously entertained in the Luther family home in Wittenberg, a couple of witnesses report Luther as declaring 1516 to be the year 'I began to write against the papacy'. But in the company of others he correctly identified 1517 as the time 'I began to write against Tetzel concerning penance'. The pastor Conrad Cordatus, in Wittenberg between jobs in 1531–2, was quite specific in remembering Luther saying that 'in the year 1517, on the Feast of All Saints, I began for the first time to write against the pope and indulgences'.

Luther's recollections of this beginning were not without strain and ambivalence. On the one hand, he was in later years painfully aware of the shortcomings of the Ninety-five Theses, almost at times disowning them. In the 1538 preface to a reissued edition, Luther claimed he was only allowing their republication 'lest the magnitude of the controversy and the success God has given me in it puff me up with pride.' The Theses, in fact, were a work in which his 'weakness and ignorance' was openly on show, for 'in many important articles I was not only prepared to yield to the pope, but beyond that I even honoured him'.[11]

This, of course, was no less than the truth. And in the Table Talk Luther is recorded at various times admitting that 'I did not yet see the great abomination of the pope but only the crass abuses'; that the Theses were originally composed not 'to attack the pope, but to oppose the blasphemous statements of the noisy declaimers' (i.e. indulgence preachers). In his fullest fragment of autobiographical writing, the 1545 preface to the first volume of the Wittenberg edition of his Latin writings, Luther begged readers to 'be mindful of the fact that I was once a monk and a most enthusiastic papist when I began that cause.' There was a great deal in his earlier writings, including the Theses, 'which I later and now hold and execrate as the worst blasphemies and abomination'. Luther freely admitted that he had expected the pope to be his protector and supporter when the excesses of the indulgence preachers were first called to his attention.[12]

Yet it was to the dispute over penance in 1517—more so than to the momentous disputation at Leipzig in 1519, the burning of the papal bull in Wittenberg in 1520, or the defiant stand at Worms in 1521—that Luther assigned foundational significance, even though by his own account he did not come to fully understand and hold the key doctrine of justification by faith alone until sometime in 1519. The indulgence controversy was indeed the moment when Martin Luther 'began to write against the papacy'.

Nor was Luther entirely apologetic about the style and content of the Theses themselves. He exhorted the clergy assembled at the Diet of Augsburg in 1530 to reflect that 'if our gospel had accomplished nothing else than to redeem consciences from the shameful outrage and idolatry of indulgences, one would still have to acknowledge that it was God's Word and power'. In 1545, Luther put it more vividly. The Ninety-five Theses, his subsequent explanation of them, and the vernacular sermon on indulgences: all these were works 'demolishing heaven and consuming the earth with fire'—or so it seemed to his opponents.[13]

Luther himself then was the chief originator of the tradition that the Reformation 'began' in 1517, and that it should moreover be linked to a precise date: the Vigil and Feast of All Saints. This, let us note, was an interpretation and a retrospective autobiographical claim, not a simple historical 'fact'. But from an early date it was a perception widely shared in the circles of Luther's supporters. It is true there is no mention of the Ninety-five Theses in the surviving version of the 'Annals of the Reformation', compiled before his death in 1545 by Luther's close ally, Georg Spalatin. The account begins with Luther's summons to face Cajetan's heresy charges at the imperial diet at Augsburg in 1518—a scene never quite fulfilling its potential for iconic status. But this was likely due to the fact that, as the manuscript's early eighteenth-century editor remarked, 'through the long passage of time both beginning and ending have been completely lost'. Other chroniclers of the first generation did emphasize the significance of the indulgence controversy, even if some, like Nicholas von Amsdorf and Johan Aurifaber, conceded that Luther still displayed 'papistic' tendencies when he composed the Theses, and had further to go in understanding the gospel.[14]

The idea that the year 1517 was a crucial turning-point in the history of Christianity, a moment of prophetic witness, and the making of a new start, became at an early date something of an article of faith among Luther's disciples and supporters. Johann Agricola was a Wittenberg scholar who was at Luther's side during the Leipzig Disputation of

1519, and for the burning of the pope's bull the following year. He wrote, in a biblical commentary of 1530, that true doctrine, persecuted and blasphemed against by popes, was 'in the year of Our Lord 1517, by the grace of God, at first reborn, by the advocacy of Martin Luther'.

This perception was encouraged by the growing popularity of printed almanacs and chronologies. Johan Carion, court astrologer to the Elector of Brandenburg, compiled an ambitious chronicle of world history, published at Wittenberg in 1532. Carion was an old school-friend of Melanchthon, who took a close interest in the progress of the work. It proved immensely popular in Lutheran Germany, going through fifteen editions by 1564. Carion's final entry for the reign of the Emperor Maximilian I was a terse but emphatic note that in 1517 'Martin Luther first wrote against indulgences, after which many disputes arose. And out of that a great divide has grown in Germany.'[15]

A more detailed and florid account of the origins of that great divide appeared in the *Historia Reformationis* of Friedrich Myconius, an early supporter of Luther and pastor in the city of Gotha, a work composed in 1541–2, though remaining in manuscript until the early eighteenth century. Like all other commentators before the mid-1540s, Myconius knew nothing of any theses-posting on the door of the Castle Church. But he had a strong sense for the dramatic setting, and saw in Martin Luther a man who was literally heaven-sent. Myconius asked his readers to visualize the humble chapel where Luther preached in the precincts of the monastery in Wittenberg: it looked 'just the way painters portray the stall in Bethlehem, where Christ was born.' It was in this poor, wretched place that in these late days God had allowed 'his dear holy gospel, and the dear child Jesus, to be born anew'.

After some preambles on the corruptions of the papacy, Myconius began his story properly in 1517, with the indulgence controversy. His account largely followed that of Luther himself, though Myconius added the intriguing detail that, before drawing up the Ninety-five Theses, Luther wrote with his concerns about indulgence preaching to four bishops—of Frankfurt, Meissen, Mersburg, and Zeitz—as well as to the Archbishop of Mainz. It was only when he saw the bishops didn't want to do anything about it that Luther composed the Theses, and allowed them to be printed, though his intention at this stage was only for a debate about indulgences among 'the learned of Wittenberg'. To Luther's own recollection that, within two weeks, the Theses had gone through all of Germany, Myconius added an arresting sequel: within four weeks they had spread across the whole of Christendom, 'as if the angels themselves were the message-runners'.[16]

There was no suggestion of angelic assistance in another account of the Reformation and its origins composed at around the same time. This was a biography of Luther which began by reporting how many people believed 'he enjoyed an occult familiarity with some demon'. The author was Johannes Cochlaeus, canon of Breslau Cathedral, and sometime chaplain at the court of Duke George of Saxony, cousin and rival to the Elector Frederick. Cochlaeus was an educated man, a humanist, and personally acquainted with Luther. But from an early stage he revealed himself as one of the reformer's most relentless and effective denigrators. By the time his *Commentaria de actis et scriptis Martini Lutheri* (Commentary on the deeds and writings of Martin Luther) was published in 1549, Cochlaeus was already an old hand at anti-Luther polemic. His biography of Luther was a work of considerable research and erudition, as well as copious quantities of vitriol. It was written primarily to disabuse deluded fellow-Germans: 'the majority of people living today think, by the crudest of errors, that Luther was a good man and his gospel was a holy one'.[17]

As a humanist attuned to the importance of verifiable sources, Cochlaeus quoted in detail from the letter Luther wrote to Archbishop Albrecht, 'from Wittenberg, on the Eve of All Saints, in the year of our Lord 1517'. But Luther was not genuinely moved by concerns about abuses in the preaching of indulgences; instead, he was motivated by 'envy' and the arrogant desire to display his intellect which was already characteristic of his career as a monk. The indulgence controversy was simply an occasion, rather than the cause, for a long-brewing rebellion against the Church. Like other Catholic critics of Luther in the first half of the sixteenth century drawing attention to the attack on indulgences—Johann Eck, Kilian Leib, Hieronymus Emser—Cochlaeus did not mention any posting of the Ninety-five Theses to the church door in Wittenberg as the symbolic form this rebellion took. Nonetheless, Luther, in Cochlaeus's telling of events, was not content to send his letters privately to the Archbishop, 'but also he publicly announced ninety-five theses'. Cochlaeus added—perhaps to make Luther seem still more unstable and inconsistent—that 'in the first draft he had written ninety-seven'.[18]

Melanchthon

Melanchthon's 1546 short *Life of Luther* was composed around the same time as Cochlaeus's much longer biography. It might have been describing an entirely different man. Melanchthon laid equal emphasis on the events of 1517, but placed an entirely contrasting construction on their meaning. Before that date, Luther was a faithful and conscientious monk, though one positively influenced by the classical studies of Erasmus, and already teaching a sincere doctrine of faith and penitence 'not found in Thomas, Scotus, and others like them' (the scholastic theologians Thomas Aquinas and Duns Scotus). It was the 'shameless', 'impious', and 'execrable' teachings of Tetzel, bursting onto the scene in 1517, that virtually forced him into taking a public stand. Luther, in this sequence of events, was the pure and proximate instrument of God, in no respect driven by his own desires or ambitions. It was thus no ostentatious or vainglorious act on Luther's part, when, having written ninety-five theses against the delinquencies of Tetzel, he 'publicly attached these to the church attached to Wittenberg Castle, on the day before the feast of All Saints, 1517.'[19]

Any competent historian needs to pause, and take a very deep breath, before dismissing outright this testimony for the authenticity of what came to be seen as the seminal public event of Luther's career as a reformer—even despite its relatively late arrival on the documentary scene. Melanchthon could not have witnessed any such posting in 1517, but he arrived in Wittenberg in August of the following year and began a close collaboration with Martin Luther that would last for almost three decades. The simplest explanation is surely that Luther informed Melanchthon he had undertaken this action on 31 October 1517, and that Melanchthon remembered the incident and included it in his biography.

Luther's younger friend was, moreover, no slapdash or deceitful chronicler of events. At the beginning of his biography he put on record how he had 'several times' asked Luther's mother Margarita about the date and circumstances of her son's birth.[20] It is unlikely that Melanchthon deliberately fabricated a story about the posting of the Theses which he knew to be untrue. Melanchthon almost certainly believed, or had come to believe, that such an episode took place. It is worth noting that there is no record of anybody who was in Wittenberg in 1517, and still alive in 1546, coming forward to contradict Melanchthon's memory of events—though it is a little hard to imagine what form such a public contradiction of Wittenberg's leading reformer might have taken.

What is certain is that if Luther himself did not consider the episode worthy of public report, neither, prior to 1546, did Philip Melanchthon. In a letter of 1519, Melanchthon made reference to Luther proposing a disputation about indulgences, but said nothing about church doors. A couple of years later, in a work defending Luther against the Italian Dominican Thomas Rhadinus of Piacenza, he spoke simply of how Luther 'modestly', and 'acting like a good shepherd', proposed difficult questions (paradoxa) about indulgences, 'according to the custom of scholars'.[21]

But what actually was 'the custom of scholars'? The mystery of the *Thesenanschlag* is perhaps resolved, perhaps deepened, by a separate and independent note concerning the posting of the Theses, one which in all likelihood predates Melanchthon's by a couple of years. Its author was Georg Rörer, a close collaborator of Luther, and the editor of several of Luther's works. Rörer first arrived in Wittenberg in 1522, and so, like Melanchthon, could not have been an eyewitness of any posting in 1517. Yet he had both a personal and professional interest in Luther's journey of faith and witness. Rörer was particularly involved, as proofreader and copyist, in the efforts leading to the publication in 1546 of a revised version of Luther's German translation of the Bible.

It was most likely in the course of this editorial work, coming to an end in 1544, that Rörer inscribed a sentence in Latin into a 1540 copy of the New Testament, used by the editors as a base-text for revisions. In 1972, the note was printed, in a supplement to Volume 48 of the vast Weimar Edition of Luther's works, but, remarkably, for thirty-four years no one really noticed. Then, in 2006, Martin Treu, exhibitions director of the Luther Memorials Foundation in Saxony-Anhalt, rediscovered the inscription in the original Bible in the University and State Library in Jena. It reads: 'On the eve of the Feast of All Saints, in the year of Our Lord 1517, theses about indulgences were posted on the doors of the Wittenberg churches by Dr Martin Luther.'[22]

It looks like a decisive endorsement of Melanchthon's account, confirmation of both the fact and the traditional dating of the *Thesenanschlag*. Yet one discrepancy immediately jumps out. Rörer has the Theses appearing on the doors—plural—of the Wittenberg churches, which must at least mean they were posted on the door of the parish church of St Mary's, as well as on that of the Castle Church. Is it likely, then, that there was no single posting of the Theses, but a general publicizing around the ecclesiastical sites of the city?

One distinct possibility is that this is what Rörer thought had happened because he knew it was what ought to have happened. In the statutes of the University of Wittenberg, drawn up in 1508, approved procedures are laid down for the initiation of academic debates. It was the responsibility of the deans of both the arts and theological faculties to ensure that theses for university disputations were publicized on the doors of the churches in the course of the preceding week. The actual job of posting was assigned to the beadles, university officials whose duties included administrative record-taking, maintenance of discipline among students, and upkeep of the buildings.

Rörer's choice of the somewhat arcane term *valvis* for a door, rather than the more common *porta*, *ostium*, or *foris*, may well indicate a direct dependence on the university statutes, which also used this word. In addition, his reliance on the passive construction 'were posted by' (*propositae sunt*) certainly allows of the interpretation 'were caused to be posted by', rather than requiring an immediate personal agency on the part of Luther. It would indeed have been unusual, a breach of procedure and etiquette, for a senior professor to have gone around nailing up his own theses.

Here it is also worth pausing to note that the idea of 'nailing', commonly used in modern scholars' English renditions of the Latin verbs *affigere* and *proponere*, may be a misleading translation. Neither the Wittenberg statutes nor the notifications of Melanchthon and Rörer make any mention of hammer and nails, whose habitual use would surely have done considerable damage to any wooden door functioning day-to-day as a university 'bulletin-board'. As the historian Daniel Jütte has established, there is considerable evidence that sixteenth-century people more commonly used glue or wax when pasting up placards and notices in public places.[23]

None of this rules out the possibility that Rörer was accurately reporting a posting of theses which took place prior to a failed disputation in Wittenberg, or that Luther personally undertook the task of fixing placards to the doors of All Saints and St Mary's. Yet had he done so, it would have been an unusual, and presumably noteworthy, gesture of personal challenge, which leaves us with the unresolved problem of why neither Luther nor anyone else made mention of it prior to the 1540s.

What is more, Rörer later changed his story. In a set of manuscript notes surviving among the papers of his estate, Rörer wrote that 'in the year 1517 after the birth of Christ, on the eve of the Feast of All Saints, Martin Luther, Doctor of Theology, issued theses against corrupt indulgences, affixed to the doors of the church which is next to the castle of Wittenberg.' As the Reformation historian Volker Leppin and others have noted, the wording here is very similar to that used by Melanchthon in 1546, and is in all likelihood directly dependent upon Melanchthon's account. If Rörer was now deferring to Melanchthon's supposedly greater knowledge of the case, it strengthens the possibility that his earlier comment, with its assertion of multiple postings, was simply based on an assumption about conventional university procedure.[24]

Another, undated, historical notice in Latin does not take us much further forward, and does not directly mention the church doors, though it deserves consideration due to the fact its author was in every likelihood Luther's disciple Johannes Agricola (c. 1492–1566), a student in Wittenberg from 1516 onwards. The note records how 'in the year 1517 Luther put forward in Wittenberg, a town on the Elbe, certain theses for disputation, according to the old custom of scholars', adding that 'his intention was not to abuse or injure anyone'. Agricola wrote that this was something to which he could attest—*me teste*—leading some scholars to suppose that here, at last, was the elusive eye-witness testimony to the posting of the Theses. But others who have examined the manuscript believe this to be a mistranscription: what Agricola actually wrote was *modeste*, modestly, indicating the manner in which Luther put forward the Theses. Even if *me teste* is correct, its placing in the sentence seems to refer to Luther's motives rather than to his action: his not intending, 'as I can testify'; rather than his putting forward, 'as I witnessed'.[25]

By the middle of the sixteenth century, a belief does seem to have been growing in Wittenberg circles that Luther posted the Theses on 31 October 1517, and that this had been a genuinely notable event, an occasion for reflection and commemoration. It is significant that Rörer's handwritten note in the 1540 Bible was inserted into a listing of *pericopes*, the portions of scripture to be read during services on Sundays and feast days. It appears after the entry for Saints Simon and Jude (28 October).[26] Paul Eber, a close friend of Melanchthon's, Professor of Latin at Wittenberg, and later preacher at the Castle Church and pastor of St Mary's, published in 1550 a calendar of noteworthy historical events, saints' days and biblical passages, arranged by days of the month. The segment for 31 October contained only one entry, printed in the red ink traditionally reserved in liturgical books for important feasts and celebrations: 'this day the disputation of Doctor Martin Luther against indulgences was publicly proposed, and fixed to the doors of the church by Wittenberg Castle'. It was, quite literally, a red letter day for Lutherans.

Eber went on to declare how, starting with the contest against the mendacities and corruptions of Tetzel, divine teaching concerning penance and remission of sins was gradually restored to the Church, 'with many other necessary things and articles of doctrine'. He added that this happened a century after the burning of the Czech reformer Jan Hus by the Council of Constance (in 1415), and that Hus had said to the bishops who condemned him, 'after a hundred years, you will have to answer to God and to me'.

The prophetic association with Hus was crucial in helping to anchor the 'start' of the Reformation in 1517. It was an association Luther himself embraced wholeheartedly in his lifetime. Luther's opponent, Eck, thought he scored a tactical success at the Leipzig disputation of 1519 by associating Luther's teaching with that of the notorious Bohemian heretic. Yet months later Luther was telling friends 'we are all Hussites without knowing it'. In a letter sent from Constance in November 1414, Hus (whose name means goose in Czech) referred disparagingly to himself as a tame bird not capable of great deeds. But he promised that other birds—sharp-sighted falcons and eagles—would follow to tear at the devil and gather and protect the true people of God. His fellow Czech reformer, and fellow martyr, Jerome of Prague, wanted to know what people would make of his own condemnation in a hundred years' time. Hus's letter was first printed in 1558. But reports of it must have been circulating orally or in manuscript, for by 1531 Luther had conflated the two utterances and decided that the 'prophecy' referred unambiguously to himself. He recounted Hus's supposed words as 'now they will roast this goose (for Hus means goose), but one hundred years hence they will hear the song of a swan which they shall have to tolerate.' In this form—the burning of a goose and the appearance of an incombustible swan—the prophecy became a fixed part of an emerging repertoire of pious reminiscences about Luther; it was repeated in funeral sermons for him in 1546 by his close associates Justas Jonas and Johannes Bugenhagen.[27]

In a very real sense, the *Thesenanschlag* was Luther's own swan song—a defining moment of his career that became talked about only around the time of his death. In October 1553, the theologian Georg Major, superintendent in Luther's hometown of Eisleben, and a former professor at Wittenberg, preached a funeral sermon for Prince Georg of Anhalt-Dessau, which he shortly thereafter published with a dedicatory epistle to Georg's brother, Joachim. The text was dated 'at Wittenberg, on the Vigil of All Saints, on which day, thirty-six years ago, the honourable and learned Dr Martin Luther, of blessed memory, at the Castle Church of All Saints in Wittenberg, while a great dross of indulgences (*Ablasskram*) was taking place there on All Saints, posted the theses against the indulgence-dross of Tetzel and others'. This, Major added, was 'the first step towards the cleansing of Christian teaching, for which let there be praise, honour and thanks to God'.

Major was an editor of the Wittenberg edition of Luther's German Works, itself an important early development in the 'memorialization' of the great reformer. He was responsible for the volume, appearing in 1557, which contained a translation of the Ninety-five Theses. Here Major added a marginal annotation: 'These theses were posted to the door of the Castle Church in Wittenberg, on All Saints' Eve, 1517.'

Major's account marks the beginnings of a more emphatic memorialization of 31 October 1517, one which wedded Melanchthon's attestation of a theses-posting to Luther's own conviction (expressed in 1541) that the quarrel with Tetzel was 'the first, real, fundamental beginning of the Lutheran tumult'. It acquires further piquancy from the fact that Major came as a schoolboy to Wittenberg in 1511, and sang in the choir of the *Schlosskirche* before being admitted to full academic study in the university in 1521. Very possibly, he remembered the *Ablasskram*, the ritual and fanfare around indulgences, which accompanied the annual display of the Elector's relics in the Castle Church each 1 November.[28] Yet Major does not actually say he was an eyewitness to Luther's posting of the Theses, and it would be rash to surmise that he was. Crucially, he did not mention the event in letters, or in several published works, prior to Melanchthon's notice appearing in the second volume of Luther's Collected Latin Works, from which Major, like Rörer, was very probably taking his cue.

Melanchthon himself quite regularly mentioned the posting of the Theses in letters written on the eve of All Saints, though only in the years after 1546. One such letter, sent in 1552 to Sebastian Glaser, Chancellor to the court of Henneberg in Thuringia, was dated 31 October, 'when Luther first, thirty-five years ago, put forth his theses on indulgences'. An accompanying letter to the Counts of Henneberg, Georg Ernst and his father Wilhelm, was written on the evening when Luther's Theses were first 'angeschlagen'. Melanchthon did not invariably invoke Luther's action in letters from the 1550s written on 31 October. But when he did, his recollections of the occasion were increasingly thoughtful and reflective.

In September 1556 Melanchthon composed a short manuscript history of the city of Wittenberg, to be sealed in a 'time-capsule' and placed in one of the newly restored towers of the city church (from which it was retrieved in 1910). Here, Melanchthon recorded that in 1517 the venerable Doctor of Theology, Martin Luther, announced (*edidit*) theses 'which were both piously and academically formulated'. They dealt with true repentance and the faith through which a person is justified, as well as refuting the deceit of indulgences. Linking the Theses-posting to the declaration of the Augsburg Confession (and thus linking himself to the legacy of Luther), Melanchthon wrote that 'it was from that time on that the abolition of superstitious abuses and the restoration of the pure teachings of the Gospel began, to which the Confession of Faith of the Saxon Congregation attests'. Melanchthon went on prophetically to say that 'books about this will be passed on to future generations'.[29]

A year earlier, Melanchthon had written to Paul Eber on the anniversary of 'the day when Luther first issued his theses which exposed the impostures of indulgences', and prayed that 'God would always unify the Church in our communities and in this region.' Signing off the same day to the Berlin pastor Georg Buchholzer, Melanchthon mused on the great examples of wrath and mercy they had seen in the space of the thirty-eight years since Luther posted those Theses which 'renewed the doctrine of penance'.[30]

Wrath and mercy indeed. In the nearly ten years since Luther's death in 1546, his German followers had crested successive waves of crisis and danger. Only a few months after the great man's passing, the long-simmering tension between the Catholic Emperor Charles and the Lutheran princes, bound together for protection in the military and political League of Schmalkalden, burst out into open warfare. The result was disastrous for the Lutherans. Charles shattered the Schmalkaldic army at Mühlberg, between Leipzig and Dresden, on 24 April 1547. Melanchthon's prince, the Elector John Frederick, nephew of Frederick the Wise, was taken prisoner, and stripped of both his territory and his electoral title. Imperial troops occupied Wittenberg, and stood in the *Schlosskirche* to gloat over the newly erected tomb of Luther. Charles, however, refused requests for it to be destroyed: 'I do not make war on dead men.'

What Charles would do, however, was impose a punitive settlement on the defeated Lutherans. The Augsburg 'Interim' of 1548 restored aspects of Catholic doctrine and practice to the evangelical territories. It was widely resisted, but Melanchthon believed it was possible to compromise without sacrificing core principles, and he worked on the creation of a Leipzig Interim for the Saxon regions, which made concessions in various areas of ceremony and ritual.

The result was a baleful schism within the schism. A movement of pastors who came to be known as Gnesio-Lutherans (original or pure Lutherans) accused Melanchthon and the 'Philippists' of betraying Luther's legacy. They also suspected Melanchthon of moving away from Luther's firm insistence on the real and literal presence of Christ in the bread and wine of the eucharist to adopt a position closer to that of the Genevan reformer, John Calvin. Gnesio-Lutherans became established at Jena and Magdeburg, while Philippists remained ensconced at Wittenberg.

The divisions were not healed when a renewed tide of war turned against Charles V after 1552. In 1555, unable to impose his will, Charles agreed to the comprehensive 'Peace of Augsburg' as a replacement for the Interims. It laid down a famous principle: *cuius regio, eius religio* ('your prince, his religion'). The individual rulers of the various German territories would decide whether Catholicism or Lutheranism was to be the sole and official faith in their territories. The Lutheran cause—at first a movement of protest and demands for reform within the Church—was now very firmly an establishment, a separate Church in its own right. But it became so amidst deep and bitter internal tensions. Small wonder if Melanchthon was petitioning God for a spirit of unity, or showing an ever greater concern over custodianship of the contested legacy of Luther's life and actions.

The posting of the Ninety-five Theses, so Melanchthon wrote to Elector August of Saxony on 31 October 1558, was 'the beginning of the declaration of Christian teaching.' 'The start of the amendment of doctrine', he called it in a sermon delivered the following day, forty-one years after the Theses were posted and printed and 'the struggles of the Church began'. In this address, Melanchthon added some further texture and detail to his earlier accounts of the event. The church where the Theses were posted was dedicated to All Saints, and there was at that time 'great impostures of indulgences' taking place there. Presumably people took notice of what was beginning to sound like a disruptive and rebellious act. The affixing of the Theses, Melanchthon now reported, happened at the time of the evening vespers service. Indulgences were things of no worth, yet out of them great events were stirred up, and are still being stirred up to this day. 'Remember, therefore, this day, and at the same time think of these same things!'[31]

Doors

There is another possible explanation for why a remembered—and quite probably misremembered and indeed imagined—door-posting of the Ninety-five Theses was in the second half of the sixteenth century assuming ever greater significance in the minds of Melanchthon and others of his circle. Increasingly, the religious conflicts and divisions of the age were themselves turning a routine method of sharing information into both a practical and symbolic gesture of protest and defiance.

As we have seen, Luther's own appeal against Cajetan seems to have been posted on the doors of Augsburg Cathedral in 1518, and the highly provocative burning of the 1520 papal bull was advertised in Wittenberg in this way. Over the following years, it is possible to point to a growing number of examples of church doors being used—by both allies and adversaries of Luther—to make contentious and combative statements to a religiously divided public.

In 1523, Thomas Müntzer, a disciple of Luther's who was shortly to turn into a bitter opponent, posted letters attacking an antagonist on several church doors in Zwickau. In Minden, a provocative set of theses by the preacher Nicholas Krage, challenging 'papists' in the city to public disputation, was posted on the doors of churches in March 1530. Similar sets of overtly anti-Catholic theses were attached to church doors in the Westphalian town of Lippstadt later the same year, in nearby Soest in 1531, and in Osnabrück in 1532, while a satirical anti-Catholic poem was posted a few years later to a church door in Salzburg.

The confrontational habit of posting written challenges was not a solely German phenomenon. Already in 1521, the authorities in Antwerp were threatening punishments and confiscation of goods to supporters of Luther who attacked traditional Catholics in ballads or libels they had 'written, distributed, or pinned and pasted to church doors or any archways'. Anticlerical verses disdaining the sacrament of confession were pinned to the door of St Peter's church in Leiden in 1526, and pamphlets and broadsheets denouncing 'idolatry' were fastened to church doors in Delft by the anabaptist David Joris at around the same time.[32]

The papal excommunication of Luther was itself pinned up on church doors across Europe. In England, a radical priest named Adam Bradshawe tore it down when it was posted at Boxley Abbey in Kent. In October 1531, an Exeter schoolmaster, Thomas Benet, posted bills on the doors of the cathedral there denouncing the veneration of saints, and the pope as antichrist. When the pendulum of religious policy swung, Catholics rather than Protestants became secret posters of subversive placards. The most notorious door-fixing of any document in sixteenth-century England was the appearance in

May 1570 of the papal excommunication of Elizabeth I on the portal of the bishop of London's palace near St Paul's Cathedral—an event which prompted an intense manhunt, and, when the culprit was found, a gruesome execution.[33]

There is no reason to think any of these were 'copycat' door-posts in response to Luther's original. In a sense, indeed, the opposite may well be true. By the middle years of the sixteenth century, several strands were fusing together: Luther's own retrospective perception of 31 October 1517 as a seminal date in his confrontation with the papacy; an institutional awareness in Wittenberg of the proper procedures mandated by the university statutes; and the wider emergence of a culture of religious conflict, involving church doors as a site of public spectacle. For Melanchthon, as well as for others, the result was the creation of a notable occasion to mark and 'remember'.

By the time of Melanchthon's death in April 1560, memories of the *Thesenanschlag* had become a fixture in Wittenberg circles, even though some details of the event remained remarkably fluid. In 1563, Melanchthon's former student Johannes Manlius published a volume of extracts and quotations from his master's lectures, reprinted several times over the course of the 1560s. Manlius wrote that Luther posted the Theses to the door of the Castle Church on the Feast of All Saints at noon, a detail conflicting with Melanchthon's 1558 recollection that it was an evening occurrence, but one which may have carried a greater symbolic resonance in tying the event to the high-point of the sun.[34]

Melanchthon's account of Luther's life, containing the foundational reference to the *Thesenanschlag*, circulated widely in the second half of the sixteenth century, not least on account of its inclusion within the covers of Luther's collected Latin works. A separately circulating edition, with various other commemorative materials, was edited by Johann Policarius, superintendent of the church at Weissenfels, a short distance south of Halle. He added various short poetic couplets, including one on the 'Year of Restoring Religion, 1517':

> You drag the work of religion out of the muck, with Christ
> As leader, O truthful Luther leaning on the right hand of God.[35]

Pollicarius's text appeared in three separate Latin editions and eight consecutive printings between 1548 and 1562. A German translation by the Frankfurt-am-Main pastor Matthias Ritter was produced in 1554, and reprinted another six times before 1561, with a further German translation in 1564. There was an early French translation, printed at Geneva in 1549 and again at Lyon in 1562, as well as a 1561 English translation, which applauded how the work had already been rendered into 'Spanish and Italian tongues by certain godly persons exiled their natural country'.[36]

This English version—*A famous and godly history containing the lives and acts of three renowned reformers of the Christian Church, Martine Luther, Iohn Ecolampadius, and Huldericke Zuinglius*—was the work of Henry Bennet, a native of Calais. Bennet confessed to readers that as soon as he perused the original volume he was 'ravished with incredible desire' to turn it into English. But Bennet's enthusiasm was not equalled by his care as a translator. Melanchthon's statement that Luther fixed his Theses to the Castle Church *pridie festi omnium Sanctorum*—that is, on the day before the feast of All Saints—was mistranslated by Bennet as 'the morrow after the feast of All Saints'.

The mistake had a lasting impact in England, as Bennet's version of Melanchthon's account was subsumed wholesale into the 'History declaring the Life and Acts of D. Martin Luther' which John Foxe included in his famous *Acts and Monuments* (Book of Martyrs) in 1563, and retained in three subsequent and expanded editions appearing in the reign of Elizabeth I. The Queen's Privy Council issued instructions in 1570 that every parish church was to acquire a copy of 'Foxe', so for English people who were paying attention it would have seemed that Luther began his campaign of Reformation on 2 November 1517.[37]

Into the 1550s, however, it was still possible to regard Luther's posting of the Ninety-five Theses as a detail of little importance, or to overlook it completely. The most important contemporary chronicler of recent events in Germany was the Strasbourg-based humanist and diplomat Johannes Sleidanus, who in 1545 accepted a commission as official historiographer to the evangelical Schmalkaldic League. Sleidanus's *De statu religionis et republicae Carolo V Caesare commantarii* (Commentaries on religion and the state in the reign of Emperor Charles V) was published in 1555. In its close attention to factual detail, its extensive use of primary sources, and its tone of objectivity (though masking a selective and deeply anti-Catholic approach), Sleidanus's work has been hailed as a landmark in the development of historical writing. Largely following Luther's own version of events, Sleidanus supplied an account of how Tetzel's extravagances provoked Luther to write to the Archbishop of Mainz and to send with the letter ninety-five theses which, for the sake of a disputation, he had lately promulgated (*promulgarat*) at Wittenberg. It is unclear whether Sleidanus believed Luther had published the theses, or merely publicized them, but of the door of the Castle Church there is in his account no sign.[38]

Biographies

The *Thesenanschlag* was mentioned, but briefly and in passing, in the first full-length Protestant biography of Martin Luther, published at Strasburg in 1556. It was the work of Ludwig Rabus, Lutheran minister there, and the nucleus of a huge multi-volume work, which—like the efforts of John Foxe in England—was intended to celebrate and commemorate the modern martyrs of the Church. Luther was not, of course, technically a martyr. But as the 'prophet of the German nation', whose proclamation of the gospel revealed that the last age of the world was underway, he was the pivotal figure of Rabus's history.

Rabus made use of Melanchthon's brief life, and did record that Luther posted ninety-five theses on the *Schlosskirche* in Wittenberg calling for a disputation in person or by exchange of texts. He noted also that this was a hundred years after the execution of Jan Hus. But the real drama of Rabus's account of Luther was elsewhere, focussing on a series of doughty confrontations with stubborn opponents. The work was accompanied by a set of eleven unsophisticated but arresting woodcut illustrations, pictures which supply for readers, in the words of Lyndal Roper, 'a basic narrative of what the pious Lutheran needs to know about the reformer's life'. The selected scenes include the encounters with Cajetan at Augsburg and Eck at Leipzig, as well as two depictions of the Diet of Worms, in one of which Luther is shown uttering the immortal, if uncertain, words, 'Here I stand, I can do nothing other'. There is also an image of Luther, resplendent in drawn-up monastic cowl, casting the pope's bull onto the flames with the city of Wittenberg in the background (see Fig. 2.2).[39] It quite evidently did not seem to Rabus, or his publisher, that a depiction of Luther positioning his Theses on the notice-board of

Fig. 2.2. Luther burns the papal bull at Wittenberg in 1520, from Ludwig Rabus, *Historien der Heyligen Außerwölten Gottes Zeügen* (1556).

Wittenberg University would add anything to the artistic or commercial appeal of the work.

The assorted claims of Melanchthon, Cochlaeus, and Rabus to be counted as the first real biographer of Martin Luther are contested by

Johannes Mathesius (1504–65), an acolyte who studied at Wittenberg, and who recorded some of the Table Talk, before taking up a post as pastor in the Bohemian silver-mining town of Jáchymov (Joachimsthal), near the border with Saxony.[40] Between 1562 and 1565 Mathesius preached no fewer than seventeen sermons on the life of the great reformer, published in a single volume in Nuremberg in 1566. The book proved hugely popular, and went through twelve editions before the end of the sixteenth century.

Mathesius's work was scarcely a biography in the modern sense. It did not seek to explore personality and elicit motive, or to trace changes in character or attitudes. Even more than Melanchthon's, Mathesius's Luther was an instrument of God's purposes, a *Wundermann* (miracle-man), sent to preach the pure Word against papal darkness in the final era of the world, a latter-day Elijah. This, in short, was a hagiography, a saint's life, of the kind which would still have been thoroughly familiar to the older members of Mathesius's Lutheran congregation. At a time of division among Lutherans, Mathesius sought to inspire and unite, devoting considerable attention to the doctrinal substance of the agreed statement of Lutheran faith, the Augsburg Confession, and very little to the actual contents of the Ninety-five Theses, with their perplexingly popish features.[41]

As to the posting of the Theses, Mathesius reported that this took place at the Castle Church on its 'Kirchmesse Tag'—that is, the feast of the church's dedication, All Saints. The implication once more is of a public disruption of a popish festivity. But in undertaking this, Luther was no gratuitous aggressor. Mathesius wrote that Luther was 'forced', by his oath and his doctoral position, to post the Theses and have them printed, in response to the 'Roman and episcopal violence' employed by Tetzel and his crew.[42]

As Volker Leppin and Susan Boettcher have acutely observed, there was an inherent ambivalence to the treatment of Luther in many of these laudatory sixteenth-century lives. On the one hand, he was the towering figure without whom the Church would not have begun to reform itself. On the other, there was a reluctance to assert that Luther himself launched or initiated the Reformation, as this was to risk making him a political figure, acting under his own rather than divine disposition. An emphasis on Luther's motivational restraint was also evident from the Eisleben pastor, and Gnesio-Lutheran, Cyriakus

Spangenberg, in sermons he preached and published on Luther, 'Man of God', at the rate of two a year (on the anniversaries of his birth and death) between 1562 and 1573. Authors like Mathesius were generally content to report both that Luther had written to Albrecht of Mainz on 31 October 1531 urging him to reform the abuses, and (following Melanchthon) that he posted a printed copy of the Ninety-five Theses on the same day at the Castle Church, without reconciling or even apparently recognizing the contradiction that this involved—though Rabus ingeniously got around the problem by redating the Albrecht letter to 1 October.[43]

We have reached and are passing the point of transition between what has been called 'communicative memory' (informal and everyday, handed on through personal recollections, shared stories, and daily interactions) and 'cultural memory' (the process of constructing and maintaining a group identity with reference to rituals, images, and texts).[44] Mathesius was the last of the major chroniclers of Luther's life to have known the man personally. Towards the end of the sixteenth century Luther was becoming a historical figure, and a magnet for myth.

The passage of time, and a reliance on earlier texts, could certainly breed carelessness. A 1586 life of Luther by the Strasburg pastor Georg Glocker reported that the posting took place 'on All Saints Day', not the eve of the feast. Georg Mylius (1548–1607), Professor of Theology in Wittenberg, no less, published a sermon in 1592 in which he said that Luther started to confute 'popish abominations', and 'publicly posted the sentences or theses of his disputation at the castle Church here in Wittenberg' in the year 1516.[45]

Yet squeamishness about admitting that Luther's action had indeed started 'the Reformation' was starting to dissipate. An updated version of the Chronicle of Johan Carion, taken in hand by Melanchthon's son-in-law Caspar Peucer, and published in German translation at Wittenberg in 1588, asserted unapologetically that the posting of the Ninety-five Theses was the 'occasion and cause' of the reform of the Church. The debate over indulgences initiated by the posting of articles on the *Schlosskirche* was, wrote the Wittenberg-trained minister Paul Seidel in 1581, 'the beginning and original cause of the Reformation and why the pure teaching of the Holy Gospel is once again among us'.[46]

For the Weimar pastor Anton Probus, preaching in 1589, 31 October 1517 was the anniversary of a spiritual liberation of consciences and souls from the 'gruesome tortures, cudgellings ("Stockmeisterei") and thief-hangings of the papacy'. For, more than seventy-two years ago now,

> Dr Martin Luther, driven and aroused by God's spirit, started to write against papistry, and in Wittenberg posted 95 propositions or theses to the door of the Castle Church, in which he answered a preaching monk, John Tetzel, and with God's Word powerfully struck down his flea market and indulgence dross.

Here, any notion of Luther writing courteously to his ecclesiastical superiors has been eclipsed by the righteous anger of an inspired prophet of God. Seidel too laid emphasis on Luther's own powers of action in undertaking the *Thesenanschlag*—his 'bountiful spirit, rigorous, just and meet'—as did the Leipzig theologian, Nikolaus Selnecker, in a biography of 1576, though Selnecker was careful to insist that when Luther posted his Theses to the *Schlosskirche* he did so 'not to defend his own person, but the truth'.

There was an added incentive, around the turn of the 1580s, to emphasize Luther's unique status as an arbiter of Christian truth, and also to anchor it in the context of the University of Wittenberg—Philip Melanchthon's town just as much as it was Martin Luther's. Selnecker and Seidel were both heavily involved in trying to win adherence to the Formula of Concord, a document drawn up in 1577 with the aim of bringing back into harmony the warring 'Gnesio-Lutherans' and 'Philippists'. In this aim it was partially, but only partially, successful.[47]

Martin Luther, like other charismatic religious figures of the later middle ages, preached reform, *reformatio*. To conservative opponents, he was another in a long line of destructive and misguided individuals who thought they knew better than the guardians of truth: a heretic. Only gradually did the notion emerge that the events of the early sixteenth century constituted some kind of unique historical watershed in the history of Christianity: *the* Reformation. But that idea was starting to receive expression in the late sixteenth century, and in the view of its advocates was closely linked with the exceptional status of Martin Luther as an inspired instrument of God.

It was, unsurprisingly, a view appealing most strongly to those Protestants who identified themselves as Luther's heirs. In the increasingly 'confessionalized' world of late-sixteenth-century Europe, Lutherans were the rivals, not just of Catholics, but of the followers of John Calvin and other Protestant leaders collectively known as 'the Reformed', as well as of various splinter groups of spiritualists and radicals. A carved stone from a domestic dwelling in sixteenth-century Wittenberg, now preserved in the *Lutherhaus* Museum there, bears an uncompromising message:

> Gottes Wort und Lutheri Schrift
> Ist des Bapst und Calvini Gift.
> (God's Word, and the writing of Luther
> Is the poison of the pope and Calvin.)[48]

For all that, non-Lutherans were often willing to acknowledge Luther's pivotal role. In England, the Calvinist John Foxe headed a section in his martyrology, 'Here beginneth the reformation of the church of Christ, in the time of Martin Luther.' But a mindset which saw God himself as the prime mover in the events of history might hesitate to attribute too much to one individual, and might lean towards alternative and longer timescales. Matthew Sutcliffe, another English Calvinist, writing at the beginning of the seventeenth century, was equally attuned to the fourteenth- and fifteenth-century dissidents John Wyclif and Jan Hus as men who 'have laboured in the reformation of the Church.'[49] Across Europe, 'Reformation' was often seen, not as a past event to be commemorated and celebrated, but as an unfinished, ongoing challenge and struggle.

The urge to commemorate past contests and triumphs is not incompatible with chronic anxieties about the present. On the contrary, it is often integral to them, as attempts are made to shore up a group identity by drawing upon a store of inherited symbols and traditions. Among Lutherans, the call to 'remember 1517' as a pivotal moment of history was by the later sixteenth century being made into a rallying-cry. The process began in the lifetime of Martin Luther, and indeed with Luther himself. But we should not fall into the trap of thinking it was the self-evident signification of that year as it unfolded in actual time.

If we could somehow stop the historical clocks in December 1517, what in fact would we have? A high-minded dispute (of a kind that had been rehearsed before) about one subsidiary aspect of the pastoral theology of penance; a moralistic friar petitioning his ecclesiastical superiors about alleged abuses within their jurisdiction; the same friar's attempts to instigate a customary kind of academic disputation; the wheels of disciplinary procedure against him starting, very slowly, to turn.

It was a still less likely eventuality that the posting of the Ninety-five Theses to the door of the Castle Church in Wittenberg would come to mark an important—ultimately, the defining—place in this historical pagination of memory. It was, as we have seen, no part of Luther's own narrative of events: most likely because it did not happen at all, or if it did, because it was an unremarkable occurrence, in no way comparable to the actual writing of the Theses, or the temerity of sending them, albeit courteously, to the Prince-Archbishop of Mainz.

In the generation after Luther's death, and largely due to the influence of Philip Melanchthon, this non-occurrence of a non-event gradually transformed itself into a verifiable historical fact—a proof of the adage that while history may repeat itself, historians repeat each other. Its meaning too was starting to mutate: a circumstantial detail of Luther's quarrel with Johan Tetzel and his backers was coming to be seen as an act of courageous defiance, and of weighty symbolic significance.

Yet this was very much still a piece of Lutheran pious reminiscence, and within Lutheranism, a largely regional one. The majority of writers and preachers who paid any attention to the event seem to have had a Saxon background, and very many of them boasted close Wittenberg connections. Even within Germany, at the close of the sixteenth century, 31 October 1517 was not widely seen as a date of towering and unique significance. An annual celebration of 'deliverance' from a benighted popish past was indeed an increasingly common feature of collective and civic life in Protestant territories. But a variety of dates were chosen locally to mark this occurrence, very often the anniversary of the moment when evangelical sermons were first preached or Protestantism was received as the official religion. In Braunschweig this commemoration was kept on the Sunday after 1 September; in Hamburg and Lübeck on Trinity Sunday, the first after Pentecost.

A number of places marked with special church services the day of Luther's birth (10 November), his baptism (11 November), or death

(18 February). Across southern Germany it was common to commemorate 25 June as the 'beginning' of the Reformation: the day on which the Augsburg Confession was formally presented to the Emperor. Publication in German of the hard worked-out Formula of Concord as the *Book of Concord*, on 25 June 1580, was timed to coincide with the fiftieth anniversary of this seminal occasion. The formal reading of the Augsburg Confession to Charles V by the Saxon Chancellor Christian Beyer at the diet of 1530 was the subject of a much-reproduced sixteenth-century engraving. It was also the theme of a magnificent painting commissioned in the early seventeenth century for the chancel of St George's church, Eisenach.[50] By contrast, no one at all had yet thought to depict the posting of the Ninety-five Theses in any kind of visual form.

In 1600, the English writer Samuel Lewkenor published a book containing lively descriptions of foreign university cities, for the benefit of 'such as are desirous to know the situation and customs . . . without travelling to see them'. In the early years of the sixteenth century, Wittenberg might have struggled to earn inclusion in such a pan-European survey of higher education, but it was now a university playing very much in the big leagues. If Lewkenor's readers were London theatre-goers, they were soon also to learn that a fictional Prince of Denmark had studied there, along with his friend Horatio. The Wittenberg doctors, Lewkenor observed, were 'the greatest propugnators of the Confession of Augsburg', and, since its foundation in 1502, the place 'in this latter age is grown famous, by reason of the controversies and disputations of religion, there handled by Martin Luther and his adherents'. In none of Lewkenor's topographical or scholarly scene-setting, however, did the Castle Church or its doors rate so much as a mention.[51] At the turn of the seventeenth century, the triumph of the *Thesenanschlag* lay firmly in the future.

3
1617: Anniversaries

Dreams

In 1617, a full century after the act he probably never performed, Martin Luther was for the first time depicted performing it. The occasion was the printing in Leipzig of a remarkable broadsheet, with an elaborate copperplate engraving by the artist Conrad Grehle, and some accompanying poetic couplets by the clergyman Peter Kirchbach (see Fig. 3.1). The same image, only slightly simplified, was at the same time circulated in a woodcut print, with prose explanations in German of what the scene depicted.

The broadsheet was known as 'The Dream of Frederick the Wise', and it told the tale of a dream in three parts which Luther's sovereign, the Elector of Saxony, supposedly experienced on the night of 30 October 1517 while staying at his castle at Schweinitz, halfway between Magdeburg and Wittenberg. Frederick went to bed that night musing on how best to assist the souls in purgatory, about to receive special remembrance at the feasts of All Saints and All Souls. In the first part of the dream Frederick had a vision of a monk, apparently a natural son of St Paul, surrounded by a host of saints. This figure begged to be allowed to write something on the door of the Castle Church in Wittenberg, and the saints assured Frederick that if he agreed to the request he would not regret it. The monk began to write the words 'Vom Ablass' (Concerning Indulgences), in a script so large that Frederick could read it in Schweinitz. And to do so he used a feather quill so enormous that it stretched all the way to Rome, where it pierced the ears of a lion (Leo X), and knocked from the pope's head the papal tiara, which kings, cardinals, and bishops fruitlessly attempted to set back on again.

Fig. 3.1. 'The Dream of Frederick the Wise', an allegorical engraving of 1617.

At this moment Frederick awoke, but the vision continued in a second dream, in which the lion summoned together all the estates of the Empire, and ordered them to take action against the monk. In the third dream, the pope's allies tried, and failed, to break the monk's pen. Frederick asked why the quill was so strong, and received from the monk the reply that it was a feather from a hundred-year-old Bohemian goose. (The goose himself—Jan Hus—is depicted being burned in the lower-right quarter of the picture.) Suddenly, other feathers started springing from the original. They were gathered up by learned men, and these quills began to grow as long and as unbreakably strong as that of the monk himself. Frederick again woke up, wondering what it all might signify. The advice he received was that, according to the Bible, God alone could unravel the meaning of dreams and revelations, and Frederick should wait to see what the future might bring.[1]

The 'dream' was in all likelihood a pious fabrication. It was documented for the first time in a 1602 sermon of the Dresden court preacher Hoe von Hoenegg, printed in 1604, and subsequently repeated and embellished. The editor of the 1617 broadsheet, identified only as 'D.K.' was almost certainly David Krautvogel, superintendent of the church in Freiberg in Saxony. He claimed that the dream was attested to by Frederick's own chaplain, Georg Spalatin, who told the tale to Anton Musa, superintendent of the town of Rochlitz, a little way south-east of Leipzig. Musa wrote the story down, and his manuscript passed into the possession of Bartholomeus Schönbach, a later pastor of Rochlitz. In 1591, Schönbach was living in Joachimsthal, where Krautvogel, temporarily deposed from his position in Freiberg by the Calvinists, also found himself stationed. Krautvogel borrowed and copied out the manuscript, appropriately enough on the Feast of All Saints.

It is a tangled and improbable tale. Musa, the supposed scribe of the story, left Rochlitz in 1544, when Schönbach was only twelve years old. He died three years later, and his manuscript does not survive. Very likely, the account was first formulated sometime towards the end of the sixteenth century.[2] This was a period when myths and pious legends about the life of Martin Luther were proliferating in Germany. Preachers like Anton Probus, Johann Lapaeus, and Georg Glocker all testified to Luther's status as a prophet, and recounted tales of how supporters were miraculously healed through the virtue of his prayers, and opponents suddenly struck down by the vengeful power of God.

There was more than a hint of the traditional powers of Catholic saints about such accounts—echoed too in the affirmative role played by the saints in 'The Dream of Frederick the Wise'. The association was still more marked in the profusion, through the seventeenth century and beyond, of popular folktales attributing miraculous powers to springs or trees associated with Luther, and also in the remarkable number of cases where images of the great reformer were apparently preserved unscathed amidst destructive fires in houses and churches. As Bob Scribner brilliantly demonstrated, the myth of 'incombustible Luther' was not just a matter of lingering peasant superstition, finding new outlets of expression in post-Reformation Lutheran lands: such tales were often avidly collected and publicized by the educated Protestant clergy.[3]

'The Dream of Frederick the Wise' thus stood squarely in an evolving tradition, which sought to vindicate the Reformation through appeals to miraculous revelation, and claims about Luther's status as a divinely ordained prophet. That tendency—as we have seen—was there already in the reformer's lifetime: Luther's own conviction that the Czech martyr Jan Hus foretold his coming was central to the arguments and imagery of the 1617 broadsheet. It has even been suggested that in the 1617 broadsheet we can see a reference to—and a refutation of—an previous revelatory vision. This was the early thirteenth-century dream of Pope Innocent III, at a time when he was trying to decide whether to give permission for the formation of a new religious order, under the leadership of the unconventional Umbrian preacher, Francis of Assisi. Innocent dreamed his basilica of St John Lateran in Rome was starting to collapse, but was saved by being supported on the shoulders of the humble friar—a scene depicted by Giotto and other medieval artists.[4]

Alongside the parade of prophecy and providence in 'The Dream of Frederick the Wise', there was also a palpable concern with historical proofs and veracity. It was evident in the elaborate explanations of how the account of Frederick's divinely sent dream originated with Spalatin, and passed down through the hands of named and reliable witnesses. And for all its complex and allegorical imagery, the engraving of 1617 functioned to locate the deliverance from papal oppression in a specific, identifiable time and place: 31 October 1517; the door of the Castle Church in Wittenberg. Luther's *Thesenanschlag* was being scrupulously historicized, at precisely the same moment it was being comprehensively mythologized, as the foundational event of the Reformation.

Centenary

It was no accident that this was happening in 1617. We have today become thoroughly accustomed to the notion that the passage of a hundred years after a significant episode or event constitutes an appropriate, almost a natural moment to commemorate it and reflect on its significance (I write these words on the sombre one-hundredth anniversary of the start of the Battle of the Somme). Yet the idea of the centenary is itself a product of history. The decision in 1617 to stage celebrations and commemorations of Luther's protest of a hundred years earlier was the very first large-scale modern centenary. It was a critical moment, not only in how the Reformation was to be understood and remembered, but in how history itself would afterwards play a role in the public life of western Europe.

Some precedents had been set by various German universities, beginning in the late sixteenth century to celebrate anniversaries of their original foundation. Tübingen marked its centenary in 1578, and Heidelberg the two-hundredth anniversary of its founding in 1587. Wittenberg itself celebrated in 1602, a hundred years after its establishment by Elector Frederick the Wise.[5]

The tendency was in all likelihood inspired and encouraged by an important development in the ordering principles of historical writing, one which itself was a product of the controversies of the Reformation. In the aftermath of the Augsburg Interim, Matthias Flacius Illyricus, a pugnacious Gnesio-Lutheran who opposed any compromise with the imperial mandate on religion, departed Wittenberg for Magdeburg. There he coordinated the efforts of a group of scholars to produce a massive new work of ecclesiastical history. It was designed to refute Catholic charges of 'novelty' against the reformers, and to demonstrate a continuous witness of true Christianity against papal corruption from the apostolic age onwards.

The work was published in thirteen volumes in Basle between 1559 and 1574. Earlier church historians tended to organize their work around the lives of saintly individuals, or to divide the history of the world along reputedly biblical lines into various epochs and ages. But the work of Flacius's collaborators assigned a volume to each hundred-year period between the birth of Christ and 1300. It was the *Ecclesiastica historia ... secundum singulas centurias*, known in English as the *Magdeburg Centuries*.

The growing concern with uniform blocks of years was scarcely a symptom of some 'modern', rationalizing way of seeing the world. Rather, an obsession with the measurement and inspection of time reflected the widespread conviction that the world was hastening towards its end, and that distinctive dates might be the markers in a continuing cosmic contest between the forces of Christ and Antichrist—a countdown to the Second Coming and Last Judgement. Luther's eminence as a prophet of the end times was hailed in his own lifetime, and endorsed in numerous Lutheran New Year's sermons for 1600: he was a born-again Moses leading the German people out of the spiritual slavery of Egypt; a David confronting and slaying the papal Goliath. Increasingly, 1517 was regarded as the year when this divine mandate was announced to the world.[6]

The anniversary celebrations of 1517 were rooted in an existing culture of commemoration, and in a powerful ordering vision of a divine plan for humanity. But they were nonetheless the product of particular contemporary circumstances, and as they took shape, distinct religious and political agendas could be identified at work in them. The first impetus seems to have come, predictably enough, from the Theological Faculty at the University of Wittenberg. In March 1617, the Wittenberg theologians wrote to the supreme decision-making body for the territorial Church in Saxony, the Upper Consistory in Dresden, and a few weeks later to the Elector, Johann Georg I. They requested permission to celebrate the last day of October as *primus Jubileus Lutheranus*, the first Jubilee of Luther.

The word 'Jubilee'—in German *Jubelfest* or *Jubelfeier*—was a carefully chosen one, and represented both a claim and a provocation. The concept's origins were biblical. In the book of Leviticus, God instructed Moses that every fiftieth year was to be kept as a holy year of Jubilee, when fields were to be left untilled, debts redeemed, and slaves set at liberty. The idea of a holy year of emancipation and restoration was revived by the medieval papacy. In 1300 Pope Boniface VIII declared a year of grace, when special plenary indulgences were offered to those coming to Rome on pilgrimage. The original intention was for these papal jubilees to occur every hundred years, later reduced to every fifty in accordance with biblical precept. In 1470, Pope Paul II decreed that they should take place every twenty-five years, so that each generation might get to experience at least one. After a crisis of morale in the middle decades of the sixteenth century, the jubilees of 1575 and 1600 were celebrated in Rome with particular splendour—a symptom of the renewed confidence of the Catholic Church after the reforms, and the zealous condemnations of Protestantism, undertaken by the Council of Trent (1545–63).[7]

Papal jubilees were inextricably tied up with indulgences, and with promises of access to the Treasury of Merits. For Lutheran theologians, appropriating the term was a daring act of theological piracy. The intention was that 1617 would be experienced, not just as a moment of historical retrospection, but as a true 'holy year' of divine favour and grace, a celebration of the triumph of the Gospel over the false promises of Antichrist. An effect was to underline still further the significance of the indulgence controversy—in itself, as we have seen, a relatively minor skirmish in the grand clash of theological arms—as the underlying 'cause' of the Reformation in Germany.

As the evangelicals' plans became clear, Rome reacted with predictable fury. The next holy year was not due until 1625, but on 12 June 1617 Paul V announced that the rest of the current year was to be kept as a period of extraordinary jubilee, a time of penance and atonement, and of prayer for God to protect the Church from its heretical enemies. Some Catholic territories fixed their main ceremonies for 31 October 1617 itself, in an effort to undercut the Protestant 'pseudo-jubilee'. In places where Catholics and Lutherans lived side by side—such as in the great imperial city of Augsburg—rival celebrations took place at the same time and fuelled simmering sectarian hatreds. Some contemporary chroniclers even dated the beginning of the Thirty Years War, which was to erupt into open conflict in 1618, to the competing jubilees of the preceding year.[8]

The rising political tensions between Catholic and Protestant states within the Holy Roman Empire were themselves an important factor in the decision to commemorate in 1617.

Through the second half of the sixteenth century there had been an uneasy religious peace in Germany. The settlement in 1555 recognized the legal rights within the Empire of princes and territories adhering to the Confession of Augsburg: they could seek redress through imperial courts, and participate fully in meetings of the estates (diets). By the beginning of the third quarter of the century, Protestantism had made spectacular advances. Three of the seven electoral territories, along with thirty-four other principalities, and dozens of smaller states and self-governing cities, had declared for the Reformation.[9]

But at the same time, German Lutheranism was, as we have seen, riven with bitter rivalries between 'Gnesio-Lutherans' and 'Philippists'. It was also increasingly facing a challenge from the alternative, 'Reformed' brand of Protestantism. Calvinism gained a strong foothold in the Empire after the Elector Friedrich III, of the Rhineland Palatinate, converted to the faith in 1561, and a handful of other rulers followed suit in the succeeding decades. A still more pressing challenge—for both Lutherans and Calvinists—was the resurgent power of Rome and its acolytes. Within the Empire, Charles V's successors—Ferdinand I, Maximilian II, and Rudolf II—proved ineffectual or indifferent in stemming the Protestant advance, and the childless Matthias II (1612–17) made concessions to smooth his way to the imperial throne. But the rising force in the early seventeenth century—his cousin and heir apparent, the Austrian Archduke Ferdinand—was a steely warrior of Counter-Reformation, as, within Germany, was the powerful Duke Maximilian of Bavaria.

The centenary of Luther's protest against Rome thus took place at a time of real anxiety for German Protestants. While the Wittenberg theologians were petitioning Elector Johann Georg for permission to host a Luther Jubilee, and thinking in terms of a local celebration along the lines of the recent university centenary, three hundred miles to the south-west, in the Calvinist enclave of the Palatinate, grander plans were being hatched at the court in Heidelberg of Elector Friedrich V.

In response to growing Catholic militancy, Friedrich's father Friedrich IV had in 1608 formed the Protestant Union, a defensive alliance bringing together Reformed and Lutheran states and cities—though Saxony held aloof, and tensions between its Lutheran and

Calvinist members continued to bedevil the alliance. In April 1617, the leaders of the Protestant Union met at Heilbronn to discuss renewal of their alliance, which was due to expire the following year. At the meeting, Friedrich V made the suggestion that across the Lutheran and Reformed territories there should be a common act of celebration to give thanks for Luther's reformation of the Church in 1517. The Union formally adopted the proposal on 23 April 1617, and ordered that, during the Jubilee, all bitterness and personal attacks between Protestants, in books or sermons, were to cease.[10]

The idea for the larger Jubilee likely originated with Friedrich's court chaplains, and perhaps particularly with the preacher Abraham Scultetus. In a New Year's sermon of 1617, Scultetus made a point of observing how it was now one hundred years since God 'looked upon us graciously and delivered us from the horrible darkness of the papacy, and led us into the bright light of the Gospel.' There may have been an English connection here. Friedrich was married to James I's daughter Elizabeth, and Scultetus visited England in 1612–13. In the messy aftermath of England's Reformation, Protestants there were pioneers in efforts to endow the commemoration of significant events with providential significance as tokens of God's favour to the state. The anniversary of the accession of Elizabeth I on 17 November was widely celebrated in the early seventeenth century as a moment of national deliverance, as, after 1605, was 5 November, the day of James I's miraculous escape from the machinations of Gunpowder Plotters.[11]

Friedrich's motives in pressing for a common 'Protestant' celebration of the anniversary were as much political as pious. Under the terms of the Peace of Augsburg, only Catholicism and Lutheranism were accepted as official religions within the Empire. Friedrich's thinking was that political pressure might persuade the emperor to decree recognition and toleration for the Reformed as well—an eventuality that would in fact come to pass only in 1648, after thirty years of bloody and ultimately indecisive warfare.

The priorities in Saxony, spiritual heartland of orthodox Lutheranism, were rather different. Elector Johann Georg hoped the centenary might help revive the flagging leadership ambitions of his princely house, facing challenges both from Calvinists and within the Lutheran fold from hold-out Philippists, rejecting the 1580

Formula of Concord, and dismissively regarded as 'Crypto-Calvinists' by their self-consciously orthodox brethren. From the outset, Johann Georg determined on a Saxony-wide celebration, rather than the parochial Wittenberg affair initially proposed by the theologians. It is no accident that 'The Dream of Frederick the Wise' drew as much attention to the prophetic role of Johann Georg's princely progenitor as it did to the scribal witness of Martin Luther. The desire for dynastic legitimation was sharpened by the fact that Johann Georg was a member of the 'Albertine' branch of the Saxon ruling House of Wettin, which had acquired the Electoral dignity from the senior 'Ernestine' branch in dubious circumstances in 1547, as a result of the defeat of Frederick's nephew in the Schmalkaldic War.

Differences of emphasis manifested themselves in the ways the Jubilee was ordered to be celebrated. The Heilbronn instruction was for festivities to take place on a single day: Sunday 2 November. This was not, of course, the anniversary of the reputed posting of the Theses and implicitly side-lined it from the central act of remembrance. The Saxon ordinance was for a three-day festival, spanning 31 October to 2 November, and evoking the high church feast of All Saints-All Souls—the lightning-rod of Luther's initial protest. The Dresden Upper Consistory recommended this as the appropriate pattern for all territories loyal to the Augsburg Confession.

In the event, the celebrations turned out to be much more than a weekend affair. Commemorative events ran over weeks in many places: in the case of Strasburg, from 31 October all the way to Christmas Eve. Across the towns and countryside of Protestant Germany, the Jubilee was marked by an outpouring of carefully orchestrated festivity, with preaching of topical sermons, holding of dedicated church services, and promulgation of special prayers. Numerous broadsheets were produced, and commemorative medals struck. Poems and songs were written, and new plays performed and printed. It all constituted, in the words of Andrew Pettegree, 'a veritable media blitz'.[12]

The Reformation, as we know it today, was in a real sense discovered or invented in 1617. The political and cultural circumstances of that year decided definitively that 'the Reformation' started in 1517, and asserted for apparent perpetuity the central and dominant role of Martin Luther in the process. Earlier, local anniversaries marked Luther's birth or death. That of 1617 focused for the first time on the actions of his life. As the first major centenary festival of a specific historical event, the Jubilee reflected a new awareness of how remembered time could be organized, celebrated, and used.

The historian Charles Zika expresses it well: centenaries 'establish a link with the past which appears to be not only "natural" but also providential, and thereby enables them to challenge and displace alternative, individual and collective memories'.[13] While focussing attention on points of origin, centenaries also reinforce the notion of time as a forwards-moving linear journey, and invite reflection—and congratulation—on how we got from there to here. Although the 1617 celebrations remained a largely German affair, an English translation of Johann Georg's Saxon ordinance did appear in London the following year. In his preface, the anonymous editor went to some lengths to justify the idea of a jubilee, and to reassure readers that 'here is no popish rite'. In fact, the occasion served to confound a prophecy of the papists that Luther's doctrine would breathe its last after a hundred years. The flourishing state of the Gospel among the Germans was ample warrant for a 'holy triumph' to mark 'the remembrance of their manumission from the thraldom of Antichrist, by the hand of God upon Luther, and through Luther, just a hundred years before.'[14]

For all that, it is premature to suppose that the Jubilee of 1617 fetishized the *Thesenanchlag* itself as the symbolic focus of spiritual celebration. During the festivities, preachers reiterated the role of Martin Luther as a heaven-sent witness, commissioned to bring about the fall of Antichrist, and they hailed the hundred-year continuance of Luther's teaching as compelling evidence of its essential truth. But they rarely, if ever, picked out the Theses-posting as the defining prism through which to view these truths.

Even the date of 31 October was not of overwhelming importance in the course of the anniversary celebrations. Certainly, the townspeople of Wittenberg marched in festive procession on 31 October 1617 to the door of the *Schlosskirche*, and in a cycle of sermons preached in that church by the Wittenberg professors Friedrich Balduin, Nicolas Hunnius, and Wolfgang Franz, the importance of the Ninety-five Theses as the starting-point of the Reformation loomed large. But elsewhere the exact time and place of the Reformation's initiating moment seemingly mattered less. Well over a hundred of the sermons given as part of the 1617 commemorations were printed, and of these most supply the date on which they were preached. Twenty-one sermons were delivered on Friday 31 October, as compared to twenty on Saturday 1 November, thirty-four on Sunday 2 November, and a further sixteen over the course of the ensuing week.[15]

Yet more remarkable is the fact that, while the 1617 Jubilee produced a rich harvest of visual materials, none of it depicted Luther in the act of posting the Theses. This is true even of 'The Dream of Frederick the Wise'—an allegorical representation of Luther's indulgence protest, rather than an attempt at a realistic portrayal of it. Luther's image was endlessly reproduced in and around 1617, often with metaphorical implements such as the swan and goose, or the so-called 'Luther Rose', which placed a red heart bearing a black cross at the centre of a white rose on a blue field, and was supposed to symbolize death and suffering, the peace of justification, and the joy of heaven beyond.

In addition to portraits, illustrated broadsheets depicted Luther as the angel of the apocalypse, who according to scripture (Rev. 14:6) flew through the midst of heaven 'with an eternal gospel to proclaim to those who dwell on earth.' A rather more sober broadsheet, published at Nuremberg in 1617, and reproduced in variant forms, depicted Luther and Melanchthon standing with Frederick the Wise and Johann Georg I around an altar, with Luther pointing to the words in an open Bible: *Verbum Domini manet in aeternum* (the Word of the Lord abides forever). The imagery here reinforced that of 'The Dream of Frederick the Wise' in reminding viewers that Luther's mandate as a divine messenger was carried out under licence from a godly ruler. This was an important take-away message from the Jubilee celebrations as a whole, which in Saxon territory at least were as much about underscoring the credentials of the current ruling house as they were about canonizing the events of the preceding century.

Another widely circulated broadsheet, again with an etching by Conrad Grehle, dramatized an imagined confrontation between Luther and Tetzel. The latter, with bulky indulgence paraphernalia and a swarm of wasps (representing heresy) buzzing around his head, is seen skulking away from a church. But it is not by writing on the church door that Luther drives Tetzel off and discomforts the roaring papal lion covering his retreat; rather, he emerges from it like a chivalric champion, a burning torch in one hand and an open Bible in the other.

A relatively new visual medium, the commemorative medal came into its own in 1617—its use had, in fact, been pioneered by papal jubilees. Around ten of these medals, celebrating Luther and his deeds, were minted in the later sixteenth century, and a further forty-five were cast for the Jubilee of 1617. The medals bore a variety of Luther portraits and motifs, but absolutely none of them depicted a posting of the Ninety-five Theses, or even bore the date 31 October 1517.[16]

One might have expected greater attentiveness to the Theses-posting in the spate of Luther-themed plays written and performed around 1617, works which combined knock-about entertainment with the imparting of serious religious messages. A trail-blazer here was the government official Andreas Hartmann, whose *Erster Theil des curriculi Vitae Lutheri* (First Part of the Life of Luther) was first published in 1600 with financial support from the Saxon court, and went on to inspire other biographical plays. Hartmann unashamedly presented Luther as both a divinely blessed *Wundermann* and as a heroic chivalric knight. His work dramatized the meeting between Luther and Cajetan at Augsburg, as well as Luther's appearance before the Diet at Worms. Prior to this (having passed over the disputation with Eck at Leipzig), Hartmann inserted an entirely fictional confrontation between Luther and Tetzel over the issue of indulgences. But the Theses-posting itself is something which is merely reported later in the drama by a narrator-like character.[17]

Hartmann's themes and approach were recast in a series of plays written and published around the Jubilee year by a clergyman from the vicinity of Eisleben, Martin Rinckhardt. Some of his work was overtly allegorical, but his *Indulgentiarus confusus* (Indulgences Confounded) of 1618 was a rollicking historical pageant, with Tetzel in the role of pantomime villain. An encounter with Luther ends with the reformer saying that he will go to his room, and set down theses 'to dispute against your indulgences'. Luther later invites 'Myconius' to come and see the Theses 'which I have posted against Tetzel, and already publicly defended'. Rinckhardt also included a scene of Frederick the Wise telling, not Spalatin, but the theologian Johann Staupitz about his puzzling dream in which he saw a monk write in huge letters 'on our church door at the Castle in Wittenberg'. But in all this the *Thesenanschlag* itself remains an off-stage and somewhat marginal event. In contrast, Rinckhardt supplied a detailed and dramatic rendering of Luther's appearance at Worms before the emperor, and of his heroic refusal to recant: 'That is my heart; I can do no more. Just here I stand; God's help I implore!'

The Theses-posting, it seems, was quite literally not a dramatic episode, and there was likewise no attempt to portray it on stage in other plays produced in the anniversary year: Heinrich Kielmann's *Tetzelocramia* (Tetzel's dross), Balthasar Voight's *Echo Jubilaei Lutherani* or the *Lutherus Drama* of the Frankfurt-am-Main schoolmaster, Heinrich Hirtzwig.[18] By the early seventeenth century, German Lutherans largely knew that the posting of the Ninety-five Theses had taken place in Wittenberg a hundred years before, and they understood that it was a significant point for dating the origins of their own religious tradition. But there is surprisingly little to suggest it was seen as a remarkable and inspiring act in and of itself, or that most people could have formed any abiding mental image of what the action entailed.

Bicentenary

This state of affairs was remarkably slow to change. The significance of 31 October 1517 was firmly fixed in the German Protestant psyche, though it had competition in the middle decades of the seventeenth century from other notable anniversaries: the centenary of the Confession of Augsburg was celebrated in several evangelical territories in 1630, as was that of the Peace of Augsburg in 1655—the latter following relatively soon after the 1648 Treaty of Westphalia which brought the Thirty Years' War to an end and finally granted recognition to the Reformed within the Empire. Individual territories staged events to mark the centenary of their own adoption of 'true religion': Brandenburg in 1639, Osnabrück in 1643.

Celebration of the one-hundred-and-fiftieth anniversary of the Reformation in 1667 was relatively restrained and small-scale, though in its immediate wake, the Saxon Elector Johann Georg II decreed that there should be an annual commemoration of 31 October 1517 through to the bicentenary of 1717. For the first time, a 'Reformation Day' was instituted as a regular annual part of the Lutheran calendar of worship, albeit in only one part of Germany, and with the actual commemoration often moved to the preceding or following Sunday.[19]

In the later seventeenth century, broadsheet illustrations depicting individual episodes from the life of Luther began to become a popular genre. One (undated) example, now in the German National Museum in Nuremberg, was made up of sixteen scenes, from Luther's birth through to his death and funeral. It included depictions of Luther's trial before Cajetan in 1518, and of his burning of the papal bull. Images of Luther receiving his invitation for, and then travelling to, the Reichstag at Worms substituted for his actual appearance before the emperor—perhaps because the artist also included a depiction of the reading out of the Augsburg Confession, which would have looked very similar. Yet there was as yet no iconographic tradition at all for the posting of the Theses, and the artist did not attempt to invent one. The events of the indulgence controversy are alluded to only in a picture showing Luther confronting a figure in secular garb (perhaps the papal nuncio) across an altar laden with coins and bearing the inscriptions '1517' and *Peccata Germanorum* (sins of the Germans).[20]

The first illustration actually to depict the *Thesenanschlag* taking place seems to date from 1697, 180 years after the putative incident itself (Fig. 3.2). It was the work of a Nuremberg publisher, engraver, and art dealer named Christoph Weigel, and appeared in a volume of *Sculptura historiarum et temporum memoratrix* (Engravings of the histories, and memorial of the times). This was an ambitious universal history, with text supplied by the scholar Gregor Andreas Schmidt. But its principal appeal to readers likely lay in the pages of engravings, one allotted to each century in the eras before and after the birth of Christ, and filled with ten small engravings of major episodes. The pictures were explicitly *aides-mémoire*, intended to help readers remember, in order, the critical events of world history. Among the ten selected episodes for the sixteenth century were the capture in battle of the French King Francis I; the award of the Electoral title to Maurice of Saxony; the Massacre of St Bartholomew in Paris; and the occupation by the Turks of the Hungarian town of Györ.

Among these, an image of Luther and the Ninety-five Theses is the only scene not to involve monarchs or soldiery. It is labelled *Reformationis sacrae initia*, or, in an alternate printing, *Reformationis Lutheri initia*: the beginning of the holy Reformation, or the beginning of the

Reformationis sacræ initia.

Fig. 3.2. *Reformationis sacrae initia*: the start of the holy Reformation, by Christoph Weigel (1697).

Reformation of Luther. A mnemonic link between the posting of the Theses and the religious transformations in Europe is firmly established. Weigel's picture made no attempt to capture a realistic likeness of the neo-Gothic *Schlosskirche* in Wittenberg. The door stands in the centre of a neo-classical church façade. Nor is Luther posting the Theses himself. In a measured and didactic way, he calmly beckons onlookers to come and read them, while they are affixed (not hammered) to the door by another monk.

In this—as we have seen—Weigel may accidentally or otherwise have hit upon an accurate depiction of scholarly procedure in the late medieval University of Wittenberg, where professors were not expected to carry out their own administrative chores. But the scene depicted is evidently not the routine announcement of an academic debate. Groups of lay people—men, women, and children, of different classes and occupations—hurry to inspect what is being displayed.

Something remarkable is clearly taking place. Here, Weigel's engraving was somewhat at odds with Schmidt's main text, which spent very little time on Luther's posting of the Theses. It remarked merely that it had been undertaken 'with the aim of discussing them with learned persons', and that 'from this very slight beginning' the mighty work of Reformation had grown.[21]

At the time of the bicentenary in 1717, images of Luther posting the Theses began to be seen a little more regularly. An elaborate commemorative broadsheet produced for the occasion by the Augsburg engraver Johann August Corvinus employed a central standing portrait of Luther, flanked by scenes of 'Merkwürdigkeiten'—remarkable events, ten each from the sixteenth and seventeenth centuries. The first of the sixteenth-century scenes was a reworking of Weigel's 1697 engraving. Although, perhaps in the interests of clarifying who exactly was whom, the placard was now being fixed to the door by a smartly dressed youth, rather than a monk, while Luther encouraged the crowd forward. The decorous scene was accompanied by an incongruously bellicose motto: 'Luther fights with Tetzel, so that indulgences will be destroyed.'[22]

Still, images of the *Thesenanschlag* scarcely dominated the iconography of Luther and the Reformation as the celebrations of 1717 approached. It was a theme conspicuous by its absence from a comprehensive illustrated survey of Luther-honouring coins and medals, compiled by the Saxon historian and educationalist Christian Juncker, and printed at Frankfurt and Leipzig in 1706. More than 180 new commemorative medals were struck in 1717. Of these, only three depicted the Theses-posting, though a couple more copied the central motif from the 'Dream of Frederick the Wise' broadsheet of 1617. In a medal cast at Augsburg, Luther is for the very first time depicted as doer of the deed, with a large mallet in his hand.[23]

Luther likewise wields the hammer in an interesting image, created in Denmark and included in the *Hilaria evangelica* (evangelical joys) of the German Lutheran theologian Ernst Salomon Cyprian, a work published in three volumes in 1719 and representing a bumper compilation of accounts of the commemorative festivities taking place across the Lutheran lands (see Fig. 3.3). The scene forms part of a composite and compacted narrative tableau, which also shows the burning of the papal bull, Luther's translation of the

Fig. 3.3. Luther burning the bull, translating the Bible, and wielding the hammer, from Ernst Salomon Cyprian, *Hilaria evangelica* (1717).

Bible, and a symbolic confrontation with the pope. In contrast to Corvinus, Luther is not only shown posting the Theses himself, but is dressed in the doctor's robe familiar from his later years, rather than in authentic monastic habit. An emblematic and didactic feel to the scene is reinforced by the realization that what Luther is actually nailing to the door is not a list of ninety-five theses, but placards bearing the mottos *verbum dei vera fecit* (the Word of God is true) and *sola fides justificat* (faith alone justifies).[24]

Visual cycles on the life of Luther produced in the early eighteenth century did not invariably accentuate the *Thesenanschlag*, or even feature it at all. A series of copper engravings from 1730 by the Augsburg artist Johann Michael Roth began, for example, with Luther before Cajetan (in the guise of St Paul before the court of King Agrippa). Yet a pattern was starting to emerge in which the posting of the Theses was enshrined as a key episode in the reformer's biography. Another Augsburg picture series from 1730, produced by Elias Baeck, aimed to chart a complete life-course in fifteen scenes, from birth and childhood to death, each paired with a symbolic motif. The *Thesenanschlag* scene exudes the cool rationalism we associate, rightly or wrongly, with the eighteenth century. Luther, in his doctor's robes, gestures towards the placard containing the Theses which has just been fixed to the church door. Four well-dressed laymen look on with exemplary discipline and attention. The matched scene is an emblem for the start of the Reformation: a cherub plants a small sapling, above a motto promising that God will raise it to a mighty tree, and protect it through all the storms to come.[25]

Such intricately constructed prints were tokens of Protestant piety, but they were also commercial artefacts, produced for profit and collected for pleasure. Another symptom of the incipient 'commodification' of the Theses-posting is a beautiful silver-gilt beaker, now in the Victoria and Albert Museum in London, into which several commemorative medals have been set. One of these depicts the Theses-posting, with the inscription 'initium Reformationis 1517 31 Oct', and a quotation from the Prophet Isaiah, 'aperite portas'—open the doors. A similarly collectible memento, preserved in the *Lutherhaus* Museum in Wittenberg, dates from the anniversary of the Augsburg Confession in 1730, and comprises a dozen soldered-together miniature medallions with painted scenes from Luther's life, set in rows beneath a roundel containing a half-length-portrait. The *Thesenanschlag* is the first of the episodes depicted, suggestive of its foundational significance.[26]

In Wittenberg itself, there are scattered hints that by the start of the eighteenth century Luther's posting of the Ninety-five Theses was entrenched in local folklore. A history of the *Schlosskirche*, by the clergyman Matthaeus Faber, was published in Wittenberg in 1717. The eminent theologian Gottlieb Wernsdorff supplied its preface, and took occasion to wax lyrical about the significance of the church's doors. He reported that it was believed locally that still stuck in them were 'the very same nails . . . which the blessed Herr Doctor Luther used on 31 October 1517 to post his first theses against the notorious indulgence-peddler, Johan Tetzel'. Wernsdorff was not prepared to endorse this pious belief himself. But it was enough that one could truly say that 'through these doors Jesus with his Gospel had entered anew into his Church.' From Wernsdorff's Wittenberg perspective on things, there was little of Gregor Andreas Schmidt's cautious perception that the Theses-posting was a 'slight' and almost accidental beginning to the Reformation. Rather, with these hammer-strikes, Luther dealt the pope an 'irreparable blow, and made a blessed beginning to the success of our healing Reformation'. Wernsdorff also thought it was a remarkable circumstance that the very doors had remained to this date intact in their place, undisturbed by 'mighty revolutions, as well as nearby and terrible fires'. As events would prove, these were unfortunately premature words.

Faber's book contained an attractive fold-out image of the church, as it appeared in 1717, in a copper engraving by Johann Georg Schreiber. Looked at closely, this contains a visual suggestion that the doors of the *Schlosskirche* were becoming a site of interest to visitors. A smartly dressed man is shown paused in contemplation in front of them, while another points towards the wooden panelling with a stick.[27]

The bicentenary of 1717 was celebrated enthusiastically in Wittenberg as in much of Germany, but it took place in profoundly altered circumstances. It was less of a pan-Protestant and more of an explicitly Lutheran occasion. The return of a broad religious peace, and the advent of official toleration for Calvinism within the Empire, reduced the imperative to make common cause. In Brandenburg-Prussia, the Calvinist ruler Friedrich I (who in 1701 had upgraded himself from Elector to King) decreed a one-day celebration, but exempted Reformed subjects from having to take part. Indeed, it was in the Lutheran Kingdom of Denmark-Norway that the anniversary seems to have been most lavishly and extravagantly celebrated. The Danish king Frederik IV presented himself as the political mainstay of the

Lutheran cause, after a spectacular and demoralizing defection. In 1697 the Elector of Saxony, Friedrich August I, successfully put himself forward as a candidate for election to the throne of the powerful Polish-Lithuanian Commonwealth. The price was conversion to Catholicism, and to ensure his succession to the Polish throne, his son, who would succeed to the Electoral dignity as Friedrich August II in 1733, also converted to Rome in 1712.

The Elector guaranteed the rights of the Lutheran Church in Saxony, but there was clearly no question of the Jubilee serving, as it had in 1617, to underpin the honour and dignity of the ruling house. Rather, it would be a more narrowly ecclesiastical and cultural affair. Responsibility for organizing the festivities was entirely devolved to the Dresden Upper Consistory, which announced it intended to celebrate the occasion 'just as it had 100 years ago'—the early eighteenth century aimed at a commemoration of 1617, as much as of 1517 itself.[28]

Either way, it meant much focus on the person of Luther. It was fortuitous that, in 1717, 31 October fell on a Sunday, though in their published sermons preachers focussed less on what he actually did on that day two hundred years earlier, and more on the symbolic significance of the date for the renewal of true piety. Despite the pleas of some princes for a moderate and restrained celebration, a great deal of Protestant triumphalism and pronounced anti-Catholicism remained on display. In light of the Elector's Catholicism, the Dresden Upper Consistory decreed there should be no provocative anti-Roman polemic, but preachers were hardly constrained. The official programme of festivity produced by the University of Leipzig even suggested a new form of calendrical reckoning: 'In the year since the birth of Christ 1717; since the revelation of the Antichrist, 200'.[29]

In a Germany still deeply divided along confessional lines (despite the cessation of overtly religious warfare), this created an inevitable backlash, and a long-standing tradition of Catholic anti-biography of Luther received a paradoxical fillip from the commemorations of 1717. One highly successful publication of that year, reprinted numerous times through the eighteenth century, was the work of Johann Nikolaus Weislinger, parish priest of Waldulm in the Black Forest. It was evocatively entitled *Friss Vogel oder Stirb!*—the literal translation of which is 'eat bird, or die!', though the phrase means something like 'there is no alternative'. Weislinger recycled Catholic slurs against Luther going back to Cochlaeus and his contemporaries, noting that 'highly respected men and trustworthy authorities took Luther for a changeling and a child of the devil'. Weislinger defensively presented his work as a response to an incessant outpouring of attacks and libels on the Catholic Church, frequently mentioning the Lutheran bicentennial celebrations in this context.[30]

Catholic polemicists against Luther had, over the course of the sixteenth and seventeenth centuries, in fact paid very little attention to the *Thesenanschlag*. They had no reason to think it did not take place, but posting his grievances on a church door must have seemed almost the least objectionable act of rebellion on the part of a renegade monk, who took an ex-nun as his wife, rejected the traditional sacramental system, and denounced the pope as antichrist.

Enlightenment

Even as Luther's *Thesenanschlag* was becoming firmly established as a landmark moment of history, an understanding of the meanings and patterns in history that the event exemplified was itself starting to change. From the earliest records of the event, through the first centenary of 1617 and on to the second, Luther seemed to his heirs and admirers a key player in a cosmically scripted drama. History was the unfolding of a divine plan leading to a pre-ordained end; it was 'apocalyptic' history in the original meaning of the Greek word *apocalypse*—a revelation or uncovering. When Luther was cast as the angel of the Book of Revelation, this was no mere whimsical analogy. His significance—and the significance of the episode in Wittenberg that signalled the beginning of a divine assignment—was to announce to the Church the true meaning of the Gospel in preparation for the end of history itself.

Yet by the turn of the eighteenth century, a good many Protestant writers, as well as some Catholic ones, were being influenced by the intellectual currents of the early Enlightenment, the broad movement in European thought which prioritized reason and experiment over the unquestioned authority of tradition. In terms of historical reflectiveness, this involved thinking about the events of the early Reformation as genuinely human processes, rather than as the supernatural workings out of a preordained divine destiny, or as a prelude to the end times. It also meant taking Luther more seriously as an agent with his own noble or ignoble motivations, instead of seeing him as either the angelic instrument of God's providence, or the sinister setter of Satan's snares.

A significant contribution here was the *Histoire des variations des Églises protestantes* (1688) by the renowned French bishop and controversialist, Jacques Bénigne Bossuet. The background to the work lay in Bossuet's involvement in campaigns to persuade French Calvinists (Huguenots) back into the Catholic fold, after Louis XIV revoked the 1598 Edict of Nantes which had given them toleration within the realm. Luther looms large in Bossuet's first volume. He is not the spawn of the devil, but an all-too-human creature, and a man of genuine talents: 'a strength of genius, a vehemence in his discourses, a lively and impetuous eloquence'. Crucially, and in a clear departure from the interpretation established by Cochlaeus, Bossuet admitted that at the start of his protest about indulgences Luther was sincerely motivated and attacking genuine abuses—a point that had already been conceded in a 1680 *History of Lutheranism* by the French Jesuit Louis Maimbourg. According to Bossuet, Luther grew up in a world where 'many preached nothing but indulgences, pilgrimages, almsgiving to the religious, and made those practices, which were only the accessories of piety, the foundation of religion.' It was small wonder if Luther seemed almost to be 'the only preacher of the Gospel' and 'captivated men of wit'.

Bossuet's attention to Luther's potentially noble traits had its own polemical purpose: it served to underline the magnitude of his subsequent fall, a personal tragedy with catastrophic social and religious consequences. Luther was ultimately a victim of his own passions, 'always in extremes', and someone who came to appear to his erstwhile allies as a veritable tyrant, 'another pope'. Bossuet made a point of playing Luther off against Melanchthon, 'the most eloquent, the most polite, and at the same time the most moderate of all the disciples of Luther'. In suggesting throughout that Luther's heretical theology was an extrapolation of his flawed character, Bossuet produced a tendentious but brilliant deconstruction of the Reformation for the age of the Enlightenment. His suggestion that, in the conflict with Tetzel, there was much a Catholic might say in Luther's defence placed a distinct question-mark over any providential account of the origins of the Reformation.[31]

In the same year as Bossuet's history, an equally significant new account appeared from the Lutheran side. This was the *Commentarius historicus et apologeticus de Lutheranismo* (Historical Commentary and Defence of Lutheranism) by the Saxon court official Veit Ludwig von Seckendorff, a landmark in historical accounts of the Reformation and its origins. The work was reissued in an expanded format in 1692 to take account of Bossuet's criticisms, and translated into German in 1714 by the Ulm preacher Elias Frick. Seckendorff was a pious Lutheran, convinced that the Reformation was indeed a work of God. But he was also a scrupulous citer of historical sources, and his account of Luther sought to delineate a living, and at times flawed, human being, rather than the celestial *Wundermann* of earlier histories. Seckendorff's anti-Catholicism was tempered by a recognition that the Church of Rome had made progress since the days of Tetzel, and by genuine dismay about the continuing divisions of Christendom.

The *Thesenanschlag* was certainly acknowledged in Seckendorff's description of the beginnings of Luther's protest, though without particular fanfare or triumphalism. Indeed, in his brief account of it, Seckendorff emphasized how the Theses had been publicized on the eve of the feast of All Saints, 'not as if they were things certain and true', but as matters 'to be examined by legitimate disputation'.[32]

Elias Frick's German edition of Seckendorff found greater room for the direct intervention of the divine, by giving prominence to the 'Dream of Frederick the Wise'. But this was accompanied by some distinct defensiveness about the status of the tale. Frick admitted that some wanted to cast doubt on the account, because there was nothing about it in the extant writings of either Luther or Spalatin. He surmised it was likely that these men resisted recording it on paper 'so that the opponents would have no opportunity to cry out that Luther's teaching was based on dreams', rather than on the Word of God.[33]

Dreams, special revelations, and miracles remained important components of the worldview of ordinary Christians, Catholic and Protestant alike, throughout the eighteenth century. But they were now coming to be seen as something of an embarrassment by the intellectuals writing histories of the Reformation. Although versions of the woodcut image of 'The Dream of Frederick the Wise' continued to be produced through the first half of the century, scholars increasingly had their doubts about it. In a work published in the anniversary year 1717, the Göttingen theologian Christoph August Heumann devoted an extensive chapter to demonstrating that the dream was a fable without historical foundations.[34]

Some orthodox Lutheran theologians, Ernst Salomon Cyprian among them, were dismayed by an apparently growing tendency to treat the Reformation as a human and historical event, with discernible causes not necessarily requiring intervention from the providential hand of God. Yet as Scott Dixon has insightfully demonstrated, such relativizing of the origins of the Reformation was an ever more pronounced characteristic of eighteenth-century history-writing, even in Protestant circles. This had a paradoxical effect on perceptions of the events of 31 October 1517. On the one hand, the *Thesenanschlag* was accepted as a significant historical fact, with a documented basis in sixteenth-century sources. No eighteenth-century scholar seems to have questioned that it took place. On the other hand, it was now often seen as a link—indeed, the first link—in a chain of historical causes, rather than as a manifestation of the preordained divine will.

Conceivably, this configuration of interlocking causes might have led in some different direction. Already in the later seventeenth century, the renowned German jurist Samuel Pufendorf, son of a Saxon Lutheran pastor, was prepared to remark that 'it was a big mistake on the part of Leo X that he was so quick to take the side of the indulgence peddlers, and that he responded to the emerging disputations with the new Bull of November 1518.' In this way, the pope 'eliminated all paths to accommodation and removed any hopes Luther may have had about a consensual solution.' The Reformation was not inevitable.

Yet even rational and 'enlightened' commentators on the origins of the Reformation hesitated to abandon completely all ideas of purposeful divine design. In some ways, recognizing that the indulgence controversy represented an unlikely start to a Reformation of the Church actually strengthened an underlying providentialism. Johann Georg Walch (1693–1775), Professor of Theology at Jena, editor of Luther's works, and the author of a biography of the reformer, was cheerfully prepared to admit that Luther did not intend a Reformation, and that his quarrel with Tetzel was something of a private matter. 'If this difference of opinion had been a mere human act, how soon it would have been solved and the controversy settled.' And yet, 'the hand of the Lord was engaged . . . and Luther was driven by power from on high to go through with that he had begun.'[35]

Directed by a hidden hand or not, there was still relatively little indication, through the middle decades of the eighteenth century, that Luther's posting of the Ninety-five Theses on the door of the Castle Church was yet a tableau to grab and stir the imagination of most European Protestants, or even most German Lutherans. Only in Electoral Saxony was a 'Reformation Day' celebrated annually on 31 October in the years after 1717, and there was not much enthusiasm for commemoration of the Reformation anywhere in the two-hundred-and-fiftieth anniversary year of 1767. After 1717, and before 1817, none of the dozens of Luther coins and medals which continued to be minted in Germany chose to depict the *Thesenanschlag*. Prints and engravings on the theme of Luther's life in the later eighteenth century seem to have shown little interest either: the preferred themes were the more intrinsically dramatic ones of the burning of the papal bull, Luther's 'kidnapping' to the Wartburg, or poignant deathbed scenes.[36]

As for Wittenberg itself, it was hardly a vibrant centre of Protestant pilgrimage, though it had developed into a minor place of interest for wealthy travellers undertaking central European variants of the formative cultural experience known as the 'Grand Tour'. A 1749 guidebook for English travellers, by the Irish writer Thomas Nugent, recommended Wittenberg as a convenient stop between Leipzig and Potsdam. It was hailed as 'a fair, large, populous town', its university the place 'in which Luther preached first the Reformation'. Nugent noted that 'the principal church, called St Ursula's [sic], and the Castle deserve to be seen.' But there was no mention for the doors of the Castle Church. A few years before this, in 1734, the English clergyman John Swinton passed through Wittenberg with two companions on his way from Venice to Hamburg. His account of the visit duly noted that 'this town and university are famous on many accounts, as will appear to everyone in the least conversant with the German historians'. But nothing further—other than the breadth and cleanliness of the streets, the clientele of the posthouse, and the town's strength as the headquarters of a military garrison—caught and held Swinton's attention.[37]

Lying on the plain of the Elbe, Wittenberg's strategic importance as a military fortress proved its undoing during the Seven Years' War (1754–63), a conflict which pitted a rising Prussia, under its warrior king Frederick the Great, against France, Austria, and a coalition of German states including Saxony. Prussia occupied Wittenberg in 1756, and in October 1760 Austrian forces recaptured it. During the artillery bombardment, a stray round hit an ammunition depot, starting a fire which lasted for several days and destroyed much of the centre of the town. The most notable casualty was the Castle Church, reduced to ashes and rubble. Priceless paintings by Cranach and Dürer were destroyed, along with the pulpit where Luther once preached. Only the stone tomb of Luther, spared centuries earlier by Charles V, again survived this second and more destructive Imperial onslaught.

The wooden doors of the church, however, boards in which pious Wittenbergers believed Luther's nails were still embedded, were no more. For the theology professor Christian Siegmund Georgi, who lived through the bombardment, it was quite simply heartbreaking. 'The mother church of all evangelical Lutheranism . . . the beautiful temple whence the teaching of the Gospel had first rung out and spread to the rest of the world' now lay in ruins.

Repair work was relatively slow to get underway, and not completed until 1771. The university organized collections within Saxony, across other Protestant territories of the Empire, and in Lutheran Scandinavia—even the Russian Czarina Catherine II contributed. In the end, though, the principal costs of restoration were borne by the Saxon government and the (Catholic) Electoral ruling house. An initial set of designs submitted by the university was in the end passed over in favour of those of the Elector's architect Christian Friedrich Exner, who provided a plan for the rebuilt church in an up-to-date baroque style suiting current princely taste. No one seemed particularly concerned with reconstruction of the doors in anything like a modern 'heritage' sense. The university's designs proposed replacing the recessed 'jambs' or side-posts around the door with Corinthian half-pillars. In the final work, the jambs were retained, which preserved something at least of the original neo-Gothic feel, but the intention was scarcely the creation of any kind of historic memorial to the *Thesenanschlag*.[38]

The church and the town of Wittenberg were still 'sadly ruined by the late war' in September 1764, when another English traveller took a detour and recorded his impressions of the place. James Boswell, friend and biographer of Samuel Johnson, seemed considerably more interested in Wittenberg's Reformation heritage than John Swinton had been a generation earlier. He made a point of visiting Luther's convent, as well as 'the old Church where he first preached the Reformation'. In the wake of the bombardment, Boswell found it 'miserably shattered', but Luther's and Melanchthon's adjacent tombs were still intact, under large plates of metal.

Once there, Boswell discovered himself 'in a true solemn humour, and a most curious and agreeable idea presented itself, which was to write to Mr. Samuel Johnson from the tomb of Melanchthon.' His guide supplied him with pen and ink, and Boswell laid himself down so that 'my paper might literally rest upon the monument, or rather the simple epitaph, of this great and good man'. Interestingly, the nearby site of Luther's posting of the Theses formed no part of Boswell's reverie, and neither, indeed, did the reformer himself. 'I said nothing of hot-headed Luther'—a man who, in Boswell's view, compared distinctly unfavourably with 'the mild Melanchthon'.[39]

That invidious comparison—which we have seen already suggested by Bossuet—was not uncommon in the era of the Enlightenment, which valued reason in religion, as well as dignity and deportment in debate. Luther's vehemence and frequent coarseness of expression provided ammunition for Catholic critics, but was quite often also commented on unfavourably by Protestants, especially from outside the Lutheran fold. The Anglican bishop of Rochester, Francis Atterbury, wrote a work defending Luther from papist attacks, but nonetheless conceded that Luther's debates with Protestant opponents were 'managed with a fierceness not exactly warrantable'. Pierre Bayle, a French Calvinist and an early advocate of Enlightenment values of toleration and free thought, disapproved of Luther's impetuous temper. It was a mistake, he believed, ever to publish the Table Talk, a work full of 'such sayings as highly deserve to be condemned'.[40]

To Voltaire, French 'high priest' of Enlightenment anticlericalism, Luther was a distinctly unappealing figure. In a work published in English in 1733, Voltaire characterized him, along with Calvin and Zwingli, as a 'wretched author', and the founder of a 'sect' comparable with Muhammed's. Frederick the Great of Prussia, whose military ambitions led directly to the destruction of the site of the *Thesenanschlag*, was scarcely more enthusiastic. He recognized the value of the Reformation for breaking the political and economic power of the priesthood, but in a letter to Voltaire of 1737, the then Crown Prince of Prussia blithely dismissed Luther as 'nothing but a blustering monk and a crude writer for somewhat unenlightened people.'[41]

On this, as on much else, the Enlightenment did not speak with one voice. In direct response to Voltaire, the Saxon jurist Justus Möser produced in 1750 a spirited defence of Luther, addressed principally to a French audience. It was not so much the fact that Luther rediscovered true doctrine that spoke in his favour, as that he had improved morality, and promoted the unity and smooth functioning of the state. A spate of eighteenth-century writers, including Gotthold Ephraim Lessing, Johann Gottfried Herder, and Johann Wolfgang von Goethe, hailed Luther, not as the prophet of God's Word, but as an apostle of freedom and progress. Luther, gushed the 'enlightened' Prussian pastor Friedrich Germanus Lüdke in 1774, was 'a veritable guardian angel for the rights of reason, humanity, and Christian liberty of conscience'.[42]

The meaning of the Reformation, in intellectual circles at least, was being reinvented once more at the end of the eighteenth century, and the foundations laid for a powerful and enduring set of historical myths. Luther's Reformation was the harbinger of economic progress, reason, toleration in religion, emancipation from irrational belief, and the ability of each person to 'think for themselves'. All these were proposals which, had he lived to hear them uttered, would almost certainly have horrified Luther, whose own conscience was always 'captive to the Word of God'. The indulgence controversy was something which fitted easily into this emerging pattern of interpretation. Challenging theological issues around the meaning and nature of repentance might simply be laid to one side in order to emphasize how a corrupt and oppressive Church exploited popular 'superstition' in pursuit of monetary gain.

To illustrate just how the Reformation could be portrayed as a crucial milestone in a progressive human history of emancipation we can turn to a *General History of the Christian Church*, composed at the turn of the nineteenth century by the English scientist, political theorist, and Unitarian minister, Joseph Priestley. Having been driven from England after expressing sympathy for the Revolution in France, Priestley took up residence in Philadelphia in 1794. Twenty years earlier, the city had been the cradle of revolution against British rule in America, which Priestley's *History* saw as a kind of finishing line in the human march of freedom. The work devoted considerable attention to Luther's quarrel with Tetzel, and quoted extensively from the Ninety-five Theses, whose arguments Priestley simply regarded as 'plain good sense'. Still, the potential of the posting of the Theses as a symbol for freedom or enlightenment remained distinctly unfulfilled. Priestley said nothing at all about the nailing of the document to the door of the Castle Church, noting merely that 'having maintained these propositions in the University of Wittenberg, Luther sent them to the archbishop of Magdeburg'.[43]

Yet as the meanings of the Reformation itself changed, the potential of the envisaged events of 31 October 1517 to encapsulate and express those meanings was slowly but surely edging its way to the fore. Once a pious Wittenberg and Saxon tradition, the myth of the *Thesenanschlag* was at last escaping the confines of Germany. This chapter can aptly close with an extract from an English-language religious education textbook, published in 1797 by Johann Gottlieb Burckhardt, a former professor at the University of Leipzig, who from 1781 served as minister to the German Lutheran congregation meeting at the Savoy Chapel in London:

> Albert, the Elector of Mainz, having been empowered by the pope to promulgate such indulgences in Germany, employed Tetzel, a Dominican friar, to retail them in Saxony. Luther finding the evil effects of that traffic in the immoral lives of his parishioners, was the first that opposed it, by publishing and fixing ninety-five theses on the great church at Wittenberg, October 31st, 1517. This bold step of Luther was the signal for vast multitudes of people in all countries to shake off the yoke of spiritual tyranny.[44]

The coming decades, in Europe and in other parts of the world, would see repeated attempts to shake off yokes of tyranny, and to invoke symbols of freedom. The nineteenth century was to be the century of the *Thesenanschlag*, and with it, of the modern invention of the Reformation.

4
1817: Heroes

Glorification

In 1806 the Berlin-based artist Johann Erdmann Hummel produced a painting entitled 'D. Martin Luthers Verherrlichung'—the glorification or 'apotheosis' of Dr Martin Luther. The work, which he turned shortly afterwards into an elaborate copperplate-engraving, consisted of a large central composition, framed by eleven smaller illustrations depicting episodes from the life of Luther. The individual scenes were made to seem like panels, set into the pillars supporting a grand triumphal arch. Beneath the arch, on a field of clouds, stands Luther, in the guise of a haloed saint, and a posture of pious prayer. He is surrounded by angels, some of them singing and playing lutes. It is a spectacle to raise the eyebrows—if not the hackles—of any sixteenth-century Protestant transported forwards in time to behold it. In fact, its imagery owed as much to classical motifs as to the Catholic iconography of the Baroque. Luther is presented with a victor's palm by an allegorical figure of Grace. Hummel describes her in his notes as a heavenly Venus. Behind her stand three female figures who are at once the three graces of classical antiquity, and the biblical virtues of Faith, Hope, and Charity—a felicitous union of reason and religion.

Apotheosis, a Greek word meaning deification, originally referred to the reception onto Mount Olympus, home of the Gods, of some worthy ruler or of the guardian spirit known as a 'genius'. The motif had long been used in works of art to extol the praises of kings and emperors, as well as of heroic saints like Ignatius of Loyola. It was not the kind of memorial a Protestant clergyman would expect, or necessarily welcome. But Hummel's accompanying text made clear that, as much as the person of Luther himself, what was being celebrated was 'the religious freedom, which he restored'. A rapturous review of the work, in the influential *Allgemeine Literatur-Zeitung* of Jena, rejoiced that art was finally following the lead of poetry and drama in concerning itself with the life and deeds of Luther, and agreed that 'the most splendid and momentous achievement of this great man concerns the freedom of belief'. The actual content of Luther's doctrine seemed to matter much less than that he had broken the stranglehold of a thought-suppressing system.[1]

Like some of the visual cycles of Luther's life dating from the eighteenth century, Hummel included in the work a scene of the posting of the Ninety-five Theses (see Fig. 4.1). With its linear boldness of execution, and confident command of perspective, it represents a startlingly new clarity and realism in depictions of the event. It also marks the beginning of a shift towards portraying the *Thesenanschlag*, rather than the confrontation with Cajetan at Augsburg, or the burning of the papal excommunication by the Elster Gate, as the key visual reference point for Luther's break with the Old Church. Hummel's descriptive notes here were unambiguous: this was 'the first act of the Reformation', when a man 'inspired with the spirit of God... caused the sentences against indulgences to be fastened to the church doors in Wittenberg'.

Caused to be, rather than fastened by himself. Perhaps as much for artistic as historical reasons, Hummel depicted Luther standing in profile on the church steps, angled towards a gathering crowd and pointing magisterially towards a seemingly handwritten placard on the door of the *Schlosskirche*. It is being fixed there by two youths, one holding the document in place while another hammers in the nails, perched on a ladder being steadied by a remarkably competent-looking younger boy. A discordant note is struck by the cowled and scowling friar, who passes by without joining in the interest or acclamation for the appearance of the Theses. The other bystanders form what is almost a stately procession to the church door, caps doffed as they approach. Their raised faces express wonder and hope, a longing for direction and clarity in a perilous and uncertain world.

The times were indeed turbulent, for Germany and for Europe as a whole. Revolution in France in 1789, followed by the execution of King Louis XVI in 1793, plunged the continent into war, as the remaining great monarchies—Austria, Prussia, Russia, Great Britain—sought to

Fig. 4.1. Luther at the posting of the Ninety-five Theses: an engraving by Johann Erdmann Hummel (1806).

stem the tide of revolutionary fervour at the borders of France. Out of that fervour arose the charismatic, authoritarian figure of Napoleon Bonaparte, who in 1804 had himself crowned Emperor of France in what seemed to many a betrayal of the egalitarian ideals of the Revolution. In Germany, Beethoven bitterly dedicated his Third Symphony (The Eroica) 'to the memory of a great man'.[2]

The leading German power, Prussia, came to terms with France in 1795, and stayed out of the coalition against Napoleon which ended in the crushing defeat of Austrian and Russian armies at Austerlitz in 1805. But Napoleon's subsequent decision to dissolve the Holy Roman Empire, and to subsume allied German states into a subservient 'Confederation of the Rhine', pushed Prussia towards renewed war in 1806, the year of Hummel's artistic endeavour. Although Germans were on both sides in this conflict, the struggle with France increasingly took on a national and patriotic aspect.

In this context, the historical figure of Martin Luther, the inspired prophet of God, the harbinger of Enlightenment rationality, began to be reinvented once again as the eternal symbol of German freedom and nationhood. Already in 1766, overcoming some of his youthful cynicism about the reformer, Frederick the Great remarked that 'Luther, as liberator of the Fatherland, deserved to have altars erected to him'. That feeling of gratitude intensified in the early nineteenth century. The philosopher Johann Gottfried Herder, in a work of 1802, stated that he did not believe Luther's legacy should be a narrowly German national Church. But he was nonetheless certain that Luther was the man who brought back to a nation asleep 'under the yoke of foreign words and customs . . . its authentic speech, its authentic religion, which is belief, faith, mind and heart'. To continue Luther's work was nothing less than to 'lay upon the altar of the fatherland pure intentions, to whatever effect they may be'.[3]

The idea of a non-dogmatic, liberating, patriotic Luther was a compelling one. It received further popular exposure in a highly successful play by the Prussian poet and dramatist Zacharias Werner. *Martin Luther oder die Weihe der Kraft* (Martin Luther or the Consecration of Strength) was written and performed in 1806, as the country rallied for resistance to Bonaparte. Werner, an enthusiastic adherent of the budding Romantic movement, explained that his aim was 'to present to the Germans a German hero, at a moment when, if they are not to succumb, heroic souls must consecrate themselves to the forces of the times'. In the play, niceties of doctrine are distinctly secondary to the struggle for freedom and nationhood. The *Thesenanschlag*, and the whole indulgence controversy, is related second-hand, through the testimony of Luther's father, Hans—portrayed as a bluff and honest miner, on a visit to see his son in Wittenberg, 'the big city':

> The parson got a letter, where it was written about what you posted before witnesses on the Castle Church at Wittenberg—about the mass, about indulgences, good works, and I don't know what else! And how you disputed over there with the Dominican—Tetzel, I think he was called.

Receiving this news thoroughly disconcerted the elder Luther's parish priest, who to Hans' amusement, became so confused that he pulled the spectacles from his red nose and threw them across the room. This, the younger Luther interjects, is precisely 'what I do too . . . I tear away from people the spectacles, with which the pope has slyly pinched the noses of the poor folk.' Romantic passions could, however, flow in unpredictable directions, and Werner shortly afterwards began to see things differently himself. Within five years he had travelled to Rome and converted to Roman Catholicism, becoming ordained as a priest in 1814. He sought to make amends for his earlier work with a long poem of 1813, *Die Weihe der Unkraft* (The Consecration of Weakness).[4]

Prussian strength received a hard lesson on 14 October 1806, when Napoleon crushed Friedrich Wilhelm III's armies at the battle of Jena-Auerstadt. Prussia was knocked out of the war, and reduced to the status of French satellite. For the town of Wittenberg, it meant occupation by French troops. The Elector of Saxony, Friedrich August III, now declared himself an ally of Napoleon, and was rewarded with Saxony's promotion to the status of kingdom. But the fortunes of war turned again after Napoleon's disastrous invasion of Russia, and ignominious retreat from Moscow in 1812. The following year saw the start of a patriotic 'War of Liberation' in Germany, with Prussian forces again taking to the field. Wittenberg was regarrisoned and fortified three times in the course of 1813, with the French turning the castle and its church into their citadel. The castle was gutted by fire in the course of a Prussian bombardment in September 1813. The town was forcibly retaken by the Prussians in January 1814, but, all things considered, the *Schlosskirche* escaped with relatively light damage: the doors installed after the fire-storm of 1760 survived this second siege and seizure.[5]

The fall of Napoleon and Prussian victory in the War of Liberation had local political consequences with considerable symbolic and cultural ramifications. In May 1815, having backed and stuck with the wrong side, the King of Saxony was forced to cede territory to his victorious neighbour, and Wittenberg found itself situated in a new Prussian province of Saxony.

A leading architect, Karl Friedrich Schinkel, recently appointed general director of building operations in Prussian territories, was commissioned to report to the Interior Ministry on the state of the Castle Church. His memorandum was an impassioned plea for architectural conservation, one of the first of its kind anywhere in Europe. It seemed to Schinkel quite evident that this 'first church of the Reformation' must be preserved and repaired 'as a treasured memorial'. He submitted proposals for substantial restoration work in order to give the church a renewed late Gothic appearance, which would 'correspond with the character of Luther's own time'. Yet the suggestions, including reconstruction of the destroyed pre-1760 interior and complete replacement of the roof, were too ambitious for the local Lutheran clergy to countenance, and in the event only minor repairs were undertaken.

The end of the Napoleonic Wars was in fact hardly a golden new dawn for the Saxon birthplace of the Protestant Reformation. Wittenberg's university, which had in effect ceased to function during the French occupation, was in 1817 amalgamated with the University of Halle, and relocated to that town, leaving its former buildings as a seminary for pastors. The Castle became a military barracks, and the Castle Church its chapel.[6]

Nonetheless, the town and the church which were linked indelibly to a great national hero of Germany's past were now absorbed politically into the kingdom which seemed to represent Germany's future. After the dissolution of the Holy Roman Empire, the question of how, or whether, its assorted territories should be reconstituted as a unified German nation-state would dominate the rest of the century. For many German nationalists, it seemed axiomatic that such a state must have a Protestant religious identity. Luther, and the events of 31 October 1517, offered possibilities for the foundation myth of a German religion and a German state—a 'klein deutsch' (small

Germany) state that would exclude Catholic Austria and anchor itself on the Prussian monarchy.

The third centenary Reformation jubilee thus arrived at a moment hungry for rich political symbolism and resonant with cultural promise. On the second day of the celebration in 1817, King Friedrich Wilhelm III of Prussia travelled to Wittenberg, where he ceremonially entered the recently (if modestly) restored Castle Church through the famous north door and attended divine service. On the same day he laid in the main market square the foundation stone of a new monument to Luther, designed by the renowned sculptor, Johann Gottfried Schadow. It would be the first statue of a commoner to be erected anywhere in Germany.[7]

On 'Reformation Day' itself, however, Friedrich Wilhelm was in Potsdam, attending a communion service designed to mark the healing of centuries of religious division—not between Catholics and Protestants, but between Lutherans and Calvinists of the Reformed Church. The princely house of Prussia had since 1613 belonged to the Reform, while its subjects were largely Lutheran in religion. Friedrich Wilhelm was himself a devout Calvinist, whose popular queen-consort Louise (died 1810) had been a pious Lutheran. The impending anniversary of Luther's protest against Rome seemed to the king the ideal moment to instigate a 'true religious unification'. The Lutheran and Reformed churches were really 'only divided over external matters'. Unity between them, he believed, 'conforms to the original intentions of the Reformers'.

As the anniversary approached, Friedrich Wilhelm issued, on 27 September 1817, a proclamation summoning representatives of the Lutheran and Reformed churches to a joint service of worship, the first step towards a full union between them. This 'evangelical' Church would not require Lutherans and Calvinists to drop their individual beliefs (they could continue, for example, to interpret the eucharist in their own distinctive ways). But an institutionally fragmented body of believers was to be gathered together under the leadership of the crown. This would bring religion, as one of the king's ministers put it, 'into harmony with the direction of the state'. Political expediency aside, Friedrich Wilhelm's outlook was influenced by Pietism, a movement for religious renewal which had swept through the Lutheran and other Protestant churches over the course of the eighteenth century. Its instinct was to downplay the significance of specific doctrines, and to accentuate spiritual experience and the importance of ethics among all the heirs of what was now conceived of as 'the Reformation'—a distinct era of religious history whose achievement was to overthrow the grip of rigid dogmatism.[8]

The 'Prussian Union' was broadly welcomed in the king's territories, and more widely across Germany. It was endorsed by the governing body of the Lutheran Church in Prussia, the Berlin Synod, and although entry into the Union was optional for individual congregations, by 1825 nearly 70 per cent of Prussian churches had adopted it. Similar unions were effected in other principalities. The Duchy of Nassau introduced one in 1817, and the Rhineland Palatinate in the following year. Anhalt, Baden, Rhenish Hesse, Hesse, and Württemberg followed suit in the 1820s. To many pastors and lay people, a shared Protestant and Reformation heritage—in the face of a Catholic Church which showed disappointingly few signs of collapsing under the weight of its own corruptions—now seemed much more important than narrow doctrinal wrangling.

The tendency was exemplified by the leading Protestant theologian of the age. Friedrich Schleiermacher was a Calvinist on the faculty of the new University of Berlin, an institution whose statutes expressed only the very loosest Lutheran orthodoxy—the requirement was not to teach anything contrary to scripture, the creeds, or the Augsburg Confession. In his address to the university on the occasion of the 1817 anniversary, Schleiermacher stressed the importance of remembering not just Luther, but all the things Luther and Zwingli had in common: justification by faith, the sole authority of scripture, a disdain for ritualism and superstition, the abolition of intermediaries between humanity and God. The times also seemed propitious for what Schleiermacher had fervently hoped for during the dark days of the struggle against Napoleon: 'my greatest wish after liberation is for one true German Empire, powerfully representing the entire German folk and territory'.[9]

Nationalist sentiment was energized by the embrace of Luther as a true German hero. But not all celebrations and demonstrations inspired by the anniversary of 1817 saw the future in terms of a submissive and obedient Protestant flock, faithfully shepherded by a sanctified Prussian monarchy. Two weeks before the formal festivities at Wittenberg, several hundred students, members of fraternities from various German universities, gathered at the Wartburg Castle near Eisenach—the place where Luther sought refuge after the Diet of Worms and translated the Bible into German. The date of assembly—18 October—was close to Reformation Day but was in fact the fourth anniversary of Napoleon's defeat at the Battle of Leipzig. Many of the students were veterans of the War of Liberation, but they had become deeply disillusioned when the 1815 Congress of Vienna crushed hopes of democratic and liberal reform and re-established the old order and the power of the ancient monarchies across Europe. As one student lamented, 'everything is different from what we expected'.

In a series of enthusiastic rallies, speeches, and declarations, the Wartburg students called for the unification of Germany, but under a liberal constitution. In the process, they reinvented Luther in their own image. The reformer, whose own political attitudes were decidedly conservative if not downright reactionary, was celebrated as a fellow citizen and democratic patriot. The students intoned Luther's great hymn, 'A Mighty Fortress is our God', as well as songs of their own devising, wishing long life to Dr Luther and defiance to the pope: 'Rise, rise, my German Fatherland / Your brothers extend to you their hand!'

The details of Luther's doctrinal teachings were of relatively little importance. His significance was as a liberator, who freed the German people from spiritual bondage, just as the liberal idealists hoped to free them from political oppression by reactionary princes. The heroic action of Luther's which resonated most with the participants in the Wartburg Festival was not, in fact, the *Thesenanschlag* of 1517, but the 1520 burning of the papal bull of excommunication—undertaken, of course, under Luther's direction, by Wittenberg students. In conscious emulation of the act, some of the Wartburg demonstrators gathered around a bonfire, where names of 'reactionary' authors and texts were read from a list, and bundles of paper bound to resemble books were cast into the flames—an episode prompting alarmed investigation on the part of the Prussian authorities.[10]

In 1817 there was no precisely agreed meaning of the event of three centuries earlier, even among those identifying as Protestants. But the excitement in Germany was palpably higher than it had been in 1717. Leopold von Ranke, then a student at Leipzig, would in later life make his mark as the founding father of objective, source-based historical writing, with a mission to report the past 'wie es eigentlich gewesen' (as it actually happened). His *German History in the Age of the Reformation*, its first volume published in 1839, contained a fairly neutrally formulated factual notice of the *Thesenanchlag* of 31 October 1517, with the comment that it was the moment at which contradictory conceptions of faith and conscience came openly into conflict. But in 1817 the young Ranke composed a fragmentary, and highly emotional, essay on Martin Luther. In it, he reported how, in the face of popish attempts to rob both the bodies and souls of the people, Luther 'wouldn't tolerate the wretchedness any more, but stood up and nailed the Ninety-five Theses against the abuses to the Castle Church in Wittenberg'. As a result, the forces of evil and ignorance united to crush his opposition, but against them he stood unshaken, 'like a rock in the sea'.[11]

Many Germans felt that Luther's achievement, irrespective of his exact views on individual questions of faith, was to light a torch for freedom and enlightenment in a time of benighted superstition and darkness. Social, cultural, and political consequences of the Reformation were prioritized over its doctrinal ones. At the same time, the jubilee of 1817 was a self-consciously historical celebration, in a way the earlier ones, focused on religious questions, had never quite been.[12] Many agreed with the Prussian king that the intra-Protestant theological debates of the ensuing centuries were a distraction from the core tenets of belief that Luther and other reformers of his generation held and taught in common. For the communion celebration at Potsdam special coins were minted, depicting Calvin and Luther side by side.[13]

Yet to some orthodox German Lutherans, all this felt like a dilution, if not a betrayal, of the actual ideals for which Luther had stood. Claus Harms, a pastor and theologian from Kiel, was a vociferous opponent of the Prussian Union, and of any kind of 'progressive' understanding of the meaning of the Reformation. His contribution to the anniversary celebrations of 1817 was to publish a new edition of the Ninety-five Theses. Harms lamented that little attention to the contents of the Theses was to be found in recent writings about Luther, even though they were 'the cradle and swaddling clothes in which our Lutheran Church was laid'. Admittedly, the Theses were 'not free of papistical error', as Luther himself had come to see, but they had a more than merely historical importance: 'the occasion, indeed the start, of the Reformation is to be found in them.'

Harms appended to the edition ninety-five new theses of his own—an indication of the iconic status ascribed by Lutherans, not just to the act of posting the Theses, but to the actual text itself. Several of these upheld orthodox Lutheran doctrines against the ideas of the Reformed: 'just as at the Colloquy of Marburg, 1529 [where Luther had disputed with Zwingli], bread and wine are the body and blood of Christ, so it is in 1817' (no. 78). But Harms' main purpose was to launch an attack upon Enlightenment readings of Luther, and of Christian faith more generally. Belief in reason, he alleged, had become 'the pope of our times, our Antichrist' (no. 9). Under the old faith, God created man, but 'by the new faith man creates God' (no. 27). All this was to take the occasion of an anniversary, not joyously to celebrate, but to issue a stark warning, a call-to-arms. The result was a publishing furore that recalled the response to the original Ninety-five Theses in 1517. Dozens of pamphlets were published in support of, or in opposition to, Harms' position; Schleiermacher was among those who weighed in against him.[14]

An aggrieved Lutheran possessiveness was not, however, the predominant tone to the 1817 celebrations in Germany. They were usually more benevolent, and in places even ecumenical occasions. Overt expressions of anti-Catholicism were hardly lacking, but mindful that German Catholics had also taken part in the liberation struggle against Napoleon, some, generally pro-Union, preachers suggested that bitterness and recrimination was now out of place. A spirit of brotherly reconciliation, in a shared love of the Fatherland, was the most appropriate way to recall Luther and the Reformation. A few even dared to envisage an ultimate reunification of evangelical and Catholic churches.

At Bamberg, Trabelsdorf, and Küps in Upper Franconia, a historically Protestant part of the majority-Catholic Kingdom of Bavaria, local Catholics joined in with the festivities, some even attending Reformation Day services in the evangelical church. There was a similar pattern at Mühlhausen and some other parts of Thuringia, absorbed into the Prussian state in 1815. Shortly before the anniversary of 1817, Goethe expressed the hope that 'every right-thinking Catholic' would feel able to participate, and in the event he rejoiced that a celebration jointly hailing the beginning of the Reformation and the victory at Leipzig had proved to be 'a festival of the purest humanity'. In Austria, where the reign of the 'enlightened' Emperor Josef II (1780–90) had already witnessed an end to the harassment of Protestants, his successor Franz II sanctioned public, empire-wide celebrations of the Reformation centenary as a token of the state's commitment to toleration. Many Austrian Catholics, especially in Vienna, cheerfully participated.

In some places in Germany, Jews also took part in Reformation festivals, despite the anti-Semitism hovering around expressions of German nationalism, and distinctly audible in the student demonstrations at the Wartburg. Luther's own ferociously anti-Semitic writings were largely unknown in early nineteenth-century Germany, and the prevailing idea of Luther as an advocate of liberty and freedom of conscience must have appealed to members of a long-disparaged religious minority.[15]

If the centenary of 1817 was less narrowly confessional than those of 1617 and 1717, neither was it so purely a German or Scandinavian affair. Similarly to the official Prussian stance, celebrations in the Netherlands emphasized the common origins of Protestant denominations. Here too, in a religiously diverse state, there was an effort to involve Catholics. Established in 1815, the Kingdom of the Netherlands incorporated under the Protestant House of Orange the Catholic territories of the formerly Austrian Netherlands (present-day Belgium).

Interest in the occasion in England and Scotland, both of which largely ignored the anniversaries of 1617 and 1717, was more muted. There was, however, a smattering of commemorative sermons—in England, preached more often among non-conformist communities than in the established Anglican Church, which took a somewhat haughty view of its genealogical relationship to Martin Luther. One such sermon, delivered to a dissenting congregation at Harlow in Essex, was entitled modestly 'The Reasonableness of Protestantism', though another, preached at a meeting house in Hackney, laid its emphasis on the corruption and perfidy, then and now, of the Church of Rome.[16]

There was apparently little interest in timing such sermons to take place on 31 October. Indeed, William Ward, preaching in commemoration of 'The Reformation from Popery' at Stowmarket in Suffolk on 9 November, preserved a longstanding British confusion—dating back to John Foxe—about the actual date of the posting of the Theses. Ward was aware that Luther's 'first remonstrances against some abuses in the Church of Rome' were sent to the Archbishop of

Magdeburg on the eve of All Saints, though he believed that it was another two days before he 'affixed the same to the doors of the Great Church at Wittenberg'. This was, nonetheless, the beginning of 'that great change which set part of the world free from ignorance and superstition'. Ward gave his listeners a rousing account of Luther's conversion, beginning after he 'accidentally found a Bible in the monastery where he lived, a book then little known'. Here, Protestant mythologizing about the status of the Bible before the Reformation is in full flow: medieval theology was, in fact, largely a matter of laborious biblical interpretation, and the monk Luther was professor of scripture at the University of Wittenberg.[17]

There was rather more interest in the three-hundredth anniversary of Luther's Reformation in the fledgling American Republic, not least because, unlike Britain, the United States contained significant numbers of actual Lutherans. These were immigrants, and the descendants of immigrants, from Germany and Scandinavia, frequently divided among themselves along doctrinal, ethnic, and linguistic lines. Members of other American Protestant denominations sometimes took part in anniversary services in 1817, but only the Lutherans organized formal events.

In contrast to the sometimes ecumenical character of the anniversary in Germany, Austria, or the Netherlands, American Catholics did not participate. The fear and hostility occasioned by large-scale Catholic immigration to the United States would reach full flood only later in the century. But anti-popery was wired deep in the early American psyche, and preachers like David Frederick Schaeffer of Frederickstown, Maryland, instinctively contrasted the 'gross corruption and spiritual tyranny of Rome' with the free air of America, where 'each may choose that method of worshipping God which appeareth most consistent and satisfactory'. In a set of three anniversary sermons, the president of the New York pastors' association, or Ministerium, Frederick Henry Quitman, marvelled at how 'three hundred years have now elapsed, since Doctor Martin Luther raised the standard of religious liberty in Saxony, and by one bold stroke laid the foundation for the deliverance of his country from ecclesiastical despotism.' Quitman combined the preconceptions of a Lutheran theologian with the enthusiasms of an advocate of the Enlightenment. 'The ages, which immediately preceded the Reformation by Luther, are properly denominated ages of ignorance and oppression.' But once Luther took his stand, inestimable numbers of his countrymen immediately embraced his new doctrine:

> Assisted by this light, they broke the fetters which superstition had forged, and under its influence arts and sciences revived. Roused from the fatal lethargy, which had depressed the human mind for many centuries, many thousands successfully attempted to shake off the humiliating yoke, to recover their natural rights, and thus to restore human nature to its original dignity.

In the current age, Quitman was pleased to reflect, 'the influence of the pope has been declining, and the thunderbolt of the Vatican has lost its terrors'.[18]

In reflecting on the blessings of the Reformation, American Lutherans generally did consider its precise date of inception to be a significant matter. 'Would it not be shameful indifference in us', Quitman asked on 31 October 1817, 'to let this memorable day pass, without taking honourable notice of that great man, to whom we are so much indebted'? In 1815, the New York Ministerium urged Synods from Pennsylvania and North Carolina to prepare for a joint commemoration on the Sunday 'nearest to October 31st, 1817', though it was only in September of the anniversary year that the New York Ministerium determined to have its own celebration on 31 October. This followed a resolution from the Pennsylvania Ministerium to the effect that they were happy to unite with their New York brethren 'in so far that we would hold the said celebration on the 31st day of October, it being the exact anniversary of the Reformation . . . and they must be requested to keep with us the very anniversary itself, and not the Sunday following'. The president of the Pennsylvania Synod, George Lochmann, later declared 31 October 1517 to be a day which must be held in grateful remembrance 'as long as the world exists'. He added that 'what the 4th day of July, 1776, is and must be to our precious political liberty, that the 31st of October of the year 1517, should be, in respect to our religious liberty'. It is a revealing pairing of dates, suggesting the emergence of multiple 'sites of memory' (see pp. 14–15) in the construction of a national narrative, as well as the capacity of public commemorations to reinforce a collective view of history.[19]

Concern with the 'exact day' was not universal—the Special Conference of Evangelical Lutheran preachers in Ohio and Western Pennsylvania resolved to hold their commemoration of 'the Reformation by the blessed Luther' in 1817 over the first three days of October. But it testifies nonetheless to the perception that one specific action of Luther's was the original wellspring from which a veritable river of blessings flowed. Among the works published by American Lutherans at the time of the anniversary was a translation of a popular biography of Luther by Johann Friedrich Wilhelm Tischer, superintendent of the Lutheran Church in Saxony. Tischer made much out of Luther's 'bold step' in posting the Theses. Everyone, he claimed, was simply 'astonished at the intrepid undertaking'. Reports of it spread through every country 'with incredible rapidity'. The crucial role played by printing in this process went silently unacknowledged: 'the greatness of the undertaking itself, and the general complaint against indulgences, but which none had dared to attack, were the cause of the rapid circulation of this news'. Yet at the same time, Tischer's account betrayed some uncertainty about the meaning of the *Thesenanschlag* in Luther's own day. He recognized that Luther's intention was to provoke an academic debate, and while suggesting that the public posting was an act of 'direct opposition to the pope', Tischer immediately contradicted himself by noting that Luther at that time had no intention to oppose the pope himself, but only to put an end to the trade in indulgences; he even sent a respectful letter to Rome.

Tischer's account confidently, if confusedly, affirmed the significance of the *Thesenanschlag*, but in common with most of the earlier accounts, it did not provide many colourful or incidental details. Luther simply 'posted them up at the Palace-Chapel at Wittenberg'. This action, while often recognized as the initiating act of the Reformation, was still not invariably acknowledged as its defining moment. In the early and middle decades of the nineteenth century, American history textbooks were strongly influenced by the *General History of Civilization in Europe* of Francois Guizot, a French Protestant professor and politician. Guizot dated the true beginning of the Reformation, not to Luther's posting of the Theses in 1517, but to his burning of the papal bull of excommunication in December 1520. This was a political rather than theological point of departure, which reinforced the case for seeing the Reformation as an emancipation of reason and liberty of conscience against the power of an overweening spiritual authority.[20]

The posting of the Theses also still sometimes struggled to compete with other, more visually realizable, and intrinsically dramatic, episodes from Luther's biography. At the laying of the corner-stone of a new English-speaking Lutheran church in New York in 1821, several items were chosen to be buried alongside it in a box: a Bible, a Lutheran catechism, a hymn book and liturgy, three American coins, and 'an engraving, faithfully representing the great Luther, of blessed memory, before the Diet of Worms'. This scene, long the subject of illustration, and accompanied with its instantly memorable motto—'here I stand, I cannot otherwise, God help me. Amen'—evidently represented a more powerful focus of reflection than the posting-up of the Theses, its solemn interment a more appropriate way to 'manifest our respect and gratitude to Luther'.[21]

A few years later, in 1839, the first biography of Luther by an American was published at Boston. *The Life and Times of Martin Luther*, by the popular and prolific author Hannah Farnham Sawyer-Lee, was—in addition to being deeply anti-Catholic—a piece of decidedly free and imaginative writing, which had no difficulty telling the reader exactly what the young Luther was thinking as he walked the fields around Erfurt, under 'the moon, with its refulgent beam, evening with its waning light, the summer shower with its "arrowy rain", the howling tempest and wintry blast'. Yet remarkably, though Lee discussed the composition of the Ninety-five Theses, their sending to Cardinal Albrecht of Mainz, and their dissemination throughout Germany, she did not mention at all their posting to the door of the Castle Church at Wittenberg.[22] The memory of Luther—even a literary, commercial, and popularized Luther—was by no means yet synonymous with thoughts of his encounter, on 31 October 1517, with a set of obedient and obliging doors.

Tourists

For that to happen, the doors themselves would have to try harder to capture the imagination of the public, both travelling and reading. In the years subsequent to the jubilee of 1817, Wittenberg was increasingly put on the international map. Visitors journeyed to the actual site of the Reformation's origins and afterwards wrote and published their impressions of it. A trickle of tourists at the start of the nineteenth century never became a torrential flood, but the number of visitors inspired to view the historic sites of the Protestant Reformation undoubtedly grew over the succeeding decades.

Some of the earliest nineteenth-century travellers to record their impressions of Wittenberg didn't actually mention the church doors or the *Thesenanschlag* at all. The English journalist and political radical, Thomas Hodgskin, visited the town in December of the anniversary year 1817, in the course of a long European walking tour. He was deeply conscious of being in 'the first seat, and the very high place of the Reformation', the town from whose pulpits Luther 'thundered his masculine and powerful eloquence against the corruptions of Rome'. Hodgskin had hoped to see the tombs of Luther and Melanchthon, but arrived too early to do so 'without waiting longer than was pleasant to me'. Perhaps he stood in frustration outside the locked doors of the *Schlosskirche*, but if so, he did not mention them. Neither did another British journalist, and commentator on German character and customs, the Scot John Strang, who visited in 1831. He was more interested in the *Schlosskirche*'s pulpit, from which Luther 'zealously laboured to instil the principles of Protestantism'. To the well-travelled, if conventionally prejudiced, Strang, it seemed self-evident these labours were not in vain: 'the people of Protestant, compared with Catholic Germany, are as superior in intelligence and worth, as Europeans are to Asiatics.'[23]

An early American visitor, Henry E. Dwight, recorded appropriate feelings of awe in a letter sent from Wittenberg in May 1826. The town itself was not much to look at, but 'to a Protestant, and to everyone who loves mental freedom, it will long remain a hallowed spot'. Evoking the struggle of the Ancient Greeks against Persian oppression, Dwight saw in the town of Wittenberg 'a moral Marathon, where the fetters of tyranny and superstition were broken, when millions, catching the song of triumph, forgot that they had been slaves.' Dwight visited the tombs of Luther and Melanchthon, and was properly impressed with Schadow's 'colossal bronze statue of Luther', set up in the town square in 1821.

But Dwight's reflections on Wittenberg, and the significance of Luther and Melanchthon's labours, contained no mention of the posting of the Ninety-five Theses. The historical event which the topography of Wittenberg summoned to mind for Dwight was rather Luther's burning of the papal bull, on what was now a piece of fenced-in meadow land just outside the city gate on the road to Dresden: 'It is difficult for us', he wrote, 'accustomed as we are to laugh at papal anathemas, and knowing how harmless they are now, to form an adequate conception of the courage that thus bade defiance to the pope'. Another American, the New York pastor Henry Hiestand, visited the town in 1835, and was similarly convinced that this deed, marking a complete repudiation of papal authority, was 'the most important act that ever Luther performed at Wittenberg'. Hiestand recognized the significance of Luther's 'ninety-five propositions, given to the world October 31, 1517', but he had nothing to say about the circumstances of their gifting.[24]

International visitors to Wittenberg in the early nineteenth century were thus not journeying there primarily, or even at all, to view the site of the *Thesenanschlag*. Travel guides, such as the *Itinerary of Germany* printed in London in 1819, might recommend a visit to the town without even mentioning the event.[25] But by the middle decades of the century, this was starting to change, as an ever greater number of visitors made Wittenberg a stopping point on German or European tours. The exercise was facilitated by the opening of the town's first railway station in 1841. By taking the early morning train from Berlin, so the Church of Scotland minister John Aiton advised in 1842, it was possible to visit 'the Protestant Mecca, as it has been called', and to return to the capital the same evening.

It was also in 1842 that the publisher Karl Baedeker published, in his series of famous travel guides, the first volume devoted to excursions around Germany. The book was to go through countless editions and within a few years would appear in both English and French versions. After noting the current population, and that Wittenberg was until 1542 the seat of the Elector, and then a fortress (besieged in 1760 and 1814), Baedeker's guide offered readers its first significant fact about the town: 'At the Castle Church, on 31 Oct. 1517, Luther posted his famous 95 Theses, the beginning of the Reformation.'

Other guidebooks of the 1840s and 1850s led off with the same distillation of fact.[26]

Increasingly, the imaginations of tourists to Wittenberg opened themselves to the doors. The American Unitarian minister Theodore Parker visited in 1844, and 'entered the church by the door where Luther put up the 95 Theses.' He was able inside to buy a copy of them, and later that evening Parker returned and 'walked in front of the door to meditate. The evening star looked down. A few persons went and came. The soft air fell upon my head. I felt the spirit of the great Reformer. Three centuries and a quarter, and what a change!'[27]

A more notable American visitor, in 1853, was Harriet Beecher Stowe, author of the recently published and internationally sensational *Uncle Tom's Cabin*—the powerful anti-slavery novel which Abraham Lincoln is supposed to have said to her, only half-jokingly, caused the American Civil War. On leaving the Castle Church, Stowe found herself looking curiously 'at the old door where Luther nailed up his theses'. She knew it was not the original: 'that was destroyed by the French'. It was, in fact, destroyed by the Austrians, in 1760—Napoleon, like Oliver Cromwell in England, frequently took the blame in the nineteenth century for earlier waves of destructiveness. Nonetheless, Stowe could effortlessly summon up the scene with a practised novelist's eye:

> under that arched doorway he stood, hammer and nails in hand; he held up his paper, he fitted it straight; rap, rap, - there, one nail—another—it is up and he stands looking at it. These very stones were over that head that are now over mine, this very ground beneath his feet. As I turned away I gave an earnest look at the old church. Grass is growing on its buttresses; it has a desolate look, though strong and well kept. The party pass on, and I make haste to overtake them.

For all her elegiac musings, Stowe shared with other visitors of these years a sense of real frustration at the condition of the town and its venerable Luther sites: 'why do the Germans leave the place so dirty? . . . the Catholics enshrine in gold and silver the relics of their saints, but this Protestant Mecca is left literally to the bats and the voles'. Her brother Charles was even more blunt, declaring in his diary that any spark of hero worship he felt towards Luther had been extinguished in Wittenberg by 'the gloom and dirt and destitution of all beauty in the surroundings'.[28]

Wittenberg's loss of 'all life and animation' was attributed by another mid-century American visitor, Mary S. Griffin, to the removal of its university. Yet she was excited by the opportunity to make 'a pilgrimage to Wittenberg, the so-called Protestant Mecca', and to stay near to the church on whose gates 'Luther hung his ninety-five theses, or arguments, condemning the doctrine of papal indulgences'. Enthusiasm also won out against cynicism and distaste—just—in the case of an English visitor, John Howard Hinton, who stayed in Wittenberg, at 'the only tolerable inn in this place, the London Hotel', during a tour of Holland and Northern Germany in the summer of 1851.

As a Baptist minister, Hinton was repelled by the ceremonialism of Lutheran worship, but also, somewhat illogically, by the shabbiness with which he saw it conducted in the Castle Church: if it was necessary to 'give me candles, and choristers, and crucifixes, then, at least, do the thing in style.' It also seemed to Hinton that in Wittenberg, 'you see Luther everywhere in form, but nowhere in spirit.' He counted almost a dozen statues and portraits of him in the town, 'as though subsequent generations would compensate themselves for losing the substance by multiplying the shadow'—almost certainly not a pun on the name of the sculptor (Johann Gottfried Schadow) who created Wittenberg's famous and foundational figural image.

Nonetheless, Hinton confessed to his correspondent that while in Wittenberg, 'my eyes have often filled with tears'. He was impressed with the Luther House, and with the spot outside the Elster gate where Luther burned the pope's bull. His most intense feelings were experienced standing over Luther's tomb, but he was moved too when his guide took him to the 'very door' where Luther affixed his Ninety-five Theses. Hinton noticed that 'an old nail is still in the place', but he did not think that his guide, a 'respectable matron', presumably speaking in German or heavily accented English, had reported it to be 'one of those employed by the reformer.'

As Wittenberg matured and developed as a site of Protestant pilgrimage, it did not exactly generate a renewed trade in fake relics. But such accounts contain premonitions of a familiar modern pattern for how the past is experienced and enjoyed. A sense of historical authenticity is reliably, if paradoxically, produced by replicas and replacements. Hinton remembered how history reported Luther to have burned the papal excommunication under an oak tree: 'an oak stands on the spot now, but not the same oak'.[29]

The north doors of the Castle Church were likewise at once the same, and not the same, as those on which Luther had placed his Theses in 1517. The potential of what had become known as the *Thesenportal* as a site of memory and reflection was hugely enhanced by the programme of restoration and rebuilding taking place there between 1845 and 1858, a programme picking up the mantle from the frustrated designs of Karl Friedrich Schinkel of thirty years earlier. The refurbishment was a pet project of the Prussian King Friedrich Wilhelm IV, son and successor of the instigator of the Prussian Union. After his accession in 1840, Friedrich Wilhelm announced that 'if it is no longer possible to restore the church to its original state, then I will focus on the Theses Door.'[30]

Responsibility for the project devolved to the architect and art historian Ferdinand von Quast, who in 1843 was appointed as Prussia's first 'State Conservator'. Quast's design trod a fine line between authentic reconstruction and creative invention. His declared philosophy was as far as possible to restore the original condition of the site, mindful that 'the same stones, in their still existing arrangement, were witnesses to the great deed of God's which took place here.' But at the same time Quast had no interest in producing a straightforward imitation of the original form of the doors—apart from anything else, that would involve putting back statues of bishops and saints into the surrounding niches. Rather, his intention was to refashion the doors as 'a monument of honour to the Reformation'. The adjacent jambs or columns were kept, but the rest of the *Thesenportal* became a canvas on which memory might be painted afresh. Above the arch, new statues were positioned—not of saints, but of the Saxon Electors Frederick the Wise and John the Constant. In the tympanum filling the archway above the doors themselves, the Berlin painter August Klöber produced in 1850 a vibrant scene, employing the novel, durable, and expensive medium of enamelled lava. It depicted Luther and Melanchthon kneeling before the crucified Christ, the one holding a Bible, and the other a copy of the Confession of Augsburg, with a silhouetted townscape of Wittenberg in the background.

The doors themselves, ceremonially inaugurated on 10 November 1858, the three-hundred-and-seventy-fifth anniversary of Luther's

Fig. 4.2. The restored doors of the Castle Church, designed by Ferdinand von Quast (1858).

birthday, were now rendered in solid bronze. On them was inscribed the Latin text of the Ninety-five Theses, in six parallel columns (see Fig. 4.2). The lettering aped the appearance of the original printed version, complete with abbreviations. The intention was not so much to make the text available for public reading as to proclaim the monumental character of the site, and to literally cast in bronze a mnemonic symbol for the great 'deed' which took place there.

The restored Theses-Doors honoured Martin Luther, but they also celebrated Friedrich Wilhelm, whose responsibility for creating the monument was recorded in a Latin inscription, accompanied by a crest of the Prussian eagle, placed above the door lintel. The sword-bearing, sentinel Electors, Frederick and John, were witnesses to the facts that political patronage of the Reformation had passed from the Wettin princes to the royal House of Hohenzollern, and that the *Schlosskirche* was now as much a monument to the future of the Prussian monarchy as to the glorious Reformation past. The point was made explicitly by the official record of the opening, which hailed the king as 'patron by birth of the evangelical Church of Germany'. The pastor of the *Stadtkirche*, and superintendent of Saxony, Immanuel Sander, remarked in his address on the occasion that Friedrich Wilhelm 'followed in the footsteps of Frederick the Wise'. In his sermon, the theologian Heinrich Eduard Schmieder saw the doors as a gracious token for 'what we can in the future expect for the advancement of God's Kingdom from pious Princes and Kings'.[31]

Germany's future contained a great deal that neither theologians nor pious princes could foresee in 1858. But for the moment, the gleaming bronze doors did much to enhance the experience of visitors to Wittenberg, and were frequently commented on with approbation. The American agricultural journalist and Presbyterian elder, Richard Lamb Allen, stopped there in 1868. A memorial volume compiled by his children described how 'we see him still as he gazed, all absorbed, on the bronze doors which will carry down to ages yet to come, in the primitive text, as Luther wrote them on the original doors of wood, the ninety-five theses'.[32]

Others, standing in the same spot, were inclined to reflect on the present as much as the past, and to conclude that Luther was without doubt proved to have been on the right side of history. Henry W. Bellows, a Unitarian minister from Boston, visited in 1867, at a time when the anticlerical nationalist Giuseppe Garibaldi, having helped unite Italy, was leading a renewed campaign to overthrow the residual political power-base of the papacy: 'it seems as if the news from Rome today must flatter Luther's ashes here in Wittenberg, or even brighten the letters on these bronze gates'. Within a couple of years, Chancellor Bismarck's Protestant Prussian state triumphed over the Catholic French empire of Napoleon III in the Franco-Prussian War. This victory, and the creation of a unified Germany which followed it, seemed yet further confirmation of an impending resolution in the clash of civilizations which began at the doors of the *Schlosskirche* three-and-a-half centuries earlier. It was surely logistic practicality, rather than religious symbolism, which in the aftermath of the Franco-Prussian War led to five thousand French soldiers being interned at Wittenberg. A chronicler of the incarceration nonetheless wrote of the town as the place where 'on the bronze gates of the temple are still engraved the ninety-five theses against the dogma of indulgences'.[33] It sounded almost as if they were an antique survival, rather than a recent addition. Authentic or not, the visual, tangible, and material served as a prompt to historical memory, and to the invocation of a past that could be consumed for pleasure in the present.

Well-informed Protestants still knew, in the middle of the nineteenth century, that the Ninety-five Theses were far from a fully developed alternative to Catholic doctrine, and that their posting by Luther represented a conventional invitation to academic debate. In a biography of the reformer first published in 1841, the British Methodist minister George Cubitt remarked that the theological insight found in the Theses was 'mingled with much obscurity, and even error'; that in publicizing them Luther had no inkling of where things would lead; and that if it had not been for the unexpected capacity of the printing press, 'the whole matter would have subsided into its former quiescence'.[34]

Yet the evolving legend of the *Thesenportal*, and its growing status as a shrine to Protestant cultural identity, demanded a more emphatic version than this. 'It was against the doors of this church' announced a best-selling American guidebook for travellers in Europe, 'that Luther hung up his ninety-five arguments against the Church of Rome'—not, we might note, against some misconceived Catholic teachings about indulgences. In 1875, the British Congregationalist minster John Stoughton produced a literary travel guide specifically to orientate travellers around Luther's 'homes and haunts' in Germany. Stoughton knew of course that of the original doors 'no fragment of the panelling even remains.' The whole of it was (repeating a popular misconception) 'burnt by the French'. But that scarcely detracted from the significance of 'this sacred spot', site of 'one of the boldest acts of Luther's life'. The place evoked for Stoughton the ancient cathedral of Milan, whose bishop St Ambrose closed the doors against the tyrannical Emperor Theodosius. Luther's action was 'a gauntlet thrown down before the Romanized world . . . the trumpet-note which rolled over Germany from end to end'. Far from being the conventional first step in a rarefied scholarly discussion, Stoughton imagined Luther's posting of the placard bearing the Theses as a popularizing, democratic disclosure: 'There it appeared before the public gaze. There it was read. There it was pondered.'[35]

The survival, embellishment, and increasingly magnetic attraction to visitors of the physical site of Luther's *Thesenanschlag* helped endow the imagined act with ever richer metaphorical and symbolic possibilities. The door of the *Schlosskirche* may have been a display board, but it was also precisely a door—a portal to a different future. The action of placing Theses there—now universally understood to have involved nails and a hammer—was a knocking which could readily be conceived of as a plea for admission, or as a succession of blows against a corrupt and tottering edifice. If a sacrament—in the traditional Christian understanding—was a material action outwardly and ritually symbolizing the thing it actually effects, then by the mid-nineteenth century the *Thesenanchlag* was on its way to becoming the historical sacrament of the Protestant Reformation.

Particularly influential was an account in the hugely popular *History of the Reformation of the Sixteenth Century* by the Swiss clergyman Jean-Henri Merle d'Aubigné. Its initial volume was published in 1835, and swiftly translated into English and other languages. D'Aubigné remarked how 'the feeble sounds of the hammer' were soon followed throughout Germany 'by a mighty blow that reached even the foundations of haughty Rome, threatening with sudden ruin the walls, the gates, and the pillars of popery, stunning and terrifying her champions, and at the same time awakening thousands from the sleep of error.' Rather than struggle to find his own words, an American biblical professor, Milton Spenser Terry, quoted this stirring passage in a late-nineteenth-century account of his visit to 'the place of the great reformer's principal labours'.[36]

In a further thickening of metaphor, the Ninety-five Theses themselves could be represented as reverberating blows. Preaching in Philadelphia on Reformation Day 1872, the scholarly Lutheran clergyman W. J. Mann invited listeners to join him in doing honour to the great figure who 'in the centre of Germany and Christendom, on that 31st of October, with those ninety-five powerful strokes, knocked at the gates of the Roman Catholic Church'. Mann depicted the heart of Luther as a place where waters had been gathering in deep channels. The *Thesenanschlag* was the moment when 'the rock was rent, the spring gushed forth, the living waters poured out into the lands, and earth, old and withering, was refreshed and rejuvenated.' In Mann's judgement, Western civilization was locked in an epic conflict between Romish and Evangelical churches, whose resolution would decide whether 'it will be an absolving and liberating, or a binding and fettering, of the world.' The spirit of freedom had been breathing for 350 years, in defiance of 'poisonous, miasmatic exhalations from putrid sepulchres'. The conflict, in which 'the Germanic and Latin nationalities are the standard-bearers', was working towards its conclusion, and Mann was confident of final victory.[37]

References to the epoch-making episode of 31 October 1517, in German, American, and British histories and textbooks of the mid- to late nineteenth century could be multiplied almost ad infinitum. They testify to further evolutions of purpose and method in the writing of history: the growing concern, in the age of Leopold von Ranke, with history as a professional business of identifying and verifying seminal events and key causal factors, through supposedly rigorous analysis of documentary sources. But nineteenth-century historical writing was rarely as neutral and objective as it fancied itself to be. Interest in the *Thesenanschlag* noticeably intensified in the approach to 1883, when the Protestant world celebrated the four hundredth anniversary of the birth of the great reformer, and a kind of 'Luther-mania' reached its peak on both sides of the Atlantic.[38]

Some German authors, Protestant as well as Catholic, continued to register the qualifications that Luther was observably 'popish' at the time he wrote the Ninety-five Theses, and that in issuing them he had no intention to cause a schism within the Church.[39] But the predominant trend was to maximize rather than minimize the significance of the *Thesenanchlag* as a moment of breach and rupture. It was this action, according to a school textbook published at Münster in 1861, 'that set the powder suddenly alight'. Luther's 'delicate hammer strokes', declared a Darmstadt Church newspaper in 1866, 'drew forth mighty lightning bolts' against him. To Ernst Jäkel, author of an 1871 biography of Luther, the posting of the Theses on the door of the *Schlosskirche* was simply 'the first cock-crow of spiritual freedom, the first rays of a rising sun. Luther himself did not know the enormous consequences which this important event would have. But the arrow, once shot, is no longer in the hunter's hand'.[40]

If anything, a tendency to allege that the strokes of Luther's hammer 'rang through Europe' and 'shook all Christendom' was yet more marked among English and American authors.[41] Accompanying this was an increased readiness to evoke for readers a fully realized mental picture of the scene. That Luther timed his protest for a moment when the church of All Saints would be thronged with curious pilgrims, and that the posting of the Theses took place 'in the presence of an excited crowd' were details which—without any real basis in evidence—could now almost be taken for granted.[42]

An example of such historical scene-painting, not to say historical licence-taking, is the Presbyterian pastor Charles Dickey's address to his congregation in Philadelphia in 1883:

> It was All Saints' Day. Crowds were gathering at the door of Wittenberg Church. The relics of the Saints were expected to quiet the consciences of worshippers. With the courage of a lion, on the evening of the 31st of October, 1517, Luther pushed through the crowd, and in their presence, nailed ninety-five theses against indulgences upon the door of the church. These hammer strokes sent terror to the heart of a corrupt Church, roused all Germany, reverberated around the world, stirred the spirit of the Reformation, and, after nearly four hundred years, their echoes awaken joy in the whole earth.[43]

Equally evocative was an imagined version of the event produced around the same time by the popular British historian, Thomas Archer:

> The main street, running in a line with the river Elbe – and having at one end the palace of the Elector and the Castle Church, and at the other, near the Elster gate, the university founded by Frederick of Saxony – is thronged with men and women, in whose faces there is a

> look of earnest expectation, as though they were about to witness some strange and serious event. Such an event is indeed about to happen. By the time that the last of the crowd has reached the church, the man who is already standing there, hammer in hand, will have nailed to the church door a declaration which will do more to determine the future history of the world than any document or proclamation which may be issued by pope, king, or emperor.

Like a good number of other nineteenth-century commentators, Archer showed himself cheerfully unconcerned by the fact that the Ninety-five Theses were written by Luther in Latin, the language of churchmen and of technical scholarly debate. He continued his account by reporting that the paper Luther fixed to the church door was one 'for everyone to read'.[44]

Painters

If such descriptions felt like life, or at least historical writing, imitating art, that was exactly what they were. Archer's vignette was part of a volume on *Decisive Events in History . . . Illustrated*, which ran an ambitious chronological course from the battle of Marathon to the restoration of the German Empire—both of them episodes which, as we have seen, lent themselves to a Protestant, providential interpretation of the onward march of time. The accompanying illustration for the section on Luther (see Fig. 4.3) depicts the reformer, hammer in hand, perched on the raised steps of the church door. He stands at the centre of a bustling and excitable crowd, containing knights, beggars, fine ladies, and halberd-carrying men-at-arms. It is a scene of pure Victorian neo-Gothic medievalism. It is also one which provides evidence of how, over the course of the nineteenth century, the *Thesenanschlag* had belatedly conquered the European visual imagination, and in the process decisively secured the place of the episode in the cultural memory of the continent.

As we have seen, there appear to be no illustrations of the Theses-posting at all in the sixteenth century, virtually none in the seventeenth, and surprisingly few in the eighteenth. This was not due to intrinsic unwillingness to depict the figure of Martin Luther, who even in his lifetime was the focus of a rich culture of visual representation. But the emphasis was on portraiture, on allegorical representations, or

LUTHER NAILING UP HIS THESES.

Fig. 4.3. A Victorian version, from Thomas Archer, *Decisive Events in History* (1878).

on other episodes from Luther's biography, such as the burning of the papal bull, or the defiant appearance of the reformer at Worms.

The jubilee of 1817 marked the start of greater enthusiasm among artists and illustrators for the possibilities of the *Thesenanschlag*. With respect to the memorial coins and medallions produced for the occasion, it continued to be a subsidiary theme: the study of the genre by Thurman Smith identified only two medals from 1817 depicting the Theses-posting. One shows Luther, his hand on the nailed text, turning as if to face and address a group of spectators. The other depicts the immediate aftermath, with a large crowd pressing around the Theses-Doors.[45] This suggestion of an event with a highly public, performative character was to be a characteristic, even defining, note of nineteenth-century depictions.

The posting of the Theses was sometimes omitted from earlier visual cycles of Luther's life, but it had an assured place in various multi-image 'memorial tables' printed in 1817, such as that produced by the Nuremberg engraver Friedrich Campe (see Fig. 4.4). There was still no standard template. Campe's take on things was a fairly cool and classical one, showing, in the immediate aftermath of the posting of the Theses, small groups of people forming rationally to discuss them—in what appears to be a large piazza, and before a Palladian-style church bearing strikingly little resemblance to the Wittenberg *Schlosskirche* in any of its architectural incarnations. Others took a more 'romantic' view. In the comparable compartment from the 1817 memorial table of Georg Paul Buchner, Luther wields the hammer himself, in the close physical presence of a crowd of riveted onlookers. There was a similar look to the engraving by Friedrich Rosmäsler, included in a volume on 'Memorials of the Reformation of the Christian Church' by the clergyman Heinrich Kreussler (see Fig. 4.5). Kreussler's actual account of the *Thesenanschlag* was muted and factual, but Rosmäsler's accompanying illustration, like Buchner's, depicted a decisive man of action, and an unambiguously Protestant one. Luther wears the robes of an evangelical preacher, rather than the habit of an Augustinian, and is unmistakably the portly Luther of later years.[46]

Other artists in the early nineteenth century (like Hummel in 1806) preferred a more 'authentic' look, with Luther in monastic habit. They combined this with a plausible attempt at realism in their

Fig. 4.4. A Luther 'Memorial Table' from 1817, engraving by Friedrich Campe.

depiction of the doors, and with showing the actual nailing of the Theses being undertaken by a university beadle. These were features of a succession of lithographs on 'the beginning of the Reformation', undertaken in the late 1820s by the little-known soldier-artist Wilhelm Baron von Löwenstern. They themselves drew upon an 1825 etching

Fig. 4.5. An emphatically 'Protestant' Luther, by Friedrich Rosmäsler (1817).

Fig. 4.6. An 'authentic' reconstruction: lithograph by Adolph Menzel (1833).

by Campe. This bore an inscription informing readers how, although all Christian minds were outraged by Tetzel's effrontery, until 31 October 1517, 'no one had the courage to step up publicly'. Löwenstern's design was reworked in 1833 by the young Adolph Menzel (see Fig. 4.6), later to establish a reputation as one of the outstanding German painters of the nineteenth century.

Menzel's print graced a short life of Luther subtitled 'a picture book for the youth'. From the middle years of the nineteenth century, the increasing presence of images of the Theses-posting in German children's books and educational texts points to the deep cultural roots the motif was starting to lay down. In works such as Heinrich Eduard Maukisch's *Germania* ('Germany's most important events and lives of its most famous men in easily understandable stories for the youth'), first published in 1835 and frequently reissued, or in an 1851 illustration from one of the popular coloured picture broadsheets produced in the Prussian town of Neuruppin, a mild-faced and youthful Luther expounds the Theses at the church door before an audience of children, looking for all the world like an unusually charismatic Sunday School teacher. The 1862 children's textbook 'A History of Germany in Pictures' contained a contrasting image: Luther is standing thoughtfully alone, with the Theses rolled under his arm, about to step across the street and nail them to the door. The accompanying caption is nonetheless at one with the underlying assumption of other artists: 'here we see portrayed the most important moment in Luther's life'.[47]

A crucial landmark for the artistic representation of the *Thesenanschlag*, and for Luther in general, was arrived at right in the middle of the nineteenth century. Inspired by Leopold von Ranke's *German History in the Age of the Reformation*, the Thuringian artist Gustav König determined to undertake something he believed had never been attempted before: an artistic cycle not selectively but comprehensively illustrating the life of the great reformer. In late 1844, he began work on an ambitious sequence of forty-eight pictures. The project was completed in 1847, though extensive negotiations with publishers meant it did not appear in book format, with accompanying historical outline by Heinrich Gelzer, until 1851. In the meantime, the illustrations had been widely viewed, and enthusiastically discussed in newspapers and magazines. Reviewers acclaimed König for emulating the skill of the sixteenth-century old masters. He became known in his lifetime as 'Luther-König', the regal echoes of his surname (König means king) bolstering his claims to sovereign mastery of the genre. *Dr Martin Luther, The German Reformer* was reprinted in numerous German editions through to the end of the century and beyond. An English version was produced in London in 1853, and a second one in 1855, with notes by the Archdeacon of Lewes, Julius Charles Hare, a renowned British Luther scholar. An American edition, published together with Merle d'Aubigné's *History of the Reformation*, appeared in Philadelphia in 1883.[48]

The posting of the Ninety-five Theses (see Fig. 4.7) was the sixteenth illustration in König's set, placed between a depiction of Luther's work as regional vicar of eleven Augustinian houses in Meissen and Thuringia, and one of his appearance before Cajetan at Augsburg. The central pane of the picture shows a grim-faced and determined reformer, stepping up to the church door with theses-placard in one hand and mallet in the other. In freezing the moment just prior to the first hammer-strike, the image crystallizes the solitary,

Fig. 4.7. Gustav König, *Dr Martin Luther, The German Reformer* (1851): the central illustration.

heroic character of Luther's deed, with the suggestion of a momentary suspension between a world as was, and one about to be changed forever. The impression is underlined by the insertion of an eight-page 'introduction' between illustrations fifteen and sixteen. To the left of Luther we see Tetzel touting his indulgences, and to the right, the Wittenberg students burning the papal bull—a juxtaposition intended to represent, in the words of König's accompanying note 'the already kindled struggle'. In a panel beneath the *Thesenportal*, as if in a crypt, Luther is hearing the confessions of penitents, and refusing absolution to those putting their trust in indulgences. In a roundel above his head, in a reference to the prophecy of Hus, a swan emerges from the flames.

The composition of the image, with its multiple scenes, and its stylized architectural framing, distinguishes it from others in the cycle, which are generally executed in a more realist manner, as snapshots of various lived historical moments. In contrast, the representation of the Theses-posting is imbued with a literally iconic character: it was clearly intended to serve as the hinge for Luther's story as a whole. König explained that 'the artist in symbolic fashion makes the church door of Wittenberg serve also as the great door of the common Christian Church, at which Luther, urgently and harrowingly, pounds with his theses.' The only other images in the series to employ a comparable visual technique are the final three dealing with Luther's death and burial, and one depicting the 1530 presentation to Charles V of the Augsburg Confession—a kind of 'Pentecost' moment of birth for the Lutheran Church in Germany.[49]

The monumental, architectonic attributes of König's rendering of the *Thesenanschlag* draw one's attention to, and were perhaps even intended to compensate for, a pronounced absence in the visual memorial culture of nineteenth-century Luther. Beginning with Schadow's 1821 monument in the Marktplatz in Wittenberg, statues of Luther multiplied in towns and cities in Germany, and even beyond: the pinnacle of the 1883 Luther celebrations in the United States was the erection of a public statue of the reformer in Washington DC. Yet in no case was the posture chosen for such statues that of Luther wielding the hammer and posting the Ninety-five Theses. The reasons for this were more likely aesthetic and practical than religious or cultural. Without the presence of a door, the action of nailing the Theses would be rendered incongruous or comical, and with one, the requirements of a three-dimensional statue for all-around public viewing would be irreparably impaired. Schadow had in fact originally intended for a carving in relief of the Theses-posting (in characteristic early nineteenth-century fashion, undertaken by a beadle) to adorn the plinth of the Luther memorial in Wittenberg, but this got no further than a detailed design drawing, which eventually came into the possession of the Prussian king.[50]

In the presence of this absence, illustrations in books, with their intimate appeal to the individual reader, and with the amplifications of explanatory text ready at hand, made good the cultural shortfall. Gelzer's essay, which immediately followed König's picture of the *Thesenanschlag*, left owners of the volume in no doubt as to the significance of the image they had just viewed:

> The first act of Luther and of the Reformation was, therefore, the rescuing of Christianity from its deep degeneration; a cry of pain from the Christian conscience against the most scandalous disfigurement and perversion of the religion of the Crucified—this is the imperishable glory of that 31 October 1517, the day on which Luther affixed his ninety-five theses against the misuse of indulgences, on the Castle Church at Wittenberg.[51]

It is a mark of how self-evident this reading of the event now seemed to be that the editor of the first English version was able to remark approvingly on how Gelzer, a man living in a country with a large number of Roman Catholics, was 'necessarily tolerant, like the rest of his countrymen'. His work was careful 'to avoid all bitterness of spirit towards the members of that creed which waged war and persecution against Luther'. Catholics, hearing their ancestral religion described as the degeneration of Christianity, may or may not have agreed.

The accompanying commentary of Archdeacon Hare, in the second English edition of 1857, was a little more guarded than Gelzer's original. Hare observed (accurately) how in 1517 Luther did not completely reject the value of indulgences accompanied by sincere repentance, and how the call for a debate on indulgences 'echoed more widely than Luther expected or desired.' But Hare was far from half-hearted in his admiration for the person of Luther. In an earlier work he remarked how 'no man ever lived whose whole heart and soul and life have been laid bare as his have been to the eyes of mankind.

Open as the sky, bold and fearless as the storm, he gave utterance to all his feelings, all his thoughts: he knew nothing of reserve'. If Hare thought this all sounded rather un-English, he did not say so. Indeed, his laudatory study earned him the award of Prussia's gold medal of science from Friedrich Wilhelm IV. The Lutheran minister Victor L. Conrad, editor of the third English-language edition of König, produced in the United States in the anniversary year 1883, began matters by declaring flatly that 'there is no greater name in human history than that of Martin Luther'. He went on without hesitation to describe Luther as the 'great Leader of the greatest liberating movement among men since the advent of Christ'.[52]

The tendency to construct the Theses-posting as a deed of boldness and valour, both mirroring and defining the heroic greatness of the man who undertook it, was not confined to illustration in books. It emerges too through an artistic fashion which reached its pinnacle of success and popularity in the nineteenth century: the depiction of decisive, 'narrative' moments from the past, in the genre known straightforwardly as 'history painting'. The life of Luther was a veritable treasure-trove of incidents for history painters, principally though not exclusively German ones.[53]

A leading painter of the so-called Düsseldorf school, Julius Benno Hübner, completed in 1878, towards the end of his life, a fine study of the *Thesenanschlag*, now in the *Lutherhaus* Museum in Wittenberg. Its themes and composition are in some ways untypical for this date. Luther stands on the steps before the *Thesenportal*, in front of a large and socially mixed crowd, gesturing towards the Theses behind him as a couple of angry and embarrassed monks skulk away.[54] He is accompanied by a group of be-gowned university officials, who are successfully calling for order so that Luther can address the spectators. It is clearly a moment of patriotic jubilation. Festive wreaths bedeck the outside of the church, and caps are raised in celebration. But, here, Luther is not so much the dashing romantic hero as the paternal instructor of the people, an older visual motif with seventeenth-century roots. The Theses themselves are being fixed to the door by a youth mounted on a ladder—a convention disappearing from artistic depictions of the *Thesenanschlag* in the second half of the nineteenth century. One wonders in fact whether, in art, the ladder was more than a historically conscientious or merely incidental detail. Its visual effect is to dilute the individuality and potency of the figure using it, who for no very evident historical reason is nearly always portrayed as a youth rather than a grown man. Luther himself is never depicted climbing a ladder.

A very different treatment of the scene is to be found in an 1852 oil painting by the Hessian artist Georg Cornicelius.[55] He likewise took as his thematic moment the immediate aftermath of the posting. But rather than addressing the intrigued spectators who are gathering around the door, Luther walks away, as if in a mystical trance, his great and noble mission completed. There are no colleagues or assistants, and the hammer, its work done, has been allowed to fall from his hand. This Luther is the epitome of the romantic German hero.

The depiction also has affinities with the idea that various 'great men' acted as the principal forces of change throughout history. This 'great man theory' was popularized in the years just prior to Cornicelius's composition by the Scottish writer, Thomas Carlyle. His 1841 book *On Heroes, Hero-Worship, and the Heroic in History* outlined how the course of history was shaped by the force of personality found in exceptional individuals. A chapter was devoted to Luther. Carlyle had no particular brief for Luther's theology, but nonetheless considered him a true great man, a revolutionary of the spirit, whose destiny was to serve as 'a prophet idol-breaker; a bringer-back of men to reality'.[56]

Perhaps the best known German history painter of his day was Karl Friedrich Lessing (1808–80), an artist who became particularly renowned for works based on episodes from the lives of Luther and Hus. Lessing never undertook a version of the *Thesenanschlag* in oils, but in 1856 he produced a detailed drawing of the scene, which the artist Leonhard Raab turned into an engraving for an exhibition of the Hannover Kunstverein (Art Club).[57] The depiction (see Fig. 4.8) is another 'aftermath' treatment, though it could scarcely differ more from Hübner's imagining of an orderly public exposition of the Theses. Here, the university officials are themselves in agitated discussion around the placard, while lay people rush forward to catch a glimpse of them. The central figure (a student?) points animatedly towards the door, while a soldier seeks to restrain him. In a feature shared with Hübner's rendering, two shaven monks, embodiments of the reactionary establishment, hurry away from the beacon of hope behind them.

Fig. 4.8. A revolutionary scene: the aftermath of the *Thesenanschlag* by Karl Friedrich Lessing (1856).

Only a few years earlier, in 1848, in a series of protests and rebellions criss-crossing Europe, progressive movements sought to overturn the old order restored after the defeat of Bonaparte. In a few places—notably France—they for a time succeeded. Across Germany, students and liberals tried to make a reality of the aspirations expressed at the Wartburg Festival of 1817, only to be crushed by conservative and aristocratic forces. In Lessing's depiction of a revolutionary moment in long-ago Wittenberg, it is hard not to hear an echo of, and an elegy for, these unfulfilled dreams of freedom.

Elements of a politically approved Luther and of a revolutionary one converged to create what is undoubtedly the most famous painting of the *Thesenanschlag* produced in the nineteenth century, one which to this day graces numerous book covers and websites dedicated to Luther and the Reformation (see Fig. 4.9). Ferdinand Pauwels was a highly regarded Belgian history painter resident in Germany, and a professor at the Weimar School of Fine Art. In 1871–2, Pauwels was commissioned by Karl Alexander, Grand Duke of

Fig. 4.9. Ferdinand Pauwels' painting for the 'Reformation room' at the Wartburg Castle (1871–2).

Saxe-Weimar-Eisnach, to produce a set of seven scenes from the life of Luther to adorn the 'Reformation room' at the Wartburg Castle, which Karl Alexander had dedicated as a historical memorial to the reformer. Of these, the depiction of the *Thesenanschlag* is by far the best-known.

Pauwels' treatment is at once intimate and epic. Luther, in the authentic black habit of an Augustinian friar, and wearing his professorial 'doctor's hat', has just nailed the Theses to a church door whose flaking blue paint is perhaps symbolic of the decay of the old order. Using the hammer as a pointer, he magisterially taps to draw attention to a key point in the text, or perhaps to the document as a whole. A trio of laymen, representing the people, stands close by Luther's left shoulder, but in passive and respectfully attentive manner. Pauwels' Luther is the embodiment of Germanic strength and certainty. The sharp profile of his face draws and holds the viewer's eye, as Luther stares at but also beyond the attending spectators.

As the art historian Henrike Holsing has pointed out, the profile likeness is based closely on Lucas Cranach's engraving of Luther undertaken at the time of the Diet of Worms. The form was at that time deliberately provocative: profile-portraiture evoked the popes and emperors against whose might Luther was audaciously setting himself.[58] Three-and-a-half centuries on, it retained its air of pristine authority, moral if not necessarily regal.

With Pauwels' commission, the iconography of the *Thesenanschlag* seems stabilized for the late nineteenth century. Luther undertakes the action as an autonomous, decisive individual; he wields the hammer himself; the occasion is both dignified and momentous; 'the people' are engaged and involved, but not riotous or disorderly. All these elements recur in a painting by the Magdeburg-born artist Hugo Vogel, completed in 1902–3 (and reproduced on the dustjacket of this book). The genesis of the piece is exceptionally interesting. Vogel was commissioned in 1896 to begin work on a fresco-cycle to cover the walls of the assembly hall in a new state parliament building in Merseburg, in the Prussian province of Saxony. The theme was to be a history of the Saxon monarchy, with paintings of medieval emperors stemming from the Saxon line, and culminating in a scene in which the personified figure of 'Germania' leads the victorious troops home from the Franco-Prussian War. But shortly after the work was completed, a German art magazine revealed that the representation of Germania had been plagiarized—from a recently completed bronze statue, no less, of the great national heroine of France, Joan of Arc, with the German flag substituted for Joan's trademark sword. To avoid further scandal, Vogel was ordered to paint over the entire scene. The choice of the initial event of the Reformation as a suitable replacement subject-matter for 'Germania' is revealing. It suggests how Luther's posting of the Ninety-five Theses had come to be seen as the most appropriate historical symbol for the German nation's understanding of itself.[59]

In the nineteenth century, artistic representations of the *Thesenanschlag* encapsulated for people, predominantly though not exclusively German people, a series of understandings—occasionally contradictory ones—of what Luther and the Reformation meant. They were not the sole focus of Luther commemoration, but they proved a particularly potent one, able to appeal simultaneously to the intellect and the emotions. They purported to be faithful renderings of a real historical moment, but were of course were products of the imagination: fantasies, inventions, and projections. In Wittenberg itself, at the turn of the nineteenth century, reproductions of works by Lessing, Pauwels, Vogel, and others adorned the postcards available for tourists to buy. Another of these postcards combined a reproduction of Cranach's line-drawing of the *Schlosskirche* (see p. 20) with a stirring poem entitled simply 'Der Thesenanschlag'. Its final lines epitomize an adulatory sense of the occasion, appropriate for visitors to feel:

> Brave was the deed, and sublime was his work!
> All hail to thee, Master of Wittenberg![60]

Just occasionally, artists showed some awareness of how they were participants in a myth-making process. Without doubt, the most ambitious piece of Luther-art created in nineteenth-century Germany was the magnificent memorial, funded by public contributions, opened in the Rhineland city of Worms in 1868. It was, then as now, the largest Reformation monument in the world. The structure comprises a central statue of the reformer, with eleven surrounding statues on plinths, the whole set on a large raised dais. The *Thesenanschlag* features as the theme of one of four reliefs around the base of the pedestal on which Luther stands, though, given the location of the monument, pride of place on the front of the pedestal is understandably awarded to Luther's 'Here I stand' appearance at the Diet of Worms.[61]

Principal creator of the memorial was the sculptor Ernst Rietschel, though he died in 1861, several years before the work was completed. During the period of planning, Rietschel was bombarded with advice about the design, and in 1858 exchanged a series of letters with the foremost Reformation memorialist of the time, Gustav 'Luther'

König. With reference to the choice of themes for the reliefs, König advised Rietschel against including references to Calvin or Zwingli, who were after all Luther's opponents. At the same time, any scene from Luther's family life would simply be 'too tame' for such a monument. The burning of the bull certainly characterized Luther's temperament, and was the best symbol to represent the break with Rome, but some would see it as unnecessarily offensive. Rietschel could surely use Luther at the Diet of Worms, but if he wanted an alternative, he could just as easily choose the posting of the Theses. This, remarked König, was every bit as much an example of 'dead history lending itself to the purposes of art'. Only a few years earlier, to universal acclaim, König had himself represented the *Thesenanschlag* as a transcendent moment of historical metamorphosis. Yet in his letter to Rietschel he showed he was quite aware that the posting of the Theses was nothing more than 'a quite ordinary and conventional invitation to a disputation'. Luther 'never for a moment dreamt that they could have such consequences'.[62] Artists, no less than historians, and sometimes with distinctly greater self-awareness, might retrospectively seek to improve the rough and indistinct first sketch produced by history, and aim to bring out the full vibrancy of its colours.

Fictions

Treatments of the *Thesenanschlag* in poetry and literature followed a similar trajectory to those in the visual arts. They were relatively sparse at the start of the nineteenth century, but grew in both volume and vivacity over its course. For the anniversary, Goethe composed a short three-stanza poem, 'To the 31st October 1817', which took Luther's protestation of three hundred years earlier as an inspiration for the fulfilment of personal potential:

> I too should my God-given power
> Leave never unexpressed,
> Through art and science at every hour
> I'll make sure to protest.[63]

Yet outside of Germany, in countries where the centenary had passed relatively unmarked, the deed was slower to catch the poetic imagination. There was no mention of it, for example, in an epic verse of 1825,

Martin Luther, by the English romantic poet, Mary Anne Cursham, a work which contained lavish descriptions of both the Diet of Worms and the Leipzig Disputation. Given the decidedly indifferent quality of Cursham's versifying, perhaps that was just as well.[64]

The balance of elements was changed, however, in another ambitious verse cycle based on the life of Luther and published in 1842. Its author, Robert Montgomery, was an Episcopalian clergyman serving a cure in Glasgow—one who was noted by contemporaries (not always admiringly) for cultivating assiduously a supposed resemblance to Lord Byron. Montgomery devoted an entire section of the poem to the Theses-posting, a section whose heading—'Reformation'—reveals the foundational significance with which the episode was freighted. There is more than a hint of a Byronic character to Montgomery's Luther, who undertakes the deed after anguished hours wrestling alone with God in prayer.

> Upon the door of Wittemberg's dark pile
> He fasten'd then, with hand divinely firm,
> Ninety and five of those all-fearless truths
> which shook the Popedom, and the World
> redeem'd
> From charms infernal, to the Cross alone.

Montgomery wanted his readers to see in their mind's eye 'the crowd that rush'd to read / In tumult wild, upon the church's gate, / Those Words, which dash'd Indulgences to air'. Yet the poetic intensity of the scene depends principally upon intimations of its still unforeseen consequences, its 'germs of unexpanded glory'. Who but God himself 'in this daring act / Of Luther, heard the Reformation's pulse / Of Life and liberty begin to beat?'[65]

Luther's nineteenth-century pathway of glorification ran in parallel to the maturation of the novel as the pre-eminent form of European literary art. Historical novels, like historical paintings, came into their own in the decades after 1800. In Germany, a fairly scant treatment of Luther by novelists in the early years of the century began to increase after the tercentenary of his death in 1846: in works by Wilhelm Raabe, Theodor Fontane, Gustav Freytag, Karl Gutzkow, Levin Schücking, and Ferdinand Gustav Kühne. In Kühne's *Wittenberg und Rom* (1877), a character greets with joyful excitement the tidings of

Luther's *Thesenanchlag*: 'he's the one to do it! He's the one we've been waiting so long for!'[66]

Ironically enough, the very magnitude of Luther's heroic status sometimes militated against his taking the main role in literary works. Several novelists preferred to follow the events of the early Reformation through the eyes of fictional or obscure characters, with Luther either an off-stage presence, or a dramatic force lying in wait for the novel's protagonist in some kind of life-changing encounter. Margaret, the heroine of a poignant tale by the clergyman Karl August Wildenhahn (translated into English by John G. Morris in 1856 as *The Blind Girl of Wittenberg*) is the evangelical daughter of a woodcarver. She is driven from her home by her father, angry that Luther's teaching is taking away his business. Margaret becomes hailed for her spiritual insight and wisdom. She attributes her powers to her father (who initially approved of Luther) reading to her as a child 'the ninety-five theses, which this valorous servant of Christ nailed to the church-door'.[67]

The eponymous hero of Joseph Sortain's 1853 historical romance, *Count Arensberg; or, The days of Martin Luther*, is a young German nobleman. Sortain was a British non-conformist minister and a renowned preacher, christened by the poet John Ross Dix as 'the Dickens of the pulpit'. His hero, Arensberg, is a member of the retinue of the papal diplomat Cardinal Adrian de Castello, and a pious and sensitive Catholic, whose 'earnest German soul' is shocked at the haste and irreverence with which he witnesses mass being said in St Peter's in Rome. Arensberg comes to hear about Luther through a friendship with the young Melanchthon, still in the nineteenth century, secure in his reputation as a 'meek, gentle scholar'. Sortain does not make Melanchthon an actual witness of the Theses-posting, but his enquiries about an evident excitement and agitation among the populace of Wittenberg establishes that 'our great Dr Luther had been taking some bold steps against Indulgences, and had just affixed some theses on the gate of All Saints.' On the Sunday following, Arensberg and his party attend mass at the *Schlosskirche*, where he is deeply moved by the intense devotion of the officiating priest. This turns out to be Luther himself, a man whose facial features suggest 'a mind in conflict and yet determined to maintain and triumph in that conflict'. The sermon which Luther proceeds to deliver consists almost entirely of direct quotations from the Ninety-five Theses. Arensberg is impressed by the piety and sincerity of the sermon, though still filled with doubts. The congregation as a whole, however, gives signs of 'the most entire and hearty sympathy with the preacher'.[68]

An understanding that the Reformation unleashed by Luther's posting of the Theses was no outbreak of fanaticism or zealotry, but an idea whose time had come, appealing instinctively to the most reasonable people of the age, was something of a nineteenth-century commonplace. Luther 'dared to put into words what was moving in the hearts of thousands' was the authorial judgement of a fictionalized life of Albrecht of Mainz, in which the posting of the Theses is a reported event, dismissed lightly and foolishly by the louche cardinal: 'am I to be frightened with mere monkish palaver?'[69]

The idea was similarly evident in the 1891 novel, *Monk and Knight*, by the American Frank Wakeley Gunsaulus, another preacher turned storyteller. The action takes place in England, but its characters are acutely aware of what is referred to simply as 'the event of Wittenberg'. In a foreword, Gunsaulus presented the Reformation as an inevitable culmination of the Renaissance—a perception still faintly echoed in the 'Ren and Ref' courses taught in many US colleges. The Renaissance, so Gunsaulus believed, 'quickened the human brain'. It 'created an atmosphere so resonant and withal so true that the blows of Martin Luther had promise of being heard from echoing cathedral doors.'[70]

Perhaps the fullest fictional treatment of the Theses-posting takes place in the 1912 novel, *The Friar of Wittenberg*, by the American historian and college teacher William Stearns Davis. One of its chapters, indeed, is entitled 'The Hammer Strokes'. Like Sortain, Davis chose for his main protagonist, and first-person narrator, a young nobleman, Walter von Lichtenstein zum Regenstein—a wealthy and cultivated individual in search of deeper meaning in life. By chance, Walter finds himself a witness of the key event, accompanying Dr Luther and his disciple Johann Agricola down Wittenberg's *Collegien Strasse* to the very door of the *Schlosskirche.* On the way, Agricola explains to him how the door of the Castle Church is 'the regular bulletin board for the university'. It all seemed very simple and straightforward, yet the event proves to be transcendent and transformative.

Making his way past Old Willy, the blind church beggar, 'rattling the pfennigs in his pewter mug', Luther sets to his task: 'The keen breeze would send the Doctor's papers flying, yet he pounded away doggedly, reaching to Agricola for more nails, making every corner fast, while his black cassock flapped in the wind.' Then, slipping the hammer into a pocket, he turns quietly away. The impact is immediate and explosive. At first a few students, seeking the latest academic news. Astonished mutterings of 'Jesu-Maria!', as others quickly join them, 'swarming like bees out of every tall gabled house, out of every beer and wine cellar.' Soon priests of the church, 'golden-chained and bearded ritters of the schloss', the burgomaster: all as yet 'too amazed to question him'. Walter is troubled, believing himself the witness to a hopelessly imprudent act. 'Dear Doctor', he says, 'you have awakened the dragon. Now if you are St. George, you will slay him.'

> And so it began. A windy street, a few long strips of paper, twelve firmly planted nails, a group of feather-brained students—the deed brave and holy that was to shake the world. The commonplace act of a peasant-born monk protesting against what he deemed a wrong... That night began a sound in Wittenberg that was never to cease, while Leo at Rome and all his cardinals must needs hold council long and late—the clang of the printing press spreading Dr. Luther's theses to all the world.[71]

The rendering of a scene approaching such mythic proportions undoubtedly represented a considerable artistic challenge: Davis opted for a seriocomic blend of the cosmic and the commonplace.

Arguably, it presented the playwright with still greater difficulties than it did the novelist. The action of the *Thesenanschlag* was pivotal to a festive performance of 1883, *Luther: A Historical Character Sketch in Seven Parts*, by the German actor and dramatist, Otto Devrient. It is preceded by a lengthy and portentous dialogue between Luther and Staupitz in front of the church door. By the time the latter declaims, 'do then, what you believe you must!', audience members may have been wishing Luther would just get on with it. The nailing of the placard itself is a ceremonious, even a liturgical exercise, with the actor playing Luther directed to kneel in prayer in front of the door, before drawing the first nail from his bag. Each of four hammer blows is accompanied by a solemn invocation to Jesus:

> O Crucified One! In your name I fight steady –
> (the second nail is hammered in)
> O Crucified One! Your work of salvation I make ready –
> (the third nail is hammered in)
> O Crucified One! Your nail prints I strike square –
> (the last nail is hammered in)
> O Crucified One! Vouchsafe it! Your sufferings I bear!

Correspondences between Luther's nailing of the Theses, and Christ's nailing to the cross, are here conveyed to the audience with an almost admirable lack of subtlety.[72]

A considerably greater dramatist than Devrient, the Swede August Strindberg, included the episode in his play about Luther of 1903, *The Nightingale of Wittenberg*. Strindberg also gave considerable thought to how the *Thesenanschlag* might be staged. 'Just think', he wrote to his German translator, Emil Schering, 'what effects were wrought by this solitary man with his hammer and three nails – I see him now before me, two nails in his mouth while he hammers the first one in.' Strindberg's Luther, standing before the church door, is unquestionably a man of destiny. He is also a figure of Christ himself, saying to his mother in front of the *Schlosskirche*, 'woman, what have I to do with you?' and announcing 'I have not come to bring peace but a sword!' A chorus-like figure, the magus Dr Johannes (Faustus), is on hand to declare that 'the sun now rises over the German land', and the scene ends with Luther's followers shaking hands and cheering. First staged in Germany in 1914, Strindberg's portrayal of an iron-willed German hero struck a chord with audiences filled with hopeful nationalistic fervour, in a Europe which had not yet collapsed into a hopeless sea of mud and blood.[73]

The decades either side of 1900 were a high water mark for Luther and the *Thesenanschlag*, years of culmination for the apotheosis proclaimed by Hummel's artistry at the start of the century. The imaginative hold of the episode was such that theologians and academics sometimes found themselves having to correct misapprehensions relating to it, such as that Luther defended the Ninety-five Theses at the Heidelberg Disputation, or having to rate other occurrences by explicit reference to it. Luther's replacement of the Latin mass with a German communion service, suggested J. W. Richard in 1901, was an act which 'deserves to be classed with the nailing up of the ninety-five theses'.[74]

That 31 October 1517 represented the start date of the Reformation seemed not an opinion but an incontrovertible fact. George W. Knight, American editor of an 1896 edition of Guizot's *History of Civilization*, was clearly puzzled by the Frenchman's contention that 'the precise date which may be assigned to the Reformation is not of much importance. We may take the year 1520, when Luther publicly burnt at Wittenberg the bull of Leo X'. Knight added a helpful explanatory footnote: 'this act may be considered as the logical consequence of social forces set in motion by the posting of the ninety-five theses in 1517.'[75]

Professional Protestant theologians still knew what they had in truth always known, what Luther himself knew—that the Ninety-five Theses were not self-evidently 'Protestant' statements. In an essay of 1912, George Cross, professor at Newton Theological Institution in Massachusetts, declared that 'there is nothing distinctively evangelical in the Theses'—a judgement some modern experts might dispute, but which would still have to be forensically argued either way. Cross was certainly correct to say that if any student 'turns to this document expecting to find in it a clear denial of purgatory and a denunciation of the Church's claims in relation to the future life, he is instantly disappointed... There is no distinct repudiation of the authority of the pope or the Church'. At best, there were lines between which clear-sighted people, then and now, could read.[76]

But the Ninety-five Theses, and the posting of the Theses, had long since ceased to belong to the theologians. This was recognized in 1883 by the Württemberg court preacher Karl Gerok. He found himself unhappy with the numerous biographies of Luther 'springing up like mushrooms out of the ground'. Their authors, Gerok complained, preferred to give attention to 'dramatic highlights and turning-points', rather than to the kind of material which was of interest to theologians, but not the general public.[77]

The *Thesenanschlag*, against some significant competition, had by the late nineteenth century secured its place as the ultimate highlight and turning-point in perceptions of Martin Luther, the epitome of the 'great man'. Across Europe, and in America, it had become part of the collective cultural furniture of all right-thinking people. As such, it lent itself to a variety of social and political rearrangements. Addressing the New York Bar Association in 1893, the American Supreme Court Justice David J. Brewer argued that the principal purpose of the courts was to guarantee rather than constrain liberty. To make the point, he employed a striking (if somewhat strained) historical analogy: the judiciary 'simply nails the Declaration of Independence, like Luther's theses against indulgences, upon the doors of the Wittenberg church of human rights, and dares the anarchist, the socialist and every other assassin of liberty to blot out a single word'.[78] The innate kinship of the Ninety-five Theses to the founding texts and struggles of American freedom is a striking idea. It was still more strongly asserted in an essay of 1892 by Willard F. Mallalieu, a bishop of the Methodist Episcopal Church:

> The sound of Luther's hammer nailing his ninety-five theses upon the heavy oak door of the old church at Wittenberg has never ceased to reverberate, and it is heard to-day wherever shackles are broken and yokes are riven, and wherever the strongholds and bastilles of tyranny and slavery are thrown down by the delivered peoples. It was heard in the clash of arms that emancipated our fathers in the War of the Revolution, and heard again in the awful thunders of that vaster conflict [the Civil War] that brought deliverance to four millions of our outraged fellow men.[79]

Americans like Brewer and Mallalieu hailed the Ninety-five Theses as a manifesto of political liberty. But, at the very moment they were doing so, and thousands of miles away, a rather different understanding of their significance was being enacted in Wittenberg itself. The Luther-centenary of 1883 was occasion for the initiation of yet another programme of restoration at the *Schlosskirche*, and on 31 October 1892, 375 years after the supposed posting of the Theses, the church was formally rededicated by Kaiser Wilhelm II, in a lavish pageant to which members of all the royal houses of Europe were invited (see Fig. 4.10). Luther's door, the *Thesenportal*, was the ritual centrepiece of the ceremony. The architect overseeing the restoration carried a cushion bearing a golden key to the Kaiser. Wilhelm passed the key to the president of the Evangelical Church, who 'with deep reverence and thanks' accepted it from 'Your Highness, greatest of

Fig. 4.10. The rededication of the *Schlosskirche* (1892), in the presence of Kaiser Wilhelm II.

kaisers and kings'. He in turn handed it 'by command of the emperor, the protector and high architect of this house of God' to the pastor of the *Schlosskirche*, who opened the hallowed doors so that the royal party might pass inside, while the congregation sang 'Come Holy Ghost, Our God'.

The whole pageant was choreographed to affirm the ancient connection between the Wittenberg church and its princely patron, and to realign a pre-eminent remembered moment of western Christian civilization with the power and prestige of the German monarchy. None of this seemed in any way incongruous or amiss to outside observers. The London society magazine *The County Gentleman* praised the Kaiser's happy 'combination of enthusiasm and tact'. His Roman Catholic subjects could surely be expected to commend an occasion at which 'the Reformation was made to represent the unity of Christendom rather than the triumph of a sect'. In America, the *Los Angeles Herald* approvingly quoted Wilhelm's speech at the evening banquet, at which he suggested that commemoration of the divine blessing which began centuries earlier at the *Schlosskirche* was 'a bond of peace, reaching beyond all lines of division'.[80]

The *Thesenanschlag* had travelled a long way by the close of the nineteenth century. A distinctively German inheritance, a well-spring of nationhood, had seemingly become the common property, not only of all Protestants, but of western civilization as a whole. It was an emblem of social achievement and political stability, even if these might mean rather different things under the conditions of monarchical Germany and those of democratic America. Most of all, it was an enduring symbol of how history was moving in the right direction. When people looked back towards Luther's Theses-posting, listening for the echoes of the hammer blows, they had reason to feel reassured. They could feel thankful that a capacity for initiating rational thought, for undertaking heroic and altruistic actions, for transcending the superstitions and constraints of the past, were constants of human endeavour, reverberating forward through time. In the twentieth century lying near at hand, however, all these assumptions were to falter and fail. In the killing-fields of two unimaginable world wars, in the death-camps and gulags of violent and dictatorial regimes, optimistic beliefs in continual social progress, and in intrinsic human goodness, were to be cruelly mocked and unclothed.

5
1917: Controversies

War

The people of Wittenberg always marked the day of the posting of the Ninety-five Theses, but the four-hundredth anniversary was an occasion of more than usual solemnity. Early in the morning of Wednesday, 31 October 1917, citizens gathered outside the former Augustinian monastery, the *Lutherhaus*, at the lower end of the *Collegien Strasse*. After listening to an address there, they marched to the *Thesenportal* of the *Schlosskirche*. A group of young people preparing for confirmation led the procession, followed by students from the Lutheran seminary, university faculty, and various dignitaries of church and state. Morning worship and a sermon in the Castle Church followed, before the company moved on to the *Stadtkirche* for another service. A third gathering was held in the large lecture hall back at the *Lutherhaus* Museum.

In addition to the main religious ceremonies, a special service for children took place in the city church of St Mary. The preacher didn't doubt that all the children understood the significance of the day, and of what had happened in their town four hundred years before, but he reminded them nonetheless. It was not only the birthday of 'our dear Evangelical Church', but also 'the day on which began a new era, when one man, our Dr Luther, guided by God's spirit, cleansed the temple of God'. It was the day on which, as the Kaiser had once said, right here in Wittenberg, 'the greatest of all Germans performed the great liberating deed for the whole world; the awakening sound of his hammer resonated over German lands'.[1]

The Kaiser should really have been there. A great international festival was intended for the fourth centenary of the *Thesenanschlag*, culminating in celebrations in Wittenberg, an occasion to rival and surpass the Luther birth-year anniversary of 1883. Planning and preparations were well underway at the start of the second decade of the twentieth century, but in the late summer of 1914 the world changed utterly. By the autumn of 1917, Germany had been at war with Britain and France for more than three exhausting years. Hardships endured by soldiers on the Western Front were now increasingly shared by the civilian population. The winter of 1916–17 was one marked by desperate food shortages, when Germans were forced to survive by eating crops normally reserved for animal fodder: it was remembered as the *Steckrübenwinter*, the turnip winter. In April 1917 a formidable new enemy appeared: enraged by the sinking of American ships by German U-boats in the North Atlantic, the United States entered the war. German-American Schwarzes, Schmidts, and Müllers nervously changed their names to Black, Smith, and Miller.[2]

In the emotion, adversity, and turmoil of the First World War, the significance of Luther, and of his *Thesenanschlag*, changed their meanings once again. For beleaguered Germans in the anniversary year, Luther was now not so much the harbinger of a shared modernity as the embattled symbol of a uniquely German spirit and destiny. In numerous publications of 1917 he was described simply as 'unser Luther', our Luther—a reminder of what Germans were fighting for, and an inspiration for them to continue a just struggle.[3] 'Admittedly', the Erlangen theologian Hans Preuss wrote, in a jubilee publication for the General Evangelical Lutheran Conference, 'the faith of Luther belongs to the world'. But the German spirit alone had proved able to discover this faith and receive it from God's hands. Luther's piety—heartfelt, trusting, joyful, filled with reverence for the gifts of history, and full of patience in all suffering—was of a distinctively German kind. It was a birthright preserved down the centuries without the say-so of 'an Italian pope, or the French Calvin . . . or the leader of some English-American sect'. Paul Althaus, a Luther scholar and a theologian serving at the time as a military chaplain, put it more succinctly: 'Oh, how Luther loved our German people! . . . There is one thing that even today Luther would never be: neutral!'[4]

If Luther was an inimitably German historical phenomenon, it followed that the *Thesenanschlag* was a uniquely German historical 'deed'. Adolf von Harnack, a leading theologian swept up like others in the wave of nationalist sentiment, sought to remind participants in the jubilee in Berlin that 'not the nailing of the Theses, but their content, was the deed'. But the symbolism of the hammer-wielding Luther lent itself perfectly to a mood of national struggle and defiance. 'There is no more splendid day in German history than 31 October 1517', wrote Otto Schulze, in a commemorative publication of 1917: 'light, sun, a new spring had risen up for the German people.' An essay on 'Luther, the true servant of his people', by the teacher Emil Zeissig, described the reformer pushing his way to the church doors through a dense crowd, 'his eyes shining with the courage to do battle... his mighty hammer blows echoing through the silent *Schlosskirche*'.[5]

This is how Luther appears, posting the Theses as an archetype of heroic German resistance, in a commemorative print of 1917 by the artist and illustrator Karl Bauer—the producer of a popular book of portraits of military notables, entitled *Führer und Helden* (Leaders and Heroes). The picture is accompanied by an extract from the reformer's famous hymn, A Mighty Fortress: 'Though devils all the world should fill / all eager to devour us, / we tremble not, we fear no ill, / they shall not overpower us.' Beneath, a Dürer-esque drawing shows St Michael fighting against the dragon, Satan (see Fig. 5.1). Such words and images were conventionally used to express the Christian struggle against sin, but here it is hard to avoid the implication that the devils and dragons are Germany's enemies in the current conflict.

The connection is still more explicit in a work by Osmar Schindler, an artist who studied in Dresden under Ferdinand Pauwels, creator of the most visually iconic of *Thesenanschlags*. Schindler's picture, used to decorate Lutheran confirmation certificates in 1917, shows Luther, solid and stoical, posting the Theses to a decidedly metaphorical door, set in the centre of a triptych (see Fig. 5.2). To one side, a German soldier, in the distinctive spiked 'pickelhaube' helmet, which had already in 1916 been replaced in the field by a more practical variant, does battle with the devouring dragon; to the other, the palm-bearing figure of victory steps forward beneath the dove of peace.

The idea of destinies forged by the strokes of a hammer had roots running deep in German culture and mythology. It evoked images of the creation of fabled swords and rings, of Wieland, the legendary smith of Northern European folk-tales, and the subject of an unfinished opera by Wagner, as well as of the hammer-wielding Norse God, Thor. There was much dipping into these deep wells of identification in works

Fig. 5.1. *Führer und Helden* (Leaders and Heroes): a commemorative print of 1917 by Karl Bauer.

Fig. 5.2. 'A remembrance of confirmation in the year 1917': Luther with images of struggle and victory, by Osmar Schindler.

published in 1917. A prime example is a printed collection of poems and songs, *Luther als deutscher Volksmann.* The compilation celebrated Luther as 'man of the German people', and was designed to provide materials for an evening of cheering patriotic entertainment. Luther was hailed by one poet as 'man of ore, fire-spirit and heart of rock', whose hammer blows at the door broke asunder the bolts of priestly oppression. Another poem from the collection, by the clergyman Joachim Ahlemann, was widely reproduced at the time. It sustained over eight heroic stanzas the metaphor of Wittenberg as a blacksmith's forge, where Luther beat into shape the defences of the German people against their enemies:

> You stand at the anvil, Luther bold, beset by angry yelpers,
> And we, Great Germany, joined with you, will be the smithy-helpers.
> From God and ash, from rage and blood,
> From gold and iron we forge our holy weapons.

With the production of such folkloric reveries, we can surely talk about the mythologizing of the Theses-posting in a virtually literal sense.[6]

Absent from Ahlemann's poem, and from a great deal of the German commemorative literature in 1917, was much in the way of explicitly anti-Catholic invective. This marked a distinct change of emphasis. German Catholics, as we have seen (pp. 122–3), participated to a limited degree in the festivities of 1817, though the tone was often still one of assured Protestant triumphalism. The celebrations for the four-hundredth anniversary of Luther's birth in 1883 took place in the immediate wake of the so-called *Kulturkampf* (struggle of cultures). This was a sustained campaign by Chancellor Bismarck to neutralize the social and political power of the Catholic Church in his newly unified Germany, through a mixture of hostile propaganda and punitive legislation. The exclusive identification of Protestantism with progress and modernity, and with the public culture of the Prussian-dominated state, was a major theme of the 1883 jubilee.

But in 1917, Germany, in alliance with Catholic Austria, was at war with the Protestant nations—the United States and Britain—who had most enthusiastically helped it to celebrate in 1883. Catholic soldiers were fighting and dying alongside Protestant ones in the German regiments on the Western Front and elsewhere. There was an incentive to 'deconfessionalize' the commemorations of 1917, to make Luther's *Thesenanschlag* count for something other than the triumph of true Christian faith over popish ignorance and superstition. Already at the war's outbreak in August 1914, the Kaiser had announced that he did not recognize different parties, classes, races, or religions, but only Germans. In the run-up to the anniversary, the Lutheran church historian Friedrich Loofs called for celebrations which would not alienate those who had 'remained our comrades throughout this long war', and public events in 1917, including the festivities in Wittenberg, made an effort to recognize Catholics as fellow Germans, and brothers-in-arms against the common enemies of the Fatherland. Still, there was a bitter pill for some Lutherans to swallow. On 31 October 1917, the very day of the Reformation anniversary, the German Chancellor Georg Michaelis was forced out of office by a coalition of centre-left parties in the Reichstag. His successor as Chancellor and Minister-President of Prussia, installed the following day, was the aged conservative Georg von Hertling, a Bavarian Catholic.[7]

To celebrate the Reformation without suggesting the intrinsic superiority of Protestantism to Catholicism was invariably something of a tall order, and not always even attempted. But the Germanness of Luther offered a way of potentially squaring the circle. In an address written on the eve of the anniversary of the *Thesenanschlag*, the Munich-based Lutheran church historian Erich Marcks did not attempt to deny that the nailing of the Theses, though seemingly an innocuous way of instigating an academic debate, was an epochal, explosive event. Even if Luther didn't himself realize it, at the time he posted the Theses he had already 'inwardly broken' with the Church. From that day to this, Catholicism and Protestantism represented 'enduring, adjoining and antagonistic spiritual directions'. Yet they formed nonetheless two parts of a greater whole, of 'Volk und Vaterland'. It was the common destiny of Germans to be 'opposed, and adjacent and together at the same time!' For Protestants, the Reformation was an inheritance rooted in their very essence, but it was equally deep-rooted in 'the inner being of the whole German world.' Even German Catholics, if they were willing to recognize reality, 'cannot get away from or past this fact.'[8]

Changing views about Luther and his Reformation manifested themselves beyond as well as within Germany's borders. There was no recurrence in 1917 of the Luther-mania which swept across the United States and the United Kingdom in 1883. In some quarters, in fact, the war prompted a frankly hostile reappraisal of the reformer and his legacy. While Lutherans in the United States struggled to find the appropriate tone in which to mark the anniversary, American Catholics went on the offensive, able for the first time to advance their longstanding critiques of Luther in a spirit of unabashed patriotism. There was a receptive audience for *The Facts About Luther*, an objective-sounding but deeply partisan and hostile publication of 1916, by a pugnacious Brooklyn-based Irish-American priest, Monsignor Patrick O'Hare. Dudley G. Wooten, a Texas law professor, congressman, and convert to Catholicism, suggested primly that 'those who indict the crimes of German autocracy and imperialism . . . should first understand their genesis and genius.' It was not only Roman Catholics who now seemed open to the idea that the crimes of modern Germany might be traced back to flaws in the character or ideas of the sixteenth-century reformer who was, above all, identified as a German. 'Lutheranism has evidently failed to Christianize Germany', declared a July 1917 review in the British magazine, *The Spectator*, 'and its failure may be traced in part at least to the arrogance and worldliness of Luther himself.'[9]

Among American Protestants, however, the more common response was a feeling that Luther, and the true meaning of his deed of 31 October 1517, needed rescuing from the Germans, or at least from the current generation of Germans. 'The nailing up of the Theses', declared the *Lutheran Witness*, English-language magazine of the Missouri Synod, was 'the starting-point of the work which still goes on, and shall forever go on, that glorious work in which the truth was raised to its original purity, and civil and religious liberty were restored to men.' It was evident that 'liberty' was something the existing German regime did not value or understand. 'The truth which Luther taught', insisted a writer in the same issue, 'was not German truth, but the truth of the Bible.' Edwin Delk, a Lutheran pastor from Philadelphia, spoke for both his co-religionists and many fellow Americans when he declared that 'nothing can be in more vivid contradiction than the Prussianism of 1917 and Luther nailing his ninety-five theses to the door of the Castle Church at Wittenberg.' The former stood for 'an imperial autocracy claiming divine sovereignty'; the latter was a symbol of 'the right of individual conscience and universal kingship.' Rather than a seminal event in the history of Germany, the *Thesenanschlag*, was, it seemed, more properly understood as a milestone on the path to American democracy, personal autonomy, and religious individualism.[10]

In Britain, too, the Reformation centenary activated a strong sense that Christianity in Germany had taken a wrong turn; that, as the Oxford historian and devout Protestant Anglican Charles R. L. Fletcher put it, 'the Germans seem . . . to have got altogether the wrong brand of God, a sort of superior War Lord who delights to drink the blood of his enemies.' There was an unpleasant irony in the fact that (just as in 1871) the German authorities had established a major prisoner of war camp next to Luther's old university town. The alleged mistreatment of inmates there produced a 1916 committee report on 'The Horrors of Wittenberg'. In April that year, a full-page cartoon in the influential satirical magazine *Punch* depicted Luther addressing Shakespeare in conversation: 'I see my countrymen claim you as one of them. You may thank God you're not that. They have made my Wittenberg—ay, and all Germany—to stink in my nostrils.' Hensley Henson, Dean of Durham, preached in Manchester Cathedral on 4 November 1917 on the theme of 'The Failure of Lutheranism, No Disproof of the Reformation'. Henson regretted the fact that the war had prevented any 'tribute of sympathy' to Germany on the occasion of the recent anniversary of Luther's nailing of the Ninety-five Theses. But he maintained that 'the Prussians were not entitled historically to represent the principles of the Reformation'.[11] Such assessments undoubtedly reflected a complacent sense that the Church of England, unlike the Lutheran Churches, had extracted and preserved the best from the Reformation.

No suspicions of insularity could adhere to the author of one of the most detailed and thoughtful British contributions to the anniversary of 1917, albeit one which also declared, 'we claim to be better disciples of Luther than the Germans are themselves.' James Stalker was a Scottish Presbyterian, Professor of Church History at the United Free Church College in Aberdeen, and a former lecturer at Yale, well known as a frequent visitor to the United States. He had been part of the British delegation present at the Luther celebrations in Wittenberg in 1883, and his reflections on how best to mark the current centenary were produced more in sorrow than in anger. Stalker had no time for the petty nationalism which would traduce Luther simply because he was a German, any more than one might want to belittle the achievement of Beethoven, Goethe, or Kant: 'Luther belongs to history'.

Appropriately, then, though Stalker began by declaring 'Luther was a hero, if ever there was one', he offered a nuanced historical appraisal of the reformer. In early writings, Luther was 'the champion of freedom and conscience, denouncing the tyranny of Rome, which wanted to enslave the whole world, and claiming for the Empire and for every German state the right to have a mind and a will of its own.' But his intemperate response to the Peasants' Uprising of 1525 was unworthy of him. Luther 'lost faith in the common man, and was too disposed to put his trust in princes.' His willingness to concede to them ever greater control over the Church was a tragic historical misstep. Its result was that, through to the present day, 'Lutheranism naturally allies itself too easily with the monarchical and the aristocratic, being afraid of the freer and more progressive forces in society'. When

Stalker declared that 'we appeal from the new Prussianized Empire to the old Land of Luther', it sounded very much as if he were also appealing from the old Luther to the young.

The posting of the Ninety-five Theses was of course the defining action of the young, freedom-loving Luther. Stalker conceded that it was 'a great event, from which the Reformation is in Germany at least usually dated'. But in a publication dedicated to commemorating that very event, Stalker demonstrated surprisingly little enthusiasm for it. He pointed out that 'there were other incidents, some of which might appeal even more to the general mind, especially in countries outside of Germany.' The burning of the pope's bull, and of the decretals, 'the very embodiment of papal tyranny', was one of these. But without doubt the most significant episode was that which Thomas Carlyle had called 'the grandest scene of modern history': Luther's defiant appearance at the Diet of Worms. His stand there on conscience and the Word of God exhibited to perfection the best qualities of both the man and his cause; 'everything of supreme importance in the centuries since was implicit in that hour'. There was a thrifty, practical aspect to Stalker's ranking of the key incidents of the early Reformation. With the commemorations of 31 October 1917 proving something of a damp squib due to the war, Stalker suggested that 'April 18, 1921, the anniversary of this scene, may well be looked forward to as a substitute.'[12] Just perhaps, there was also an uneasy sense that there might be something too elementally Germanic, too implicitly violent, about the imagery of hammer blows crashing into the splintering wood of that Wittenberg door.

Leaders

Military defeat in 1918 spelled the end of German Imperial ambitions, and the royal family who had set themselves up as custodians of the Reformation sites of Wittenberg, and guardians of Luther's memory and meaning, packed their bags for exile in the Netherlands. But nationalism, and nationalism with a pronounced religious flavour, was scarcely extinct in the Germany of the ill-fated Weimar Republic. The study of the Reformation in the interwar years in Germany is generally associated with the so-called 'Luther Renaissance'. This was a movement of intense theological analysis of the ideas of Luther, particularly the Luther of the first years of the Reformation, concerned to demonstrate their relevance to the modern world, and to engage closely with Luther's own writings in the best available editions.[13]

What the 'Luther Renaissance' did not do was cast any doubt on either the historical fact or the historical significance of the *Thesenanschlag*. Its foremost exponent, the theologian Karl Holl, believed that, though Luther had no comprehensive plan for reform when he posted the Theses, as soon as he began to expound them, discussion turned to what lay behind his view of indulgences: 'not just his teaching on justification, but also his teaching on the Church'.[14] Another of the leading lights of the Luther Renaissance, the Leipzig historian and theologian Heinrich Boehmer, provided in 1925 a description of the *Thesenanschlag* remarkable for its confident command of the details of the event, and of Luther's thinking in undertaking it.

> He well understood that he was embarking on something which could entangle him in all kinds of difficulties. And so, before he went to the task, he first threw himself to the ground, to dedicate the business to God. He then wrote the placard and caused it to be printed across the street by Johann Grünenberg. But he said nothing to any of his friends or colleagues about his intention. He did not show to anyone in advance the placard with 95 Theses on the spiritual power of indulgences. No one in Wittenberg had any idea what he had planned, when, on 31 October 1517, the Eve of All Saints, shortly before noon, accompanied by his *famulus* Johann Schneider, alias Agricola, from Eisleben, he walked the approximately fifteen minute route from the Black [Augustinian] monastery to the Castle Church, and there at the north entrance door, which had often in the past been used for similar purposes, posted up the placard with the 95 Theses.[15]

Nor was belief in Luther's quintessential, and potentially redemptive, Germanness very much shaken by the capitulation of 1918. If anything, the trauma of defeat produced a renewed and more intense engagement with it. An influential biography of 1925, by the Lutheran historian Gerhard Ritter, portrayed the reformer as the central and defining figure of German national identity: 'how very difficult it is exactly to determine the spiritual character of Germany before the appearance of Martin Luther!'[16]

It was in these years, too, that Germans were for the first time able imaginatively to experience Luther's posting of the Ninety-five Theses in a new visual medium. The first significant motion picture to deal with Luther's life, and to show him posting the Theses, premiered in 1913, and was screened again in retitled and edited versions in the early 1920s after the censors objected to historical liberties taken by the script. Those objections did not extend to the portrayal of the Theses-posting, which was depicted as a revolutionary act, accompanied by a screen-caption declaring, 'And now Luther took a step, which with mighty strength broke the power of the pope'. As in the romantic paintings and drawings of the mid-nineteenth century, the action almost immediately attracts a crowd of excited and gesticulating Wittenbergers around the church door.

The scene featured again in two films supported financially by the Lutheran Church: *Martin Luther, Der Kampf seines Lebens* (the Struggle of his Life), 1923, and a more professional feature of 1927, *Luther—Ein Film der deutschen Reformation* (a film of the German Reformation), which went on general release the following year despite vigorous protests from the Catholic Church and some further difficulties with the censors—the film contained grossly caricatured scenes of papal Rome and an almost comically villainous Tetzel. The absence of spoken dialogue in these silent-era films allowed for greater attention to be given to the actual text of the Theses themselves. The 1927 feature in particular employed choice verbatim quotations from the Theses in several of its printed 'intertitles'. The abiding message the film wished to convey, however, is placed in the mouths of the patriotic knights Ulrich von Hutten and Franz von Sickingen, reflecting on Luther's protest: 'And so there is indeed something which is stronger than Rome or any popes: the German conscience'. A flyer from the Evangelical-Social Press Association of the province of Saxony, issued to publicize the film, contained a distinctly political observation: 'we all call today for a great leader who will put an end to German suffering'. It was not yet clear whether such a figure would arise, but Luther was the pre-eminent example from the past of an outstanding individual 'from whose strength of soul and courage of convictions we are still drawing vital substance'.[17]

Such a figure was indeed coming, and Germany would pay a heavy price for wishing for him. A preoccupation, in both scholarly circles and in wider culture, with a 'German' Luther had ominous racial overtones, which had already come to the fore before and during the Great War. In 1917, a quartet of writers including the Schleswig-Holstein pastor Friedrich Andersen, and the poet and journalist Adolf Bartels, published a pamphlet entitled *German Christianity on a Pure-Evangelical Foundation: 95 Theses for the Reformation Festival.* Just as Claus Harms' reformulated ninety-five theses of 1817 had inveighed against the pollution of Lutheran Christianity by the forces of ecumenism and 'reason', the theses of Andersen and his cohorts demanded a resetting of the Reformation. They wanted a Church cleansed, not only of Roman Catholic traces, but of Jewish and 'Israelite-Old Testament' ones. In 1921, the four authors founded the anti-Semitic *Bund für deutsche Kirche* (League for a German Church). Two years later Andersen argued for the rejection of the Old Testament in its entirety, citing the authority of the distinguished historian Arnold von Harnack, who had earlier expressed the view that removing the Old Testament from the canon of scripture would represent the logical fulfilment of Luther's Reformation. Some of those seeking in the 1920s to harness religion to an ideology of extreme nationalism thought ninety-five theses were not nearly enough. In 1926, the writer and politician Arthur Dinter, an early supporter of the Nazi Party, brought out *197 Theses for Completion of the Reformation.*[18]

Many German intellectuals, including German Christian intellectuals, were complicit in the rise and consolidation of Hitler's power. Whether Nazism was intrinsically and consistently hostile to Christianity, or whether the regime, at least at first, saw potential for genuine partnership with churches in the 'renewal' of Germany, is something historians continue to debate.[19] What is not in doubt is that groups of so-called 'Deutsche Christen' (German Christians) energetically supported the Nazi party, and campaigned to get their supporters elected to Lutheran church bodies. At the same time, historians and theologians made enthusiastic comparisons between Hitler and Luther. Both these men, gushed Hans Preuss in 1933, were 'deutsche Führer' (leaders), who knew they were 'called to the rescue of their people'. Hitler himself was on record as saying that Luther, along with Richard Wagner and Frederick the Great, was one of three great historical figures to combine a grand vision with an understanding of political realities. Luther's own anti-Semitic writings, ignored for much of the nineteenth century, were now given an ominously full airing.[20]

It was the purest coincidence—though some considered it a providential conjunction—that Hitler became German Chancellor in the year of another significant Luther commemoration: 1933 was the four-hundred-and-fiftieth anniversary of the reformer's birth. Celebrations were not on the scale of fifty years earlier, and some planned events were cancelled so as not to interfere with a new round of Reichstag elections. Nonetheless, Luther's birthday (10 November) was marked in the days following by mass rallies of the Deutsche Christen, at which banners were displayed intertwining cross and swastika, while calls were issued for the completion of the Reformation Luther had started by purging everything Jewish and 'un-German' from doctrine and worship. In advance of the festivities, Hans Hinkel, editor of a Berlin Nazi magazine, argued that Luther, the German fighter, should serve as 'an example above the barriers of confession for all German blood comrades'. Yet, as in 1917, it was very difficult to detach celebration of the reformer from suggestions of Protestant triumphalism. The papal nuncio complained to the German foreign minister about excessive 'celebration of an action (the *Thesenanschlag*) which had a plainly hostile tendency towards the Catholic Church'. His concerns were brushed aside, but he was able later to report to Rome, with quiet satisfaction, that throughout Germany the Luther birthday events had eclipsed 'the anniversary of Luther's theses-posting (31 Oct.), which some Protestant pastors wanted to celebrate first'.[21]

The symbolism surrounding the composition and posting of the Ninety-five Theses was nonetheless something which lent itself all too easily to Nazified interpretation. The message of a defiant break with the corrupt old order, accompanied by an urgent call for ideological change, resonated with the self-image of those bent on establishing a Third Reich. Indeed, in the Nazi Party's official history, the first mass meeting of the newly christened National Socialist German Workers' Party, at the Munich *Hofbräuhaus* on 24 February 1920, and at which Hitler unveiled the 25-point programme of the party, was directly compared to the *Thesenanschlag* of Luther. Nazi students in Erlangen published in April 1933 an anti-Jewish manifesto in the form of theses clearly designed to recall the ninety-five. In preparation for the 'Luther Day' of that year, a pamphlet was assigned for reading in schools which declared that 31 October was justly celebrated as 'the beginning of a new age', as for the first time in German history it produced a harmony between national character and the Gospel 'which once again in our days speaks its enchanting language'. Addressing a gathering of schools in Braunschweig for the Luther Day celebration on 14 November 1933, the regional Nazi leader Dietrich Klagges declared the *Thesenaschlag* to be a revolutionary act whose significance was in no way limited to matters of the Church, but which encouraged the effort 'once again to fashion German life in German lands'.[22]

To outside observers, the attempts after 1933 to create a racialized Germanic Christianity seemed profoundly misconceived, if not positively idolatrous. In 1937, Pope Pius XI issued an encyclical in German, *Mit brennender Sorge* (with burning anxiety) which condemned increasing restrictions on Catholics in Germany, as well as the exaltation of 'race, or the people, or the state, or a particular form of state', as a perversion of the order intended by God. Hitler was furious. Reportedly, his initial intention was to give a retaliatory speech in the Reichstag which 'would greatly eclipse Luther's ninety-five theses and... complete the work of the Reformation in the German spirit'.[23]

In October the following year, members of the United Lutheran Church of America were gathered in Baltimore for their biennial convention. The occasion involved a historical pageant based around Luther's posting of the Ninety-five Theses. *Life* magazine, the best-selling American weekly, published a photograph of the (rather cheesy-looking) re-enactment of this 'epochal act', along with an accompanying caption. It linked the events in 'peaceful Baltimore' to the recent harassment of a Viennese cardinal by Nazis 'whose religion is the state'. The story ran under an eye-catching headline: 'Lutherans Mark an Old Religious War as Nazis Bring on a New One'.[24]

Within Germany, some Protestants were far from content to see Martin Luther presented as a progenitor of Adolf Hitler, and the *Thesenanschlag* reimagined as the act which laid the foundations for a de-judified, ethnic German Church. In August 1933, the dissident pastor Dietrich Bonhoeffer produced with others a document called the 'Bethel Confession'. It restated the basic meaning of the Reformation as an awareness of God's offer of free grace, and of Martin Luther as the faithful witness of this to all peoples. 'To understand his actions as a breakthrough of the Germanic spirit', the Bethel Confession declared, 'is to completely misunderstand his mission'.

The largely successful Nazi attempt to take over the institutional structures of Lutheranism in Germany led to the formation in 1933 of an 'Emergency Pastors' League', and to the appearance in the following year of a break-away 'Confessing Church' (*Bekennende Kirche*) to oppose the official *Deutsche Evangelische Kirche* (German Evangelical Church), which had by then adopted into its constitution an 'Aryan Paragraph' dismissing from office all clergy of Jewish descent, or having wives of Jewish descent. Despite government restrictions, Confessing Christians in Berlin were able to turn 31 October 1934 into a celebration of their autonomy, holding large public meetings in various venues across the city. On the same anniversary in the previous year, the leading Reformed theologian Karl Barth delivered a rousing lecture in Berlin. He urged fidelity to the true spirit of the Reformation, and condemned the 'false Evangelical Church' which sought to add to the pure deposit of faith merely human categories, such as 'culture' or 'Volkstum'—the latter was a word much used by the Nazis, its meaning encompassing folk customs and national/ethnic character.[25]

In the end, appeals to the true meaning of Luther against Nazi distortions were scarcely more successful than any other form of internal resistance at preventing the regime's ever-tightening grip on German society. Barth left the country in 1935, and returned to his native Switzerland. Bonhoeffer's Confessing Church faced increased repression in the years leading up to the war, even as the anti-Semitic writings of Luther were invoked to justify the *Kristallnacht*—the overnight wave of violent attacks on Jewish homes, businesses, and synagogues in November 1938 that left broken glass littering the streets of Germany like shards of crystal. The event took place, as some German Christians exultantly noted, on Luther's birthday. Bonhoeffer himself was arrested by the Gestapo in April 1943 and incarcerated in Tegel Military Prison in Berlin. After evidence emerged of his connections to the plotters who planned to assassinate Hitler in July 1944, Bonhoeffer was moved to a Gestapo facility and then successively to Buchenwald, Schönberg, and Flossenbürg concentration camps. He was hanged at Flossenbürg on 8 April 1945, just over three weeks before Hitler took his own life, in a Berlin collapsing before the advance of a vengeful Soviet army.[26]

In a world of barbarism and butchery, was Luther's exploit of 31 October 1517 a beacon of hope or a false light? Bonhoeffer himself wrestled with the question. A letter sent to his parents from Tegel prison in 1943 was written on 31 October, Reformation Day. It was, Bonhoeffer said, 'a feast that in our time can give one plenty to think about.' He wondered why it was that Luther's action

> had to be followed by consequences that were the exact opposite of what he intended, and that darkened the last years of his life, so that he sometimes even doubted the value of his life's work. He wanted a real unity of the Church and the West – that is, of the Christian peoples, and the consequence was the disintegration of the Church and of Europe; he wanted the 'freedom of the Christian man', and the consequence was indifference and licentiousness; he wanted the establishment of a genuine secular social order free from clerical privilege, and the result was insurrection, the Peasants' War, and soon afterwards the gradual dissolution of all real cohesion and order in society. I remember from my student days a discussion between Holl and Harnack as to whether the great historical, intellectual and spiritual movements made headway through their primary or their secondary motives. At the time I thought Holl was right in maintaining the former; now I think he was wrong. As long as a hundred years ago Kierkegaard said that today Luther would say the opposite of what he said then. I think he was right—with some reservations.[27]

These were dark thoughts for a Lutheran pastor to entertain, even for one racked by rheumatism in a Nazi cell. The nineteenth-century vision of the *Thesenanschlag* as the dawn of a bright new day for humanity was fading fast, as the sun seemed to be setting on western civilization itself.

Rehabilitation

After the deluge, the reckoning. As scores were settled with the surviving leaders of the defeated Nazi regime, to some people it seemed almost as if Luther should be standing alongside them in the dock at Nuremberg. The suspicions whispered already in Britain and America during the First World War—that Luther bore considerable responsibility for a strain of violence and coercion in the make-up of modern Germany—received full-throated expression in the years immediately preceding and following 1945. A succession of commentators, in the United States in particular, advanced the thesis that Luther's fatalistic and submissive attitudes towards political authority had removed all constraints from the development of an unaccountable and ultimately totalitarian state. The earlier rhapsodic comparisons between Luther and Hitler by German nationalist historians and theologians were mirrored in the censorious judgements of post-war British and American writers who traced a straight line in German history from one to the other—a theory popularized in the immensely successful *Rise and Fall of the Third Reich* (1960) by the US journalist and former war correspondent William L. Shirer. Worse, the undeniably virulent strain of anti-Semitism in Luther's thought and writing, which the Nazis exploited to the full, led to claims he was a historical progenitor of the Holocaust. It was a suspicion hardly dispelled by the defence case of Julius Streicher, most vehement of Nazi anti-Semitic propagandists, who complained before the Nuremberg Tribunal that his copy of Luther's *On the Jews and their Lies* had been confiscated from him. Streicher asserted that 'Dr Martin Luther would very probably sit in my place in the defendants' dock today, if this book had been taken into consideration by the prosecution.'[28]

Some Germans manifested feelings of remorse and repudiation in respect to Luther. The most famous of literary exiles from Hitler's Germany, the novelist Thomas Mann, addressed an audience at the Library of Congress in Washington DC on 29 May 1945, three weeks after victory was declared in Europe. His theme was 'Germany and the Germans', and the shadow of Martin Luther, 'a gigantic incarnation of the German spirit', hung heavily over his remarks. Mann introduced himself by noting that he was a native of Lübeck, a place whose beautiful city hall was completed in 1517, 'the very year in which Martin Luther posted his Theses on the portal of the Castle Church at Wittenberg'. That event marked 'the beginning of the modern era'—though Luther the reformer still had 'a good deal of the medieval man about him'. Mann had no desire to belittle Luther's greatness: his Bible translation created the modern German language, and his insistence on a direct connection between individuals and God 'advanced the cause of European democracy'. And yet, he added, 'I frankly confess that I do not love him. Germanism in its unalloyed state, the separatist, anti-Roman, anti-European, shocks me and frightens me, even when it appears in the guise of evangelical freedom and spiritual emancipation'. Mann supposed that as a dinner companion 'I would have gotten along much better with Leo X, Giovanni de' Medici, the amiable humanist'. Luther was a kind of liberating hero, but—a crucial qualification—'in the German style'. In fact, 'he knew nothing of liberty . . . of political liberty, the liberty of the citizen'. The tragedy of Germany, a country which had never had a successful revolution, was that it had not learned to combine the concept of the nation with the concept of liberty. Mann bitterly remembered words spoken by the first president of the Weimar Republic (the Social Democrat, Friedrich Ebert): 'I hate revolution like sin'. 'That', Mann reflected, 'was genuinely Lutheran, genuinely German.'[29]

The Germans, however, were far from done with Martin Luther, even if the four-hundredth anniversary of his death in 1946 passed with relatively little public fanfare. Hartmut Lehmann's perceptive study of Luther's reputation in the years after the Second World War shows that German theologians and academics combined to launch a vigorous campaign of rehabilitation: 'only a very few wanted to knock the reformer off his pedestal as a national hero'. It was a campaign that certainly aimed to disassociate Luther from the actions of the Nazi regime (which involved a degree of quiet backtracking on the part of several of the scholars concerned) but one which had no intention of repudiating his unique place in the grand sweep of German history. The Tübingen theologian Karl Heim, in an article written for Luther's 400th death-day, remarked that 'all the other giants of the German past, the great emperors and statesmen, could only be looked back upon with wistful feelings, because the ship they once steered between the cliffs is sunk'. But it was otherwise with Luther, who offered something 'completely independent from all mutations in political destinies, from the rise or fall of the old German empire'. There was certainly greater effort than before to 'historicize' Luther, to fix him in his own time, but his religious message was decidedly not a dusty relic of the distant past. In circumstances of defeat, drift, and disillusion, Luther's timelessness was also his timeliness: he showed what it meant to be a good Christian, and therefore a good German too.[30]

Abroad, the public culture of both Britain and (especially) the United States was still to a very considerable extent Christian and Protestant in the post-war years. It was in America in the 1950s that a complete scholarly edition of Luther's works, in 55 volumes, was produced in English for the first time.[31] For all the controversies about the cultural and intellectual antecedents of Nazism there was little real prospect of Luther being recast as a scowling villain in the popular imagination. On both sides of the Atlantic, there was huge commercial success for an affectionate biography of Luther by the British-born American church historian and Yale professor, Roland H. Bainton. *Here I Stand: A Life of Martin Luther* was first published in 1950, and went through numerous subsequent editions, becoming perhaps the single most widely read book ever written about the reformer. In his conclusion, Bainton observed that 'Germans naturally claim such a German for themselves', but he squarely maintained that Luther's stature and significance were transcendently universal.

The posting of the Theses was, of course, a part of Bainton's story, but it is noteworthy that his treatment was brief and factual, shorn of all traces of nineteenth-century rhapsodizing. Luther simply responded to Tetzel's provocations 'by posting in accord with current practice on the door of the Castle Church a printed placard in the Latin language consisting of ninety-five theses for debate.' As the title of his book might suggest, Bainton was more drawn to Luther's appearance before the Diet of Worms, an episode which 'lends itself to dramatic portrayal.' His chapter on it was the longest in the volume.[32] There was no explicit suggestion (as with Stalker in 1917) of the Worms declaration being elevated in importance above the Wittenberg 'deed'. But it makes some sense to suppose that the honest confession of conscience in front of political authority sat more easily with the post-war American religious outlook than the provocative demonstration of 'strength' which generations of German historians had seen manifested in the *Thesenanschlag*.

My own 1955 paperback copy of *Here I Stand* comes with an inducement to purchase emblazoned on the back cover: 'Subject of Widely Acclaimed Movie!' The film in question was a 1953 production starring the Irish actor Niall MacGinnis (bearing a remarkable resemblance to portraits of the middle-aged Luther), and directed by Irving Pichel, a successful and well-established Hollywood figure, but one who had fallen foul of Senator Joseph McCarthy's House

Un-American Activities Committee. It helped that *Martin Luther* was an independent European production, shot in West Germany and funded by a variety of Lutheran Church organizations in Germany and the United States. The film was not directly an adaptation of Bainton's biography, but it had pretensions to historical veracity and credited as advisers the eminent Reformation historians Theodore G. Tappert and Jaroslav Pelikan—the latter a lead editor of the American edition of Luther's works. The film was nominated for two Oscars, and proved both a commercial and critical success, even if not all reviewers were entirely won over. In Britain, *The Observer*'s long-serving film critic, C. A. (Caroline) Lejeune, commented that 'a touch less caricature in the presentation of the champion's opponents, a mite more candour in the confession of his own trespasses, could have made "Martin Luther" a better picture.' Indeed, the film's perceived anti-Catholicism stirred considerable controversy. The London-based Catholic Truth Society rushed out a pamphlet, *'Martin Luther': The Film and the Facts*, while several prominent American Catholics produced detailed printed rebuttals. In French-speaking Quebec, a Catholic-dominated film censorship board denied the film a cinematic release. Three years after its initial debut, a first television showing by a Chicago TV station was cancelled in the face of voluble Catholic protests. This bias was not just in the eye of the aggrieved beholder. A letter of 1950 from the director of the US National Lutheran Council, soliciting investment in the project, unashamedly began its pitch by pointing to the need to tackle the growing 'aggressiveness and arrogance of Roman Catholicism', and to counter 'the smearing of Martin Luther and the Reformers [which] gets more subtle and vicious all the time'.[33] Into the second half of the twentieth century, Luther's memory was far from becoming safely 'deconfessionalized'.

The treatment of the Theses-posting in *Martin Luther* represents an intriguing blend of the familiarly iconic and the playfully irreverent. The relevant segment is a fairly short one, in a film whose climactic dramatic moment is really Luther's defence at Worms. Lejeune nonetheless considered the Theses-nailing to be 'its central episode', and it is undoubtedly a memorable scene. A voiceover places the action for us: 'Wittenberg, the Eve of All Saints' Day, October 31st, 1517. Martin Luther was scarcely noticed as he passed by those waiting to worship before the relics about to be displayed in the Castle Church.'

In contrast to the solemnity of earlier literary portrayals, MacGinnis's Luther nails the Theses up in a leisurely, almost nonchalant way, before cheerfully strolling off again. The action attracts virtually no attention from the townsfolk present, who, when the doors are opened, stream through them into the church, ignoring the appended paper. The only people to take any notice are a couple of idlers passing the time in the town square. Out of curiosity, one of them gets up and wanders over to take a brief look before sitting back down again with his friend: 'Just something in Latin'.[34]

The comedy serves to upset viewers' expectations as well as to underline for a popular audience the well-established scholarly perception that there was nothing intrinsically surprising or subversive about a monk posting a notice to the Wittenberg church door. Yet the limits to *Martin Luther*'s revisionism about the Theses-posting are very quickly revealed. We cut to a scene of the door at night time, with some men reading, and copying, the Theses by torchlight, and then to another of the same men operating a printing press, followed by a quick montage of monks (in Latin) and lay people (in English) reading out the printed Theses in wonder and excitement. As the film's historical advisors must have known, there is no evidence at all for the fanciful idea that the posting of the Theses to the door of the Castle Church was the direct means of their transmission into the hands of the printers. Almost equally questionable, from a historical viewpoint, is the confident voiceover assertion that 'printers had the theses translated into the language of the people.' As we have seen (p. 46), a vernacular printed version was planned, but no copies of such an edition survive. The idea that the posting of the Ninety-five Theses was a seminal moment in the democratization of religion was, however, one that the film's sponsors were keen to promote. It was one already so grounded in western (particularly American) culture that to reiterate it was, as it were, to push at an open door.

The idea received further, and more formal, ratification in another American cultural production of 1953. That year saw the completion of work on a new War Memorial Chapel in the episcopal National Cathedral in Washington DC, the spiritual home of American government. Vibrant stained-glass windows in the chapel illustrate themes of struggle and sacrifice for the cause of liberty. The scenes depicted include Moses leading the captives out of Egypt; Paul Revere on his famous ride to warn the patriots of the approach of British troops during the Revolution; Lincoln emancipating the slaves; paratroopers landing on a battlefield during World War Two, and marines raising the Stars and Stripes at Iwo Jima. In a panel above the head of George Washington, father of American freedom, Luther appears. He is hammering his Theses to the door—not gently tapping, but vigorously pounding, his arm arched back above his head.[35]

The image of the *Thesenanschlag* as an iconoclastic blow for freedom, a modern twist on the progressivist notions of the nineteenth century, fitted with the socially emancipatory mood of the dawning 1960s. In Luther scholarship, it was heralded by the appearance in 1958 of a successful but unusual biography. Erik H. Erikson's *Young Man Luther* was subtitled 'A Study in Psychoanalysis and History'. A practising psychoanalyst, Erikson sought to understand Luther's protest against the Church as the delayed outcome of an adolescent identity-crisis, forged in youthful conflicts with his father. For Erikson, the Theses-posting was an example of Luther's characteristic impulsiveness and secretiveness at decisive moments: 'he acted without seeking the counsel of those who might have restrained him'. The wave of support and encouragement that the Theses produced among all classes of people could best be summed up, so Erikson suggested, in the phrase 'Atta boy, Monk!'[36]

Erikson's work was an inspiration to the playwright John Osborne, one of the so-called 'angry young men' who transformed British theatre in the late 1950s and early 1960s. Osborne's 1961 play *Luther* was in fact exclusively dependent on Erikson for its historical detail, and drew heavily on his general interpretation of Luther as an individual struggling to attain a meaningful sense of personal identity. The pivotal moment of the play (Act II, Scene 3) takes place on and around 'the steps of the Castle Church, Wittenberg, October 31st, 1517'. A lengthy monologue by Tetzel in a previous scene has established him as a sinister and cynical huckster. But, other than as a prop in Luther's hand, the Ninety-five Theses, and their detailed critiques of indulgences, play no real role in the action. Instead, Luther delivers a sermon describing a personal emancipation in the breakthrough that led him to understand how justification came through faith alone—a breakthrough achieved in the moment of relief from constipation on the monastic privy. At the conclusion of the scene, Luther, now able to 'see the life I'd lost', descends from the pulpit, walks up the steps to the door of the church and nails to it what is not so much the agenda for a scholarly symposium as a declaration of independence for the autonomous individual.[37]

Luther premiered at the Theatre Royal, Nottingham, on 26 June 1961, and in early July its company took the production to Paris before commencing a run at London's Royal Court Theatre. It transferred to the West End on 5 September 1961, a reviewer in *The Times* commenting, pun doubtless intended, that, as Luther, Albert Finney's delivery of the sermon was 'outstanding in its hammering in of the play's main theme'. A 2.30pm matinee and a 7.30pm evening performance went ahead as usual on Wednesday 8 November 1961.[38] On the same day, at Mainz in Rhineland Germany, a forty-six-year-old professor of church history entered the Auditorium Maximum of the University to deliver a presentation with the provocative title 'Luther's Thesenanschlag: Fact or Legend?' To the consternation of much of his audience, he proceeded to argue that it was, in fact, a legend.[39]

Iserloh

The debate ignited by Erwin Iserloh's lecture of 1961 was one of the great scholarly controversies of the post-war decades. A recent calculation is that since its inception nearly 300 publications have addressed the question of whether or not Luther posted the Ninety-five Theses to the door of the Wittenberg Castle Church on 31 October 1517, and the number—as this book bears witness—continues to rise.[40] The question is also one which, in Germany at least, has attracted the attention of the wider public to an extent the arcane disputes of academics only seldom manage to do. There is no need here to go over the arguments of Iserloh and his critics in any detail: the most pertinent evidence relating to the question is reviewed in the first two chapters of this book, where I arrive at the conclusion, broadly mirroring Iserloh's own, that it is on balance unlikely that the Theses were posted on 31 October 1517, and quite probable they were not posted at all. But the Iserloh controversy is itself an episode of considerable significance in the cultural history of the *Thesenanschlag*, a moment where history collided with culture to produce particularly sensational and soul-searching results.

Iserloh's revelation did not come entirely out of the blue. In 1957, the Lutheran scholar Hans Volz, one of the leading editors of the long-running Weimar edition of Luther's works, first advanced the theory that the *Thesenanschlag* took place, not on 31 October, the eve of All Saints, but on the day itself, 1 November. It was hardly a revolutionary thesis, and other leading Luther researchers were not convinced. But it represented for the first time a scholarly recognition that the evidence for the posting was decidedly fragmentary and open to interpretation, and that the alignment between an annually commemorated 'Reformation Day', and the historical event lying behind it, might be somewhat less than exact. Volz's elaboration of his case in a short book of 1959 prompted the historian Konrad Repgen to wonder whether, not just the dating, but the reality of the *Thesenanschlag* itself—'which until then I, like all the world, had taken for a fixed fact'—might be open to question. Repgen discussed his doubts at the end of 1960 with his friend, Erwin Iserloh, who went off to start re-examining the sources with this once unthinkable thought firmly in mind.[41]

Iserloh's 1961 Mainz lecture was published in a scholarly journal, and as a pamphlet in the following year. In 1966, an expanded version appeared in the form of a short book on 'Luther between Reform and Reformation', whose subtitle—'Der Thesenanchlag fand nicht statt' (the Theses-posting didn't happen)—showcases the expressive possibilities of the German language at its monosyllabic best. Second and third editions appeared in 1967 and 1968, with a translation into English in the latter year.[42] In Germany, the historical establishment took Iserloh's intervention, and the storm of controversy it created, very seriously indeed. At the 1964 gathering in Berlin of the *Deutscher Historikertag*, the prestigious biennial conference of German-speaking historians, a special session was convened to discuss the question. Everyone understood that this was no minor point of historical detail: it was as if an English historian were denying that King John set his seal to Magna Carta in June 1215, or an American one had produced compelling evidence to show the founding fathers did not sign the Declaration of Independence on 4 July 1776.[43]

In some ways, the controversy was more emotionally charged even than that, for Erwin Iserloh was not only a highly regarded church historian, he was also a Roman Catholic priest. To some German

Protestants, it seemed that this was all a shameless Catholic attempt, perhaps even a plot, to rob them of a corner-stone of their cultural identity. A 1968 article in the venerable Lutheran review, the *Theologische Literaturzeitung*, declared that 'it is no longer a secret that for some time Catholic theology has been seeking to conquer Luther for itself.' The leading British Luther scholar of the period, the Cambridge professor and Methodist preacher Gordon Rupp, in a review of Iserloh published the same year, scarcely sought to pull his punches:

> Since 1617, Protestants in Germany, and Lutherans everywhere, have celebrated 31 October as the day on which Luther nailed his 95 Theses to the door of the Castle Church of All Saints, Wittenberg. It can, alas, be no accident as the 450th anniversary looms up, signally pre-echoed in Germany and America by conferences and festal lectures, that it should be Catholic historians who have called in question the historicity of this event, so often recalled in pictures and purple patches.

Rupp conceded that Iserloh, and other Catholic scholars of recent times, had distanced themselves from an 'old, bad polemic tradition', in the sense that they were not gratuitously offensive about Luther, and recognized his considerable virtues: 'Yet under the surface they still exploit Luther rather than sit down under him, and support the old thesis that what is true in Luther is Catholic.'[44]

The aggrieved sense on the part of some Protestants that the Catholics were seeking to steal Luther away from them was not entirely without foundation. Catholic views about Luther—at least in scholarly circles, and especially in Germany—had undergone a quiet revolution during the first half of the twentieth century. Firmly in the 'old, bad polemic tradition' was an immensely thorough, yet extraordinarily hostile, biography by the Austrian Dominican and Vatican archivist, Heinrich Denifle, first appearing in 1904. A three volume study of 1911–12, by the Innsbruck Jesuit Hartman Grisar, moderated the tone somewhat, yet continued to present the flaws in Luther's theology, and the flaws in Luther's character and personality, as inextricably intertwined, and employed modish language of psychology and neurosis to hammer home the point. In the jubilee year of 1917, Grisar produced a detailed literature review, monitoring and rectifying an adulation of Luther that seemed to him decidedly unmerited. Denifle, incidentally, ignored the *Thesenanschlag* entirely;

free gift of God's grace, should be dated to the spring or summer of 1518—in other words, it followed rather than preceded the indulgence controversy.[48]

Leading Luther researchers of a firmly evangelical persuasion, such as Volz, Heinrich Bornkamm, and Kurt Aland, refused to be convinced. Bornkamm was inspired to greater attempts at refutation by 'the sensational effect which must follow from this shaking of one of the most famous landmarks of world history.' Aland, in his efforts to establish a precise chronology for the transmission of communications, even contacted the Westphalian Riding School at Münster for information about the accustomed speed and stamina of horses.[49]

But in the secular history departments of German universities, and in the books produced in them into the 1970s and beyond, the historical status of the *Thesenanschlag* perceptibly shifted: from a certainty to a possibility, and often to an improbability. Even scholars who defended the authenticity of the event often now did so in a way that detracted from its iconic status. They stressed the routine (and therefore probable) nature of Luther's action in affixing his Theses to the 'blackboard' of the university, and avoided overly portentous talk about the 'birth-hour' of the Reformation. For many professional historians, the very idea that the Reformation was an 'event', with a precisely identifiable point of commencement, was in any case starting to seem distinctly questionable. As more attention was given to the social, economic, and cultural factors underlying Europe's religious transformation, so the chronologies of change became longer, and the idea of focussing so much on a single day when the Reformation supposedly 'started' began to feel oddly old-fashioned. And as the Reformation came to be understood as a complex, Europe-wide phenomenon, rather than as a distinctly German undertaking which was subsequently exported elsewhere, so Luther had to concede ever more of the limelight to a varied cast of other leaders and personalities.[50]

Over the course of the 1960s, the specialist debate among historians about what Luther did or didn't do on 31 October 1517 increasingly came to the attention of a public outside the relatively restricted readership of the scholarly works themselves. Reports of the newly minted doubts about the reality of the *Thesenanschlag* circulated widely in Lutheran church newspapers and magazines (much less so in

Catholic ones, casting doubt on any idea this was some sort of Romanist 'plot'). They also made it into the German national press, with stories appearing in such publications as the popular news weeklies *Die Zeit* and *Stern*, and the TV and radio listings magazines, *Hörzu* and *Gong*. A report in *Der Spiegel*, one of Europe's best-selling weekly periodicals, was published in January 1966 under the arresting title 'Reformator ohne Hammer'—'Reformer without a Hammer'. The main body of the piece was a fair-minded summary of the points at issue between Aland, Iserloh, and Volz, but the story began with an intentionally impish presentation of the matter, set in overtly confessional terms:

> Protestants can protest again: a Catholic wants to put them straight about the fact that Martin Luther never picked up any hammer to nail his 95 Theses to the church door in Wittenberg. The Catholic claim threatens the heroic image of Luther which, from pulpits and lecterns, has been instilled into successive generations of confirmation candidates and students.[51]

Doubts about the *Thesenanschlag* notwithstanding, the four-hundred-and-fiftieth anniversary of the start of the Reformation was duly celebrated in both West and East Germany in 1967, but without much of the self-confident triumphalism which had characterized previous jubilees. Ecumenism, and improved relations with the Catholics, were prominent themes of the occasion. In Wittenberg, a service of thanksgiving in the *Schlosskirche* was preceded by the customary festive procession from the *Lutherhaus* (see Fig. 5.3). But the Lutheran Church received little support for its efforts from the government of the German Democratic Republic, and relatively few of the West Germans invited to come to commemorative events in the East were granted visas to attend.

The Communist authorities remained suspicious of Luther's bourgeois and reactionary proclivities. As a historical role model for socialist German society, they much preferred his bitter rival, Thomas Müntzer, the apocalyptic preacher who inspired the rebellious peasants in 1525. In heavy-handed fashion, the East German government tried to steer the commemoration in Müntzer's direction. In the Federal Republic, no single theme dominated the literature produced in the anniversary year, and the Reformation bestseller of 1967 was a

Fig. 5.3. Luther commemoration in Communist East Germany: a service in the *Schlosskirche* for the anniversary of 1967.

smooth but bland survey of *Luther: His Life and Times* by the German-British writer and poet, Richard Friedenthal. In reviewing it, the church historian Karl Kupisch was prompted to declare, 'Aus Wittenberg nichts Neues': 'All Quiet on the Wittenberg Front.'

Still relatively new, of course, was Iserloh's bombshell. *Der Spiegel* began its report in the anniversary week 1967 by observing wryly that the event which was about to be commemorated with great solemnity 'did not take place'.[52] *Spiegel* enjoyed something of a reputation for anticlericalism, and as with its 'Reformer without a Hammer' piece of a couple of years earlier, the journalist responsible undoubtedly took pleasure in tweaking the tail of respectable churchly opinion. But the iconoclastic 1960s, the era of student revolt and of the Vietnam War, were propitious times for dismantling heroic reputations and overturning traditional pieties of all sorts. 'Der Thesenanschlag fand nicht statt!' was hardly the chant to be heard on the lips of youthful protestors, as 1967's Summer of Love gave way to the defiant Spirit of '68. But it was very much a sign of the times to believe that parents, and the parents of parents, had got a lot of basic things wrong.

Resilience

Reactions to Iserloh's claims in the English-speaking world were more muted and less anguished. There was relatively little awareness of the debate outside of specialist scholarly circles before the appearance of a translation of Iserloh's book in 1968, though the *New York Times* did run a report in March 1966 under the headline 'Theologians Debate Luther's Hammer'.[53] Even at the end of the 1960s, responses to the suggestion that the posting of the Ninety-five Theses 'did not happen' tended to divide along religious lines. A 1968 review of a general history of Christianity, in the British Catholic weekly, *The Tablet*, spotted that in it 'Luther is still nailing his theses to the church-door'. The reviewer was inclined to be forgiving, as 'the book was produced before Iserloh had shown it to be a legend.' In a joint review of the German and English editions of Iserloh's work, published in October 1969, the American Jesuit Robert E. McNally declared: 'I do believe that the traditional representation of the debut of the ninety-five theses is a legend, perhaps the most dramatic of modern history.' By contrast, Gordon Rupp found nothing in Iserloh's new and expanded edition to persuade him to change his mind about what he thought would 'increasingly be regarded as an unsuccessful attempt to prove that Luther never did nail the 95 Theses publicly in Wittenberg.'[54]

Nonetheless, awareness of the attempted debunking filtered slowly through to the attention of the newspaper-reading public. In May 1970, the travel correspondent of *The Guardian*, making the case that 'the German Democratic Republic has much to offer to the holidaymaker', could blithely recommend a trip to 'Luther's town of Wittenberg, and the church to whose door he nailed his 95 Theses'. Yet by the time Germany was celebrating the five-hundredth anniversary of Luther's birth in 1983, a writer in the same newspaper was referring to the event as an 'unproven legend'. Rather more cautious was *The Guardian*'s reporting that year of the inauguration at the University of Sheffield of Britain's first Centre for Reformation Studies. It noted that the opening reception, attended by both Church of England and Roman Catholic dignitaries, was 'held on the anniversary of Martin Luther's reputed nailing of his 95 theses to the door of the *Schlosskirche* in Wittenberg'.[55]

Majority opinion in the Anglo-American scholarly world, as in the German one, was by the 1980s at the least highly sceptical about the historical veracity of the *Thesenanschlag*. Even historians who believed the evidence still pointed towards such an event taking place on 31 October 1517 tended now to downplay its intrinsic significance.

Yet myths are myths precisely because they are powerful and meaningful: they can prove remarkably resilient in holding on to their place in the popular imagination. If closeted academic historians ever need a reminder that the wider world has a distinctly discerning and selective interest in what they have to say to it, the recent history of the *Thesenanschlag* will be on hand to provide proof.

In 1983, the authorities in the GDR reversed the stand-offish attitude they had displayed in 1967, and decided after all that Luther could be a cultural and political asset for the state. In advance of the anniversary, the Communist Party even issued its own '15 Theses on Martin Luther', which grandiloquently claimed that 'Luther's progressive legacy has been absorbed into the socialist culture of the [East] German nation'. Erich Honecker, East German leader, and self-appointed chair of the 'Martin Luther Committee of the GDR' declared in a speech that Luther's posting of the 'famous 95 Theses on the church door in Wittenberg' was the event which brought into the mainstream of modern history 'the decisive impulse for liberation'—a blatant communist appropriation of the celebratory reveries of nineteenth-century liberalism and Protestantism.[56]

Within only a few years the corrupt and autocratic Honecker would learn at first-hand what an 'impulse for liberation' looked like. So far as I am aware, none of the protestors taking hammers to the Berlin Wall in November 1989 is on record as comparing their actions to that of Martin Luther at the Wittenberg *Thesenportal* in 1517, but many of the demonstrators in those heady days adopted as their own the words of the German reformer's greatest namesake, Martin Luther King Jr: 'We Shall Overcome'.[57] King, as we have already seen (pp. 6–7), was but the most eminent of a large number of individuals, in various countries, who since the 1960s have re-enacted Luther's posting of the Ninety-five Theses as a gesture of cultural or political protest. In Wittenberg itself, on 31 October 1989, the Lutheran pastor of the city church, Gottfried Keller, declared that 'Theses belong to Reformation Day', and drew up a set of seven propositions calling for the opening of political dialogue, which he posted in the presence of a supportive crowd of around fifteen thousand people. In a conscious adaption and redirection of the symbolism, he affixed them, not to the door of the church, but to that of the *Rathaus*, the seat of secular and political authority. With its rich accumulation of historical resonances, the *Thesenanschlag* is in the end far too valuable a cultural resource to be lightly ditched, and one which lends itself to purposes of which even the most pedantic and purist of historians might find themselves wholeheartedly approving.[58]

More mundane considerations have also contributed to the durability of the popular image of Luther hammering at the church door. Commercial and artistic treatments of Luther and the Reformation understandably struggle to do anything with the descriptive depiction of a non-event. The highly successful Italian novel *Q*, for example, by a quartet of writers merged into the identity of 'Luther Blissett', opens with an informer's letter reporting a collapse of order 'since the Augustinian monk Martin Luther nailed his notorious theses to the portal of the cathedral'.[59] Several 'biopics' of Luther, for television and the cinema, have been made since the early 1960s. Of these, only one, a stagey German TV production called *Der arme Mann Luther* (Poor Man Luther), omits the scene of Luther nailing his Theses to the door of the Castle Church. Revealingly, it was made in 1965, at the height of the furore created in Germany by the claims of Erwin Iserloh.

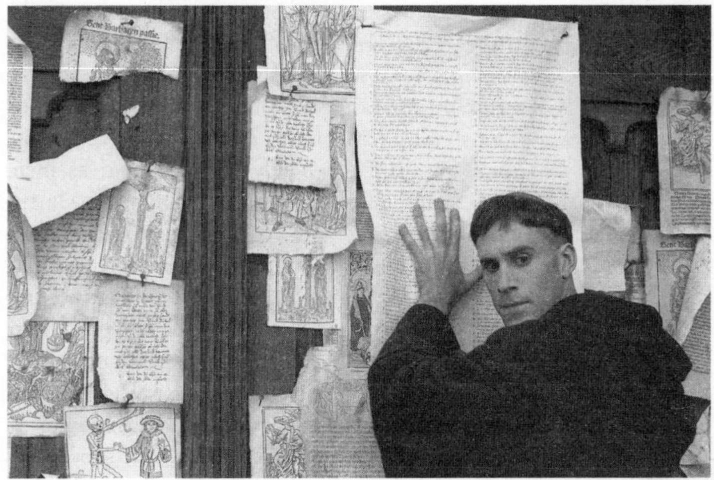

Fig. 5.4. Joseph Fiennes nailing the Theses in director Eric Till's *Luther* (2003).

There was emphatic reversion to type in the 2003 English-language film, *Luther*—a major cinematic release directed by Eric Till and starring the English actor Joseph Fiennes. Its treatment of the events of 1517 is almost a throw-back to the nineteenth-century pathos of *The Blind Girl of Wittenberg* (see p. 157). Luther writes and posts his Theses in furious, impulsive reaction to his discovery that a poor young woman with a crippled child has been conned by Tetzel into buying an indulgence with the last of her savings (see Fig. 5.4). With heavy-handed symbolism, the hammer blows are heard echoing through an implausibly empty church. We cut to a scene of two laymen, laboriously reading the text from the placard Martin has posted. One pulls the paper from the door, over the objection of his friend—'Dr Luther wanted everyone to see that'. 'And everyone will' is the reply, as the man rushes off to the printers with the explosive text of the Ninety-five Theses clutched firmly in his hand.

The film's decidedly old-fashioned portrayal of the Theses-posting as a democratic, emancipatory moment, in the face of opposition from a corrupt Catholic establishment, becomes more explicable in light of the fact that—just like the Luther films of the 1920s and 1950s—it was underpinned financially by a number of Lutheran organizations. Critics, in Germany and elsewhere, generally panned it. Luke Harding, Caroline Lejeune's successor at *The Observer*, astutely complained that 'inevitably, the film also shows him nailing the 95 Theses to the door of Wittenberg's Castle Church, something academics now believe didn't happen.' But Lutherans, and other Germans too, flocked to see the film. The timing of its release probably contributed in November 2003 to Luther coming second (behind Konrad Adenauer, but ahead of Bach, Bismarck, Einstein, Goethe, and Marx) in a much-trumpeted television poll for the title of 'greatest German in history'.[60]

Within Germany, Reformation Day is a public holiday in five separate states—Brandenburg, Mecklenburg-Vorpommern, Saxony, Saxony-Anhalt, and Thuringia—as it is also, curiously perhaps, in predominantly Roman Catholic Slovenia and Chile. Even though Reformation Day now faces stiff cultural competition from an ever-more commercialized Halloween, the holiday in itself represents an enduring head-wind against any willing acceptance of the idea that the commemoration is based on a historical mistake. There was considerable public interest in Germany, and in some quarters almost a palpable sense of relief, when in 2006 the rediscovery of the 'Rörer-note' (pp. 63–4) seemed after all to suggest a more solid historical foundation for the *Thesenanschlag*. Some, though by no means all, historians of the Reformation have considered it to be significant new evidence, but even the most persuadable now see the matter as falling somewhere along a spectrum of probabilities and possibilities.[61]

Possibilities, however, do little to sell postcards and fill hotel rooms. International tourism to Wittenberg, officially renamed Lutherstadt-Wittenberg (Luthertown) by the Nazi regime in 1938, dropped off during the Soviet occupation and Cold War, but has mushroomed since the reunification of Germany in 1990. The charming medieval appearance of the town centre draws numerous cultural or casual visitors, taking their place alongside earnest but cheerful groups of Lutherans and other Protestants, for whom travelling to the birthplace of the Reformation is an enjoyable form of modern pilgrimage. Visitor numbers were boosted, fairly shortly after reunification, by yet another in the recurring cycle of Luther commemorations: the four-hundred-and-fiftieth anniversary of the reformer's death in 1996. Numerous

Fig. 5.5. Tourists outside the Theses-Doors in Wittenberg on Reformation Day 2012, halfway through the German 'Luther Decade'.

sites in Saxony claimed association with Luther, but newspaper reports noted the particular bonanza expected at the place 'where Luther spent 38 years of his life and nailed his 95 theses to the Palace Church door'. By the start of the twenty-first century, Wittenberg was receiving around three hundred and fifty thousand visitors a year, and the number will no doubt spike again in the anniversary year 2017 (see Fig. 5.5).[62]

The tourist authorities in Wittenberg, and those promoting travel to Germany more generally, have little incentive to persuade visitors that nothing of real interest actually happened at the entrance to the Castle Church, where the engraved doors of 1858 continue to commemorate in bronze a famous turning-point in world history. The illustrious *Baedecker* guides are now a little more cautious than their predecessors of a century and more ago: the doors of the *Schlosskirche* are recommended for viewing as the site 'where in October 1517 the monk Martin Luther is supposed to have posted his 95 Theses'. But other best-selling titles for tourists, such as the *DK Eyewitness Travel Guide*, or *Fodor's Germany*, have fewer scruples about relaying the traditional version in all its rebellious glory: Luther's Theses were 'brashly nailed to a church door' according to the 2014 edition of *Fodor*.[63]

Perhaps the ultimate in having one's cultural cake and eating it is to be found on the website of the German National Tourist Board. Here, in a section specifically devoted to Luther, we read that 'it has been 500 years since Martin Luther nailed his 95 theses to the door of the Castle Church in Wittenberg. Although there is no historical proof of this happening, it was an event that changed the world'.[64] In response to such a remarkable assertion there is really nothing a historian can say, other than simply: quite so.

Epilogue: Reformations

This book has attempted to show how a historical myth comes into being, and to illustrate some of the cultural and political 'work' it can be seen to have undertaken over time. What the future will make of Martin Luther's *Thesenanschlag* is a question best left to the future to decide. The extensive and expectedly exuberant Reformation commemorations of 2017 are still pending as I write these words, and will in time deserve and acquire their own historians. The quincentenary certainly represents a welcome boost to Reformation scholarship: there have already been a great many articles, books, and academic conferences stimulated by the prospect of it, with many others scheduled for the year of the jubilee itself. There has been, and will be, intense critical reflection on the historical significance of the Reformation, and on the role played in it by Martin Luther. The extent to which this will be substantially able to shape a wider public experience and understanding of the event is, however, more open to question.

Anniversaries tend to be, almost by definition, conservative and celebratory occasions: married couples seldom (and probably shouldn't) use them to undertake fundamental re-evaluations of the nature of their relationship. The Lutheran Church authorities in Germany tasked with organizing many of the festivities will no doubt emphasize inclusivity and ecumenism—the vehement anti-Catholicism characteristic of past Reformation commemorations will assuredly not be on display. For their part, the German Catholic bishops have published a report in 2016, admitting that Rome made mistakes in the handling of Luther's case, and praising him as 'a religious pathfinder, Gospel witness, and teacher of the faith'.[1] Yet it is too much to expect that Lutherans will forgo the opportunity to express genuine pride in their own heritage, or to hail the Reformation in fairly traditional terms as an undoubted engine for social good. In a speech of 2011, launching the branding campaign for the coming events of the 'Luther decade', the Council Chairman of the Evangelical Church in Germany (EKD), Nikolaus Schneider, was decidedly upbeat. Luther, he admitted, should not be seen as the solitary hero of an all-encompassing liberation. Nonetheless, 'many modern values, like enlightenment and democracy, individualism and human rights, religious pluralism and tolerance are hardly thinkable without the Reformation, and without Martin Luther.' There are similar, very broad-brush claims about the Reformation's foundational importance to many of the most valued principles of western modernity in a short promotional film produced by 'Luther 2017', the church-advised government office charged with coordinating the events of the anniversary in Germany.[2]

In his introduction to the EKD's official commemorative publication, filled with essays on different aspects of the history and legacy of the Reformation, Nikolaus Schneider noted that all of the contributions had one thing in common: '1517 as a symbol of new beginnings and the ever fascinating narrative of Martin Luther nailing his 95 Theses on penance to the door of Wittenberg's Castle Church. This was a new beginning for an entire generation of Reformation men and women'. Legendary or not, the *Thesenanschlag* remains in both an imaginative and an institutional sense the essential point of focus for a festival of public memory. And the brand-logo, chosen by 'Luther 2017' to adorn its pamphlets, websites, and exhibition catalogues in the final year of the Luther decade? It is, almost inevitably, a stylized hammer.[3]

Whether or not Luther ever actually used such a hammer is, in one sense, a small and insignificant detail, and many historians have understandably regarded the debate over the posting of the Theses as the business of a footnote, no more. Should we not simply pick up the hammer and deposit it in the cabinet of trivial historical folklore, alongside the apple placed on the head of William Tell's son and the other falling on Isaac Newton under his tree; the cakes carelessly burned by Alfred and advocated for peasant diets by Marie Antoinette; the telescope held to Nelson's blind eye, and the arrow flying into King Harold's good one?

I hope this book will have persuaded readers that the answer here should be, no. It actually matters a good deal if we can ascertain that Luther openly publicized his Ninety-five Theses on 31 October 1517, particularly in an already printed format, or if we believe it can safely be established that on that day the handwritten Theses were not 'posted', but only posted: sent in a packet in the mail to the Cardinal Archbishop of Mainz. Films and TV shows often experiment with 'alternative endings', but this presents us with a case of alternative beginnings. The Luther in the first scenario has already initiated a movement of public agitation, setting himself up in opposition to the Church authorities, whose blessing of an execrable indulgence campaign represents a symptom of a deeper failure of leadership. Even if few now see the event in the terms it was described by an American magazine in 1892—'the official declaration by Luther of his rebellion against Rome'[4]—a *Thesenanschlag* on the Eve of All Saints is an unmistakable trigger event, the first link in a chain of causation inexorably pulling Luther and his followers away from the stultifying embrace of papal Rome.

The second Luther, who only publicizes the Theses after he believes he has been ignored and let down by his legitimate superiors, the bishops, tells a different story of origins. He is the responsible (if impassioned) Catholic pastoral theologian, concerned for the probity and reputation of his Church, and anxious for it to convey its teaching on penance in a doctrinally correct way. There is no lighted passage to the exit, but rather a disordered set of subsequent steps in the dark—steps which might well have led him in a different direction, or led nowhere at all.

At the very least, the question of whether Luther's nailing of the Ninety-five Theses to the church door in Wittenberg 'fand nicht statt' or 'fand doch statt' (did indeed happen) is an invitation to reflect on whether there was anything inevitable, or even likely, about a permanent split in western Christianity in the sixteenth century, and on the extent to which 'the Reformation' is really anything more than a tidy retrospective label for an unpredictable sequence of messily accidental events. It poses the challenge of determining whether there is much at all really distinctive and special about 1517, a year conventionally portrayed as a hinge between the 'medieval' and 'modern' worlds. And it asks us, or ought to ask us, what precisely is being remembered or commemorated in 2017. A singular and potent historical incident? The life and achievement of Martin Luther? The wider transformative effects of the European Reformation? Or—perhaps more truthfully—a social legacy of inherited cultural attitudes, standards, and values (and indeed, of conventions, assumptions, and prejudices)?

It is the contention of the subtitle of this book, as well as a theme running implicitly all the way through it, that the Reformation was 'invented'. That is, it was something discovered or constructed as an organizing category of memory, rather than something encountered and described as an objective experience of lived reality. That does not, however, make it inauthentic, fake, or unreal, a kind of impostor to be unmasked. As a historical phenomenon, 'the Reformation' is precisely whatever that term has meant to the people using it, from the sixteenth century through to our own times—there is no 'real' Reformation, waiting to be revealed like a carefully restored painting, after the stripping away of layers of varnish and grime.

For precisely that reason, whether or not Luther's *Thesenanschlag* ever really 'happened' is in the end a less interesting and important question than what the image of the friar at the door has represented and stood for, at different times and in different places. The very fact that this has always been—in one sense or another—an 'invented' image makes it paradoxically a more rather than a less reliable point of entry into historical attitudes and mentalities, and the things that were influencing or changing them. The doors of the *Schlosskirche* in Wittenberg, still hinged and hanging through various disasters and recoveries, are real and solid enough, but down the centuries they have also served as a kind of blank screen, onto which the hopes and aspirations of visitors, both actual and virtual, have been projected in vibrant and moving colours.

One important viewing of the scene is as a moment of providential declaration, a direct intrusion of God into the course of history and time, using the faithful witness Martin Luther as his instrument and messenger. This was the image that Luther's own contemporaries and immediate descendants began to cultivate, and it has retained much of its currency with faithful Lutherans and other Protestants down into modern times. The message of the Ninety-five Theses, not necessarily in their precise formulation, but in their authority and impact, is here a fundamentally doctrinal one, restoring the true Gospel of Christ to a Church which had lost its religious way.

The message too was one of liberation—initially, of over-burdened Christian consciences from the yoke of indulgences, and a plethora of other oppressive papalist traditions. Yet, increasingly, in the second and third centuries after Luther's death, the liberation for which the *Thesenanschlag* stood surety began to be reconceived in humanizing, psychological, and secularizing terms—a transformation which reflects a significant shift in the writing of history itself. Luther, so it seemed to many educated people, was an early incarnation of 'enlightened' values, a man asserting the rights of reason against irrational superstition, and of the freedom to think autonomous thoughts against the conformist weight of prescription and tradition. He may well have been divinely motivated, but the drama and inspiration of the moment by the door lay in an individual's courageous, and very human, decision to take a defining stand. As Catholicism in Europe came to be ever more associated with reactionary and repressive regimes, so the *Thesenanschlag* suggested real possibilities of social and political, as well as intellectual, liberation.

The ability of Protestantism to seize for itself the mantle of political liberalism, and to align the idea of the Reformation—almost irrespective of its actual doctrinal teachings—with narratives of social, economic, and governmental progress, is surely one of the most significant developments of west European history over the past two centuries and more. It is an idea that even in 'post-Christian' Europe still exercises a surprisingly strong imaginative grip, in historically Catholic as well as culturally Protestant societies. For many people in the United States of America, it is almost a founding article of faith. If a symbolic encapsulation of these processes did not exist, it would surely have to be invented—and in a sense it was. Luther's nailing of the Ninety-five Theses has functioned as a kind of cultural bookmark for the reading of the European past, conveniently locating the point at which the story takes a new and dramatic turn. Alongside Luther's repeat performance at the Diet of Worms—'Here I stand, I can do no other!'—it is a powerful foundation-myth of western individualism, and of a tolerant, liberal, democratic society.

There is, too, a dark side to the *Thesenanschlag*, just as the projects of enlightenment and modernity have themselves veered disastrously off-course at various times in the broad sweep of European history. From the outset, the Wittenberg door has been a symbol of division as well as triumph, separating the world into those who cheer the hammering of the nails, and those who skulk away scowling from the doors. The

Reformation's legacy of hostility and contempt towards the followers of the pope (historically, a majority of west European Christians) is the counterpart of its declared commitment to conscience and liberty, and for much of the past four hundred years and more such animosities have been sharpened and renewed by contemplation of the deed of 31 October 1517. Even into fairly recent times, discussion of the posting of the Theses has been coloured by confessional suspicions and allegiances. A matter for ecumenists to ponder, in the run-up to the more amiable commemorations we can anticipate in 2017, is that of who needs to apologize most to whom.

The ringing sound of virile hammer blows has at times also carried with it undertones of coercion and violence. Luther's status—asserted already in his lifetime—as a hero of the German people, a doer of great deeds, undoubtedly helped fuel an unhealthy and aggressive nationalism, an impulse which swelled in the nineteenth century, and in the early part of the twentieth brought the country, and the world, to the brink of disaster and beyond. Wittenberg in the 1930s had a reputation as a pro-Nazi town, and in September 1933 hosted the infamous 'Brown Synod', which many delegates attended wearing the distinctive coloured shirts of the stormtroopers of the SA.[5] Not all sets of theses drafted in tribute to the ninety-five have been wholesome or productive.

Yet the image of Luther nailing his statement of conscience to the church door—in the words of one nineteenth-century author, 'like the English captain who nailed his colours to the mast'—has long proved to be an invaluable asset of what has been termed the 'usable past', a beacon serving as a point of navigation for successive generations of courageous non-conformists.[6] In the twentieth century, in both 1934 and 1989, it helped inspire some Lutheran Germans to reclaim the best in their religious heritage and resist the forces of totalitarian oppression. Over the years, not only Protestants, but civil rights campaigners, environmental activists, atheists, and even Catholics have been drawn to its powerful symbolic possibilities for registering peaceful public protest against perceived chicanery or injustice. The witness and sincerity of these people is in no way lessened by the fact that the original of their action is more likely an elaborate fable projected onto history than a true memory drawn from it. For, at its best, a *Thesenanschlag* is a pageant of the nobility of the human spirit.

Notes

Prologue

1 Milton Viorst (ed.), *The Great Documents of Western Civilization* (New York, 1994); Brian Bonhomme and Cathleen Boivin (eds), *Milestone Documents in World History* (Hackensack, NJ, 2010); Scott Christianson, *100 Documents that Changed the World: From the Magna Carta to WikiLeaks* (New York, 2015); <http://www.mirror.co.uk/news/uk-news/how-past-wrote-future-10-3813438> (accessed January 2017).

2 Peter D'Epiro, Mary Pinkowish, and Desmond D'Epiro, *What Are the Seven Wonders of the World? And 100 Other Great Cultural Lists* (New York, 1998), xviii.

3 <http://www.reformationsa.org/index.php/component/content/article/1-latest-news/257-95-theses-for-reformation-today>; http://truthwatch.info/statements/95-theses-for-a-new-millenium (accessed April 2016); James Fowler, *95 Theses for the Twenty-first Century Church* (Fallbrook, CA, 2010); Lothar Gassmann, *95 Thesen für 2017* (Freudenstadt, 2013); T. Scott Womble, *Beyond Reasonable Doubt: 95 Theses which Dispute the Church's Conviction against Women* (New York, 2009); <http://www.patheos.com/Resources/Additional-Resources/95-Theses-for-a-New-Reformation> (accessed January 2017); Thomas F. O'Donnell, *Mainlining Christianity: 95 Theses for the 21st Century* (Bloomington, IN, 2006).

4 Anne Norton, *95 Theses on Politics, Culture and Method* (New Haven, 2004); Andrew Bushard, *A Case For Homeschooling: 95 Theses Against the School System* (self-published, 2013); Bill Basaar, *95 Theses Project: Let's Save Our Constitution* (self-published, 2014); Dieter Aebi et al, *ProGenesis: Ninety-Five Theses Against Evolution: A Scientific Critique of the Naturalist Philosophy* (Houston, 2013); *The 95 Theses of Kay's Beauty Shop* (AMB Press, 2015); Dennis J. Martin, *Theses on 95 Sexdecillion Indulgences: With Flirts and Spices* (Atlanta, 2003).

5 <http://www.postingandtoasting.com/2014/12/9/7340643/the-95-theses-of-the-knicks-rebuild>; <http://www.sbnation.com/nba/2011/8/15/2363784/nba-lockout-2011-95-theses>; <http://articles.latimes.com/keyword/djs>; <http://95theses.io/about>; <http://beekmanwealth.com/wp-content/uploads/2013/01/95-Theses-for-Managing-Wealth1.pdf>; <http://www.dezeen.com/2013/09/12/opinion-kieran-long-on-contemporary-museum-curation > (all accessed January 2017).

6 Cathy Gorn, 'Taking a Stand in History: Individuals, Groups, Movements', *OAH Magazine of History*, 9 (1995), 44; George A. Carver Jr., 'Intelligence in the Age of Glasnost', *Foreign Affairs*, 69 (1990), 147.

7 Barry Stephenson, *Performing the Reformation: Public Ritual in the City of Luther* (Oxford, 2010), 77; <http://www.history.com/this-day-in-history/martin-luther-posts-95-theses> (accessed January 2017); A. C. Grayling, *The Heart*

of Things: Applying Philosophy to the 21st Century (London, 2005), 103; Brent F. Nelsen and James L. Guth, *Religion and the Struggle for European Union: Confessional Culture and the Limits of Integration* (Washington, 2015), 85.

8 Coretta Scott King, *My Life with Martin Luther King, Jr* (New York, 1969), 282; James M. Washington (ed.), *A Testament of Hope: The Essential Writings of Martin Luther King* (New York, 1986), 279–80.

9 James F. Findlay, *Church People in the Struggle: The National Council of Churches and the Black Freedom Movement, 1950–1970* (Oxford, 1993), 201–3; *The Lutheran*, 16 (1978), 262.

10 '95 Theses Group', *95 Theses: in Vindication of Freechurchmanship, against Episcopacy and Sacerdotalism in the Covenant Proposals* (Nottingham, 1981); John Ankerberg and John Weldon, *Knowing the Truth About the Trinity* (ATRI Publishing, 2011), unpaginated e-book.

11 Matthew Fox, *A New Reformation: Creation Spirituality and the Transformation of Christianity* (Rochester, VT, 2006), 1–9; Adam Bucko and Matthew Fox, *Occupy Spirituality: A Radical Vision for a New Generation* (Berkeley, 2013), 249; <http://matthewfox.org/about-matthew-fox/a-new-reformation/95-theses> (accessed April 2016).

12 <https://mormonreformationday2013.files.wordpress.com/2013/09/the95ldstheses_2016.pdf>; https://mormonreformationday2013.wordpress.com/posting-the-95-lds-theses (accessed January 2017).

13 <http://www.sandiegouniontribune.com/uniontrib/20041128/news_z1e28louv.html> (accessed April 2016); Stefaan Blancke, Abraham C. Flipse, and Johan Braeckman, 'The Low Countries', in Stefaan Blancke, Hans Henrik Hjermitslev, and Peter C. Kjærgaard (eds), *Creationism in Europe* (Baltimore, 2014), 76; *British Medical Journal*, 340 (24 April, 2010), 894; 'The Ballyhea Theses', in Gene Kerrigan, *The Big Lie—Who Profits From Ireland's Austerity?* (London, 2012); <http://www.theguardian.com/world/2012/jan/05/irish-village-ballyhea> (accessed January 2017); Seamus Lynch, *Cast Out into the Deep: Attracting Young People to the Church* (Dublin, 2004).

14 <https://www.ibka.org/node/1329>; <http://blog.bdkj.de/category/allgemein/page/31> (accessed January 2017).

15 <http://www.gettyimages.co.uk/detail/news-photo/paper-addressed-to-limburgs-bishop-and-referring-to-the-news-photo/184349165>; <http://www.bbc.co.uk/news/world-europe-24638430> (accessed January 2017).

16 <http://www.bamberg.bund-naturschutz.de/kinder-jugend/jugendgruppe.html>; https://mikenagler1.wordpress.com/2011/10/31/thesenanschlag-und-fortsetzung-der-montagsversammlungen-angekundigt>; <https://bgereformationstag.wordpress.com/aktion>; <http://www.deutschlandfunk.de/neuzeitlicher-thesenanschlag-in-erfurt.697.de.html?dram:article_id=228475> (all accessed January 2017).

17 <https://www.stura.tu-dresden.de/webfm_send/556>; <www.tu-chemnitz.de/uk/pressestelle/aktuell/2/2279>; <https://www.freitag.

de/autoren/the-guardian/95-thesen-fur-deine-universitat>; <http://www.mz-web.de/halle-saale/martin-luther-universitaet-halle-thesenanschlag-fuer-die-erhaltung-der-bildungsvielfalt—882736> (all accessed January 2017).

18 <http://www.tagesspiegel.de/politik/lutz-bachmann-und-pegida-der-thesenanschlag-von-dresden/11381508.html>; <http://www.newslocker.com/de-de/region/leipzig/thesenanschlag-legida-chef-spielt-luther-bild/view> (accessed January 2017).

19 Martin Brecht, 'Luther, Martin', in Hans J. Hillebrand (ed.), *The Oxford Encyclopedia of the Reformation* (4 vols, Oxford, 1992), 2:462; W. D. J. Cargill Thompson, review of Wilhelm Borth, *Die Luther sache (Causa Lutheri) 1517–1524*, in *Journal of Theological Studies*, 24 (1973), 295; Volker Leppin and Timothy J. Wengert, 'Sources for and against the Posting of the Ninety-Five Theses', *Lutheran Quarterly*, 29 (2015), 373.

20 For example, Keith D. Lewis, *The Catholic Church in History: Legend and Reality* (New York, 2006), 77; Friederike Lübke, 'Placing Luther on a Pedestal', in Thomas Schiller et al (eds), *Perspectives 2017*, tr. David Dichelle (Hannover, 2013), 15–16; Gerhard Prause, *Niemand hat Kolumbus ausgelacht: Fälschungen und Legenden der Geschichte richtiggestellt* (Frankfurt, 1966; new edn 1995), ch. 3; Bernd Ingmar Gutberlet, *Die 50 populärsten Irrtümer der deutschen Geschichte* (Hamburg, 2002), 104–8.

21 Jan Assmann, *Moses the Egyptian: The Memory of Egypt in Western Monotheism* (Cambridge, MA, 1997), 14–15. Assmann warns against an 'infelicitous opposition between history and myth', and insists that 'history turns into myth as soon as it is remembered, narrated and used'.

22 On this theme, see Kerwin Lee Klein, 'On the Emergence of *Memory* in Historical Discourse', *Representations*, 69 (2000), 127–50; Peter Burke, 'History as Social Memory' in his *Varieties of Cultural History* (Ithaca, NY, 1997), 43–59.

23 Pierre Nora, 'Between Memory and History: *Les Lieux de Mémoire*', *Representations*, 26 (1989), 7–24 (quote at p. 8). See also Pierre Nora and Lawrence D. Kritzman (eds), *Realms of Memory: The Construction of the French Past*, tr. Arthur Goldhammer (3 vols, New York, 1996–8).

24 Burke, 'History as Social Memory', 46.

Chapter 1

1 K. G. Bretschneider and H. E. Bindesil (eds), *Corpus Reformatorum (Series 1: Philip Melanchthon)* (28 vols, Halle, 1834–60), 6:161–2: 'Lutherus, studio pietatis ardens, edidit Propositiones de Indulgentiis, quae in primo Tomo monumentorum ipsius extant, Et has publice Templo, quod arci Witebergensi contiguum est, affixit pridie festi omnium Sanctorum anno 1517.' My translation: see also Erwin Iserloh, *The Theses Were not Posted: Luther between Reform and Reformation*, tr. Jared Wicks (London, 1968), 73; Elizabeth

Vandiver, Ralph Keen, and Thomas D. Frazel (eds and trs), *Luther's Lives: Two Contemporary Accounts of Martin Luther*, ed. and tr. (Manchester, 2002), 19.

2 *Corpus Reformatorum*, 6: 155–70; Irena Backus, *Life Writing in Reformation Europe: Lives of Reformers by Friends, Disciples and Foes* (Aldershot, 2008), 2–9. See also Michael P. Alderson, 'Melanchthon's Authorizing of Luther: An Examination of the Narrative Origins of Sixteenth-Century Historical Life-Writing', University of Durham PhD thesis (2013), ch. 5.

3 *D. Martin Luthers Werke. Kritische Gesamtausgabe. Schriften* [WA], (68 vols, Weimar, 1883–1999), 1:528–9; Timothy J. Wengert, 'Introduction', in Wengert (ed.), *The Annotated Luther: Volume 1 The Roots of Reform* (Minneapolis, 2015), 3; Andrew Pettegree, *Brand Luther: 1517, Printing, and the Making of the Reformation* (New York, 2015), 26.

4 Martin Steffens, *Luthergedenkstätten im 19. Jahrhundert: Memoria-Repräsentation-Denkmalpflege* (Regensburg, 2008), 237–42.

5 Andreas Meinhardi, *Über die Lage, die Schönheit und den Ruhm der hochberühmten. Herrlichen Stadt Albioris, gemeinhin Wittenberg genannt*, ed. Martin Treu (Leipzig, 1986), 12; Lyndal Roper, *Martin Luther: Renegade and Prophet* (London, 2016), 81–4.

6 Paul Kalkoff, *Ablaß und Reliquienverehrung an der Schloßkirche zu Wittenberg unter Friedrich dem Weisen* (Gotha, 1907), 6–10, 64–6; Nikolaus Paulus, 'Raimund Peraudi als Ablaßkomissar', *Historisches Jahrbuch*, 21 (1900), 645–82; Norman Housely, 'Indulgences for Crusading, 1417–1517', in R. N. Swanson (ed.), *Promissory Notes on the Treasury of Merits: Indulgences in Late Medieval Europe* (Leiden, 2006), 292–8; Pettegree, *Brand Luther*, 56–7.

7 Craig M. Koslofsky, *The Reformation of the Dead: Death and Ritual in Early Modern Germany, 1450–1700* (Basingstoke, 2000), ch. 2; Peter Marshall, *Beliefs and the Dead in Reformation England* (Oxford, 2002), ch. 1.

8 The best recent assessment is supplied by the essays in Swanson (ed.), *Promissory Notes*. See also the helpful overview in Elizabeth C. Tingle, *Indulgences after Luther* (London, 2015), 1–13.

9 Robert W. Shaffern, 'The Medieval Theology of Indulgences', in Swanson (ed.), *Promissory Notes*, 33–6.

10 B. J. Kidd (ed.), *Documents Illustrative of the Continental Reformation* (Oxford, 1911), 3–4; Norman Houseley, *Crusading and the Ottoman Threat, 1453–1505* (Oxford, 2013), 181–2.

11 Robert E. McNally, 'The Ninety-Five Theses of Martin Luther, 1517–1967', *Theological Studies*, 28 (1967), 446–7; Charlotte Methuen, 'Luther's Life', in Robert Kolb, Irene Dingel, and Lubomir Batka (eds), *The Oxford Handbook of Martin Luther's Theology* (Oxford, 2014), 10–11; Richard Marius, *Martin Luther: The Christian between God and Death* (Cambridge, MA, 1999), 128–9.

12 Kidd (ed.), *Documents*, 13–17; Marius, *Luther*, 134–6.

13 Arno Herzig and Saskia Rohde, 'Reuchlin, Johannes', in Hans J. Hillebrand (ed.), *The Oxford Encyclopedia of the Reformation* (4 vols, Oxford, 1992), 3:425–6; Berndt Hamm, *The Early Luther: Stages in a Reformation*

Reorientation, tr. Martin J. Lohrmann (Grand Rapids, MI, 2014) chs 1–3; Volker Leppin, *Martin Luther* (Darmstadt, 2006), 117–18.

14 Timothy J. Wengert, 'Martin Luther's Preaching an Indulgence in January 1517', *Lutheran Quarterly*, 29 (2015), 62–75; Martin Brecht, *Martin Luther: His Road to Reformation, 1483–1521*, tr. James L. Schaff (Philadelphia, 1985), 188; Jared L. Wicks, 'Martin Luther's Treatise on Indulgences', *Theological Studies*, 28 (1967), 481–518 (quotation at 493).

15 E. G. Rupp and Benjamin Drewery (eds), *Martin Luther* (London, 1970), 7–8; Robert Kolb, *Martin Luther: Confessor of the Faith* (Oxford, 2009), 19; Alister E. McGrath, *Iustitia Dei: A History of the Christian Doctrine of Justification* (2nd edn, Cambridge, 1998), 208; Brecht, *Road to Reformation*, 170–3.

16 Paul F. Grendler, *Renaissance Education Between Religion and Politics* (Aldershot, 2006), 14; Heinrich Bornkamm, 'Thesen und Thesenanschlag Luthers', in Kurt Aland, Walther Eltester, Heinz Liebing, and Klaus Scholder (eds), *Geist und Geschichte der Reformation: Festgabe Hanns Rückert zum 65 Geburtstag* (Berlin, 1966), 211.

17 Wengert (ed.), *Annotated Luther*, 34. Quotations from the Ninety-five Theses in the following paragraphs are drawn from the translation here, at 34–46.

18 Hamm, *Early Luther*, 177; James D. Tracy, *Erasmus of the Low Countries* (Berkeley and Los Angeles, 1996), 108. For the role of Erasmus in Luther's evolving theology, see David Whitford, 'Erasmus Openeth the Way Before Luther: Revisiting Humanism's Influence on *The Ninety-Five Theses* and the Early Luther', *Church History and Religious Culture*, 96 (2016), 516–40.

19 Marshall, *Beliefs and the Dead*, 11.

20 David Bagchi, 'Luther's Ninety-five Theses and the Contemporary Criticism of Indulgences', in Swanson (ed.), *Promissory Notes*, 343; Tingle, *Indulgences*, 19–20; Wilhelm Ernst Winterhager, 'Ablasskritik als Indikator historischen Wandels vor 1517: Ein Beitrag zu Voraussetzungen und Einordnung der Reformation', *Archiv für Reformationsgeschichte*, 90 (1999), 6–71.

21 Erasmus, *Praise of Folly*, ed. A. Levi, tr. B. Radice (Harmondsworth, 1971), 126–7; *The Colloquies of Erasmus*, tr. C. R. Thompson (Chicago, 1965), 7, 627.

22 Bagchi, 'Luther's Ninety-five Theses', 346–9; Jared Wicks, 'Cajetan', in Hillebrand (ed.), *Encyclopedia*, 1:233–4.

23 Wengert (ed.), *Annotated Luther*, 51–5; Wicks, 'Treatise on Indulgences', 484–5.

24 Iserloh, *Not Posted*, 54, 76; *D. Martin Luthers Werke. Kritische Gesamthausgabe. Tischreden* [WATr] (6 vols, Weimar, 1912–21), 3:564.

25 Bernd Moeller, 'Thesenanschläge', in Joachim Ott and Martin Treu (eds), *Luthers Thesenanschlag—Faktum oder Fiktion* (Leipzig, 2008), 12–13, 18–24, 28–9; Pettegree, *Brand Luther*, 42–3, 51, 70–1. Pettegree goes too far (p. 72) in claiming the typographical evidence helps prove 'almost certainly the indulgences [sic.] were posted up on the door of the castle church, as the accepted narrative would have it, most probably in a now lost printed edition of Johann Rhau-Grunenberg.'

26 Roper, *Luther*, 98.

27 *D. Martin Luthers Werke. Kritische Gesamthausgabe. Briefwechsel* [WABr] (18 vols, Weimar, 1930–85), 1:121–2; Kurt Aland (ed.), *Martin Luther's 95 Theses*, tr. P. J. Schroeder et al (St Louis, MO, 2004), 72–4, 115n.

28 As suggested by Brecht, *Road to Reformation*, 201.

29 Iserloh, *Not Posted*, 79; Wicks, 'Treatise on Indulgences', 483–7; Brecht, *Road to Reformation*, 206–7; Aland, *95 Theses*, 112–13.

30 Richard Rex, 'The Friars in the English Reformation', in Peter Marshall and Alec Ryrie (eds), *The Beginnings of English Protestantism* (Cambridge, 2002), 38; WA 1:527–8.

31 WABr 1:118; 1:244–5. Aland, *95 Theses*, 114, dating the first of these letters to early November 1517, offers it as proof that the Theses were clearly already widely known in Wittenberg (and thus posted on 31 October 1517). But as Brecht has shown, a date in January or February 1518 is more likely: *Road to Reformation*, 508.

32 Aland, *95 Theses*, 74. A further, albeit circumstantial, argument against any announcement of a disputation on 31 October 1517 is that the day fell in the period of vacation, and students would not have been around to see the notification or take part: Hartmut Lehmann, *Luthergedächtnis 1817 bis 2017* (Göttingen, 2012), 31.

33 Whether such a disputation 'extra ordinem' fell within the rules of normal academic procedure is debatable: Daniel Jütte, *The Strait Gate: Thresholds and Power in Western History* (New Haven and London, 2015), 180; Irene Dingel, tr. Robert Kolb, 'Pruning the Vines, Plowing Up the Vineyard: The Sixteenth-Century Culture of Controversy between Disputation and Polemic', in Anna Marie Johnson and John A. Maxfield (eds), *The Reformation as Christianization* (Tübingen, 2012), 400–1; Heiko Oberman, *Masters of the Reformation: The Emergence of New Intellectual Climate in Europe*, tr. Dennis Martin (Cambridge, 1981), 148–50.

34 Aland, *95 Theses*, 76–9.

35 WABr 1:151–2; 'Christoph Scheurl's Geschichtsbuch der Christenheit von 1511 bis 1521', in J. K. F. Knaake (ed.), *Jahrbücher des deutschen Reichs und der deutschen Kirche im Zeitalter der Reformation* (Leipzig, 1872), 112, 123.

36 Roper, *Luther*, 97, 456; *Collected Works of Erasmus* (Toronto, 1974), 5: 327; Aland, *95 Theses*, 42.

37 Aland, *95 Theses*, 75, 77, 80; Wengert (ed.), *Annotated Luther*, 58–9, 64–5.

38 WABr 1:152; Wengert (ed.), *Annotated Luther*, 58.

Chapter 2

1 Andrew Pettegree, *Brand Luther: 1517, Printing, and the Making of the Reformation* (New York, 2015), 78–9; Jared Wicks, 'Roman Reactions to Luther: The First Year (1518)', *Catholic Historical Review*, 69 (1983), 521–62 (quotations at 529, 561). See Dennis Bielfeldt, 'Heidelberg Disputation,

1518', in Timothy Wengert (ed.), *The Annotated Luther: Volume 1 The Roots of Reform* (Minneapolis, 2015), 67–120.

2 David Bagchi, *Luther's Earliest Opponents: Catholic Controversialists 1518–1525* (Minneapolis, 1991), 21–2; Wicks, 'Roman Reactions', 539–56; Suzanne Hequet, 'The Proceedings at Augsburg, 1518' in Wengert (ed.), *Annotated Luther*, 121–6.

3 Michael A. Mullett, *Martin Luther* (London, 2004), 89–98.

4 Lyndal Roper, *Martin Luther: Renegade and Prophet* (London, 2016), 158–71 (quotation at 170); *D. Martin Luthers Werke. Kritische Gesamthausgabe. Schriften* [WA], (68 vols, Weimar, 1883–1999), 7:183; Mullett, *Luther*, 120. The text of the papal bull can be read at http://www.papalencyclicals.net/Leo10/l10exdom.htm (accessed April 2017).

5 *Deutsche Reichstagsakten, Jüngere Reihe*, Vol. 2 (Gotha, 1896), 555, and note 555–6; transl. in E. G. Rupp and Benjamin Drewery (eds), *Martin Luther* (London, 1970), 60. The amended account: Georg Spalatin, *Die gancz handlung szo mit dem Hochgelerte[n] D. Martino Luther taglichen die weyl er auff dem Keyserlichen Reychs tag tzu Wormbs gewest, ergangen ist* (Wittenberg, 1521), B1v.

6 Mullett, *Luther*, 130–5; text of the Edict at <http://www.crivoice.org/creededictworms.html> (accessed January 2017).

7 Peter Marshall, *The Reformation: A Very Short Introduction* (Oxford, 2009), 18; C. Scott Dixon, *Contesting the Reformation* (Chichester, 2012), 8–9.

8 WA 50:348–51; Scott Dixon, 'Luther's Ninety-Five Theses and the Origins of the Reformation Narrative', *English Historical Review* (forthcoming); Herbert D. Rix, *Martin Luther: The Man and the Image* (New York, 1983), 280–2.

9 Heinz Schilling, *Martin Luther: Rebell in einer Zeit des Umbruchs* (Munich, 2012), 127.

10 *D. Martin Luthers Werke. Kritische Gesamthausgabe. Briefwechsel* [WABr] (18 vols, Weimar, 1930–85), 4:275; Hartmut Lehmann, *Luthergedächtnis 1817 bis 2017* (Göttingen, 2012), 16; Robert Kolb, 'Amsdorf, Nikolaus von', in Hans J. Hillebrand (ed.), *The Oxford Encyclopedia of the Reformation* (4 vols, Oxford, 1992), 1:27–8.

11 *D. Martin Luthers Werke. Kritische Gesamthausgabe. Tischreden* [WATr] (6 vols, Weimar, 1912–21), 1:441; 2:376; 3:477; 2:467; WA 39/1:6.

12 WATr 5: 657–8; 5:77–8; WA 54: 179–80.

13 WA 30/2: 281; 54:180–1.

14 Dixon, 'Ninety-Five Theses'; Georg Spalatin, *Annales Reformationis Oder Jahr-Bücher von der Reformation Lutheri*, ed. Ernst Salomon Cyprian (Leipzig, 1718), A3^{v}, 1–5; Robert Kolb, *Martin Luther as Prophet, Teacher and Hero: Images of the Reformer, 1520–1620* (Grand Rapids, MI, 1999), 23–5.

15 Johannes Agricola, *Epistola S. Pauli ad Titum* (Hagenau, 1530), E3^{r-v}; *Chronica durch Magistrum Johan Carion* (Wittenberg, 1532), F2^{r}. See Robin Barnes, *Prophecy and Gnosis: Apocalypticism in the Wake of the Lutheran Reformation* (Stanford, 1988), 106–8.

16 Frederic Myconius, *Historia Reformationis vom Jahr Christi 1517 bis 1542*, ed. Ernst Salomon Cyprian (Leipzig, 1718), 22–5. See Robert Rosin, 'Myconius, Friedrich', in Hillebrand (ed.), *Encyclopedia*, 3:117–18.

17 Ralph Keen, 'Johannes Cochlaeus: an introduction to his life and work', in Elizabeth Vandiver, Ralph Keen, and Thomas D. Frazel (eds and trs), *Luther's Lives: Two Contemporary Accounts of Martin Luther*, ed. and tr. (Manchester, 2002), 40–6, 48; Gottfried Wiedermann, 'Cochlaeus as a Polemicist', in Peter Newman Brooks (ed.), *Seven-Headed Luther: Essays in Commemoration of a Quincentenary 1483–1983* (Oxford, 1983), 195–206.

18 Erwin Iserloh, *The Theses Were not Posted: Luther between Reform and Reformation*, tr. Jared Wicks (London, 1968), 68; Vandiver, Keen, and Frazel, *Luther's Lives*, 55–9.

19 Vandiver, Keen, and Frazel, *Luther's Lives*, 14–19, 55–9.

20 Vandiver, Keen, and Frazel, *Luther's Lives*, 15.

21 K. G. Bretschneider and H. E. Bindesil (eds), *Corpus Reformatorum (Series 1: Philip Melanchthon)* (28 vols, Halle, 1834–60), 1:88–9, 291.

22 'Anno do[m]ini 1517 in profesto o[mn]i[u]m Sanctoru[m] pr(. . .) Wite[m]berge in valvis temploru[m] propositae sunt pro(opositiones) de Indulgentiis a D[octore] Mart[ino] Luth[ero]': Martin Treu, 'Urkunde und Reflexion: Wiederentdeckung eines Belegs von Luthers Thesenanschlag', in Joachim Ott and Martin Treu (eds), *Luthers Thesenanschlag—Faktum oder Fiktion* (Leipzig, 2008), 59–60; Marilyn J. Harran, 'Rörer, Georg', in Hillebrand (ed.), *Encyclopedia*, 3:450; Volker Leppin, 'Der Thesenanschlag bleibt fraglich: Bemerkungen zu einer neuen Diskussion und alten Problemen', *Luther-Bulletin*, 17 (2008), 42. The Rörer note can be viewed, in digitalized form, at <http://archive.thulb.uni-jena.de/hisbest/rsc/viewer/HisBest_derivate_00001623/RN_0039_0413tif_re.tif (accessed May 2016).

23 Walter Friedensburg (ed.), *Urkundenbuch der Universität Wittenberg* (2 vols, Magdeburg, 1926–7), 1:30, 33, 54; Aleksander Gieysztor, 'Management and Resources', in Hilde de Ridder-Symoens, *A History of the University in Europe: Volume 1 Universities in the Middle Ages* (Cambridge, 1992), 127–7; Jütte, *Strait Gate*, 192; Jütte, 'Schwang Luther 1517 tatsächlich den Hammer?', *Frankfurther Allgemeine Zeitung*, 16 June 2014, online at <http://www.faz.net/aktuell/feuilleton/geisteswissenschaften/thesenanschlag-schwang-luther-1517-tatsaechlich-den-hammer-12994372.html> (accessed January 2017).

24 WA 48, Revisionsnachtrag, 116, n.3; Volker Leppin, 'Geburtswehen und Geburt einer Legende: Zu Rörers Notiz vom Thesenanschlag', *Luther*, 78 (2007), 149.

25 Adolf Brecher, 'Neue Beiträge zum Briefwechsel der Reformatoren', *Zeitschrift für die historische Theologie*, 42 (1872), 326; Hans Volz, *Martin Luthers Thesenanschlag und dessen Vorgeschichte* (Weimar, 1959), 94, 104; Iserloh, *Not Posted*, 66; Harald Weinacht (ed.), *Melanchthon und Luther: Martin Luthers Lebensbeschreibung durch Philipp Melanchthon* (Zürich, 2008), 82–3.

26 Volker Leppin, '"Nicht seine Person, sondern die Wahrheit zu verteidigen": Die Legende vom Thesenanschlag in lutherischer Historiographie und Memoria', in Heinz Schilling (ed.), *Der Reformator Martin Luther 2017: Eine wissenschaftliche und gedenkpolitische Bestandsaufnahme* (Berlin, 2014), 86–7.

27 Paul Eber, *Calendarium Historicum* (Wittenberg, 1550), 368; Scott H. Hendrix, *Martin Luther, Visionary Reformer* (New Haven and London, 2015), 83–4; Hendrix, *Martin Luther: A Very Short Introduction* (Oxford, 2010), 9; R. W. Scribner, *Popular Culture and Popular Movements in Reformation Germany* (London, 1987), 309, 326–7.

28 Timothy J. Wengert, 'Georg Major: An "Eyewitness" to the Posting of Martin Luther's Ninety-Five Theses', in Ott and Treu, *Thesenanschlag*, 93–7; WA 51:541.

29 *Corpus Reformatorum*, 7:1121, 1122; MS on display in *Melanchthonhaus* Museum, Wittenberg.

30 *Corpus Reformatorum* 8: 594–5. Cf. Volker Leppin and Timothy J. Wengert, 'Sources for and against the Posting of the Ninety-Five Theses', *Lutheran Quarterly*, 29 (2015), 377.

31 H. E. Bindseil (ed.), *Philippi Melanchthonis epistolae* (Halle, 1874), 435; *Corpus Reformatorum*, 25: 777. See also *Corpus Reformatorum*, 9: 956 (a letter of 31 October 1559, identifying the day as the start of *emendationis doctrinae*).

32 Berthold Kress, *Divine Diagrams: The Manuscripts and Drawings of Paul Lautensack (1477/78–1558)* (Leiden, 2014), 27; Jütte, *Strait Gate*, 181–2; Gary K. Waite, *David Joris and Dutch Anabaptism, 1524–1543* (Waterloo, 1990), 9, 52–3.

33 London, National Archives, SP 1/22, 207r; John Foxe, *Acts and Monuments* (London, 1583), 1037; Julian Lock, 'Felton, John (*d.* 1570)', *Oxford Dictionary of National Biography*, online edition.

34 Leppin, 'Nicht seine Person', 88–9; Ian Maclean, *Learning and the Market Place: Essays in the History of the Early Modern Book* (Leiden, 2009), 121–2.

35 Vandiver, Keen, and Frazel, *Luther's Lives*, 14, 353–5.

36 Leppin and Wengert, 'Sources', 375; *Verzeichnis der im deutschen Sprachbereich erschienenen Drucke des 16. Jahrhunderts*, searchable online at http://www.gateway-bayern.de/index.html?func=file&file_name=search_vd16: M 3416- M3430; *Corpus Reformatorum*, 20: 435; Philip Melanchthon, *A famous and godly history*, tr. Henry Bennet (London, 1561), A3r. Cf Timothy J. Wengert: 'The First Biography of Martin Luther, Compiled by Johannes Pollicarius', in Irene Dingel (ed.), *Memoria—theologische Synthese—Autoritätenkonflikt: Die Rezeption Luthers und Melanchthons in der Schülergeneration* (Tübingen, 2016), 14–44.

37 *Famous and godly history*, A2v, C1v; John Foxe, *Acts and Monuments* (London, 1563), 455; (1570), 1009–10; (1576), 817; (1583), 844. Cf. Elizabeth Evenden and Thomas S. Freeman, 'Print, Profit and Propaganda: The Elizabethan Privy Council and the 1570 Edition of Foxe's "Book of Martyrs"', *English Historical Review*, 119 (2004), 1288–1307.

38 Johannes Sleidanus, *De statu religionis et reipublicae Carolo V caesare commentarii* (Strasburg, 1556), 1r–v. Cf. A. G. Dickens and John Tonkin, *The Reformation*

in Historical Thought (Oxford, 1985), 10–19. It is revealing of modern assumptions that a leading authority writes that Sleidanus supplies 'a description of the posting of the Ninety-five Theses': Donald R. Kelley, 'Johann Sleidan and the Origins of History as a Profession', *Journal of Modern History*, 52 (1980), 592–3.

39 Ludwig Rabus, *Historien der Heyligen Außerwölten Gottes Zeügen, Bekennern vnd Martyrern . . . Der vierdte Theyl* (Strasburg, 1556), vi^{r-v}; Kolb, *Martin Luther*, 87; Lyndal Roper, 'Martin Luther's Body: The "Stout Doctor" and his Biographers', *American Historical Review*, 115 (2010), 364–6.

40 Robert Rosin, 'Mathesius, Johannes', in Hildebrand (ed.), *Encyclopedia*, 3:32–3, where he is described as 'first biographer of Martin Luther', the argument also of Hans Volz, *Die Lutherpredigten des Johannes Mathesius* (Halle, 1929).

41 Roper, 'Luther's Body', 366–7; Irena Backus, *Life Writing in Reformation Europe: Lives of Reformers by Friends, Disciples and Foes* (Aldershot, 2008), 8–12; Kolb, *Martin Luther*, 87–90; Ernst Walter Zeeden, *The Legacy of Luther*, tr. R. M. Bethell (London, 1954), 18–23.

42 Johannes Mathesius, *Historien von des ehrwirdigen in Gott seligen thewren Manns Gottes Doctoris Martini Luthers Anfang, Lehr, Leben und Sterben* (Nuremberg, 1566), xii^{r-v}.

43 Leppin, 'Nicht seine Person', 92–3; Susan Boettcher, 'Martin Luthers Leben in Predigten: Cyriakus Spangenberg und Johannes Mathesius', in Rosemarie Knape (ed), *Martin Luther und der Bergbau im Mansfelder Land* (Eisleben, 2000), 172–3; Kolb, *Martin Luther*, 46–50.

44 Jan Assman, 'Collective Memory and Cultural Identity', tr. John Czaplicka, *New German Critique*, 65 (1995), 125–33.

45 Leppin, 'Nicht seine Person', 95; Georg Mylius, *Parentatio Lutheri: Eine Christliche Predigt vom Herrn Martino Luthero* (Wittenberg, 1592), A3^{r-v}.

46 Dixon, 'Ninety-Five Theses'.

47 Anton Probus, *Renovalia Lutheri* (Jena, 1590), C1^{v}; Dixon, 'Ninety-Five Theses'; Leppin, 'Nicht seine Person', 94; Kolb, *Martin Luther*, 111–15.

48 Exhibit in the *Lutherhaus* Museum, Wittenberg: the stone was re-inscribed in the anniversary year 1717.

49 Foxe, *Acts and Monuments* (1576), 813; Matthew Sutcliffe, *The subuersion of Robert Parsons his confused and worthlesse worke, entituled, A treatise of three conuersions* (London, 1606), 92.

50 Lehmann, *Luthergedächtnis*, 18–19; Thomas Albert Howard, *Remembering the Reformation: An Inquiry into the Meanings of Protestantism* (Oxford, 2016), 12. A copy of the engraving is held by the Deutsches Historisches Museum, Berlin, viewable at http://www.dhm.de/datenbank/dhm.php?seite=5&fld_0=GR000125 (accessed January 2017). The Eisenach painting is reproduced on pp. 140–1 of Pierre Chaunu (ed.) *The Reformation* (London, 1989).

51 Samuel Lewkenor, *A discourse not altogether unprofitable, nor unpleasant* (London, 1600), 15^{v}–16^{r}. Cf. Shakespeare, *Hamlet*, I: ii, 113, 119, 164, 168.

Chapter 3

1 Hans Volz, 'Der Traum Kurfürst Friedrichs des Weisen vom 30./31. Oktober 1517', *Gutenberg Jahrbuch*, 45 (1970), 174–211; Ruth Kastner, *Geistlicher Rauffhandel: Form und Funktion der illustrierten Flugblätter zum Reformationsjubiläum 1617 in ihrem historischen und publizistischen Kontext* (Frankfurt, 1982), 278–88; R. W. Scribner, *Popular Culture and Popular Movements in Reformation Germany* (London, 1987), 301–3; Volkmar Joestel, *'Hier stehe ich!': Luthermythen und ihre Schauplätze* (Wettin, 2013), 86–9.

2 Volz, 'Der Traum', 198–207.

3 Scribner, *Popular Culture*, 309–19, 323–53.

4 Volker Leppin, '"Nicht seine Person, sondern die Wahrheit zu verteidigen": Die Legende vom Thesenanschlag in lutherischer Historiographie und Memoria', in Heinz Schilling (ed.), *Der Reformator Martin Luther 2017: Eine wissenschaftliche und gedenkpolitische Bestandsaufnahme* (Berlin, 2014), 96; Julian Gardner, *Giotto and His Publics* (Cambridge, MA, 2011), 33–5.

5 Thomas Kaufmann, 'Reformationsgedenken in der Frühen Neuzeit: Bemerkungen zum 16. bis 18. Jahrhundert', *Zeitschrift für Theologie und Kirche*, 107 (2010), 286.

6 Anthony Grafton, 'Church History in Early Modern Europe: Tradition and Innovation', in Katherine Van Liere, Simon Ditchfield, and Howard Louthan (eds) *Sacred History: Uses of the Christian Past in the Renaissance World* (Oxford, 2012), 3–26; Andrew Cunningham and Peter Ole Grell, *The Four Horseman of the Apocalypse: Religion, War, Famine and Death in Reformation Europe* (Cambridge, 2000), 19–30; Kaufmann, 'Reformationsgedenken', 291–2.

7 Kaufmann, 'Reformationsgedenken', 296; Charles Zika, 'The Reformation Jubilee of 1617: Appropriating the Past in European Centenary Celebrations', in D. E. Kennedy (ed.), *Authorised Pasts: Essays in Official History* (Melbourne, 1995), 80–2.

8 Thomas Albert Howard, *Remembering the Reformation: An Inquiry into the Meanings of Protestantism* (Oxford, 2016), 15–16; Johannes Burkhardt, 'The Thirty Years' War', in R. Po-chia Hsia (ed.), *A Companion to the Reformation World* (Oxford, 2004), 276–7.

9 Thomas A. Brady, 'Emergence and Consolidation of Protestantism in the Holy Roman Empire to 1600', in R. Po-Chia Hsia (ed.), *The Cambridge History of Christianity: Volume 6, Reform and Expansion 1500–1660* (Cambridge, 2007), 24–5.

10 Simon Adams, 'The Union, the League and the Politics of Europe', in Geoffrey Parker (ed.), *The Thirty Years' War* (2nd ed., London, 1997), 32; Hans-Jürgen Schönstädt, *Antichrist, Weltheilsgeschehen und Gottes Werkzeug: römische Kirche, Reformation und Luther im Spiegel des Reformationsjubiläums 1617* (Wiesbaden, 1978), 13–15; Zika, 'Reformation Jubilee', 78–9.

11 Howard, *Remembering the Reformation*, 13; Zika, 'Reformation Jubilee', 83; David Cressy, *Bonfires and Bells: National Memory and the Protestant Calendar in Elizabethan and Stuart England* (London, 1989), 50–66, 141–55.

12 Kaufmann, 'Reformationsgedenken', 296–9; Zika, 'Reformation Jubilee', 75–80; Andrew Pettegree, *Brand Luther: 1517, Printing, and the Making of the Reformation* (New York, 2015), 308–9.

13 Schönstädt, *Antichrist*, 304–7; Zika, 'Reformation Jubilee', 76.

14 *The Duke of Saxonie his iubilee* (London, 1618), $A2^{r-v}$.

15 Brian Cummings, 'Luther and the Book: The Iconography of the Ninety-Five Theses', in R. N. Swanson (ed.), *The Church and the Book*, Studies in Church History, 38 (Woodbridge, 2004), 224; Scott Dixon, 'Luther's Ninety-Five Theses and the Origins of the Reformation Narrative', *English Historical Review* (forthcoming); Kaufmann, 'Reformationsgedenken', 304–9; Hartmut Lehmann, *Luthergedächtnis 1817 bis 2017* (Göttingen, 2012), 20.

16 Kastner, *Geistlicher Raufhandel*, 178–90, 261–77; Zika, 'Reformation Jubilee', 87, 91–9; Thurman L. Smith, 'Luther and the Iserloh Thesis from a Numismatic Perspective', *Sixteenth Century Journal*, 20 (1989), 186–7, 194.

17 Detlef Metz, *Das protestantische Drama: Evangelisches Theater in der Reformationszeit und im konfessionellen Zeitalter* (Cologne, 2013), 673–87.

18 Martin Rinckhart, *Indulgentiarius confusus, oder Eißlebische Mansfeldische Jubel-Comoedia* (Eißleben, 1618), quotations at $E6^r$, $F2^r$, $F5^r$, $L8^r$ ('Das ist mein Herz / ich kan nicht mehr / Allhier steh ich / Gott helffe mir'); Robert Kolb, *Martin Luther as Prophet, Teacher and Hero: Images of the Reformer, 1520–1620* (Grand Rapids, 1999), 122–6.

19 Kaufmann, 'Reformationsgedenken', 295–6; Zika, 'Reformation Jubilee', 78; Lehmann, *Luthergedächtnis*, 21.

20 Joachim Kruse (ed.), *Luthers Leben in Illustrationen des 18. Und 19. Jahrhunderts* (Coburg, 1980), 26–7.

21 Christoph Weigel, Gregor Andreas Schmidt, *Sculptura historiarum et temporum memoratrix: das ist: Gedächtnuß-Hülfliche Bilder-Lust der merckwürdigsten Welt-Geschichten aller Zeiten von Erschaffung der Welt* (Nuremberg, 1697), 206–7, 209. See also Walter Goffart, 'The Map of the Barbarian Invasions: A Longer Look', in Marc A. Meyer (ed.), *The Culture of Christendom* (London, 1993), 5; Henrike Holsing, 'Luthers Thesenanschlag im Bild', in Joachim Ott and Martin Treu (eds), *Luthers Thesenanschlag—Faktum oder Fiktion* (Leipzig, 2008), 144–5.

22 Kruse, *Luthers Leben*, 32. The image is reproduced in Joestel, *Luthermythen*, 79.

23 Christian Juncker, *Das Guldene und Silberne Ehren-Gedächtniß Des Theuren Gottes-Lehrers D. Martini Lutheri* (Frankfurt; Leipzig, 1706); Jürgen Voss, 'Juncker, Christian', in *Neue Deutsche Biographie* (Berlin, 1974), 10: 660; Smith, 'Numismatic Perspective', 188–92.

24 Ernst Salomon Cyprian, *Hilaria Evangelica, Oder Theologisch-Historischer Bericht Vom Andern Evangelischen Jubel-Fest* (Leipzig, 1719), 65.

25 Krause, *Luther's Leben*, 34–44; Holsing, 'Thesenanschlag im Bild', 145–8.

26 http://collections.vam.ac.uk/item/O93433/beaker-and-cover-dockler-sigmund/ (accessed January 2017); 'Andenken-Dose mit Bildern zur Reformation', *Lutherhaus* Museum, Wittenberg.

27 Matthaeus Faber, *Kurtzgefaste Historische Nachricht Von der Schloß- und Academischen Stiffts-Kirche zu Aller-Heiligen in Wittenberg* (Wittenberg, 1717), 'Vorrede'. In a manuscript of about 1740, another Wittenberg professor referred, sceptically, to belief in the preservation of the original nail: Ernest G. Schwiebert, 'The Theses and Wittenberg', in Carl S. Meyer (ed.), *Luther for an Ecumenical Age* (St Louis, 1967), 123. The engraving of the church is reproduced in Martin Steffens, *Luthergedenkstätten im 19. Jahrhundert: Memoria-Repräsentation-Denkmalpflege* (Regensburg, 2008), 241.

28 Harm Cordes, *Hilaria evangelica academica: Das Reformationsjubiläum von 1717 an den deutschen lutherischen Universitäten* (Göttingen, 2006), 304–9; Kaufmann, 'Reformationsgedenken', 318–19; Howard, *Remembering the Reformation*, 24–6.

29 Lehmann, *Luthergedächtnis*, 21–2; Cordes, *Hilaria evangelica*, 273–85; Hans-Jürgen Schönstädt, 'Das Reformationsjubiläum 1717: Beiträge zur Geschichte seiner Entstehung im Spiegel landesherrlicher Verordnungen', *Zeitschrift für Kirchengeschichte*, 93 (1982), 58–118 (quote at p. 91).

30 Johann Nikolaus Weislinger, *Friss Vogel oder Stirb!* (Strasburg, 1726), A2^{v}, Q4^{v}, 35 (quotation), 336, 358, 369, 376, 381.

31 Jacques Bénigne Bossuet, *History of the Variations of the Protestant Churches* (2 vols, Dublin, 1836), 1. 11–229 (quotes at 23, 169, 44, 90); Volkmar Joestel, *1517: Luthers 95 Thesen, Der Beginn der Reformation* (Berlin, 1995), 38–9.

32 Veit Ludwig von Seckendorf, *Commentarius historicus et apologeticus de Lutheranismo* (Frankfurt, 1688), 31–2; Ernst Walter Zeeden, *The Legacy of Luther: Martin Luther and the Reformation in the Estimation of the German Lutherans from Luther's Death to the Beginning of the Age of Goethe*, tr. Ruth Mary Bethell (London, 1954), 55–64; Lewis. W. Spitz, 'Veit Ludwig von Seckendorf and the "Historia Lutheranismi"', *The Journal of Religion*, 25 (1945), 33–44.

33 *Herrn Veit Ludewigs von Seckendorff, Ausführliche Historie des Lutherthums*, ed. and tr. Elias Frick (Leipzig, 1714), 74–5.

34 Cummings, 'Luther and the Book', 228; Christoph August Heumann, *Lutherus apocalypticus, hoc est historia ecclesiae christianae ad nostra usque tempora* (Hannover, 1717), 73–116.

35 Dixon, 'Luther's Ninety-Five Theses'; Zeeden, *Legacy of Luther*, 110–14.

36 Lehmann, *Luthergedächtnis*, 22; Smith, 'Numismatic Perspective', 194; Kruse, *Luthers Leben*, 46–52.

37 Thomas Nugent, *The Grand Tour: or A journey Through the Netherlands, Germany, Italy and France* (2nd ed., 2 vols, London, 1756), 2: 425–6; 'The Travels of Three English Gentlemen, from Venice to Hamburgh', *The Harleian Miscellany, Vol. 11* (London, 1810), 330–1.

38 Herbert J. Redman, *Frederick the Great and the Seven Years' War, 1756–1763* (Jefferson, NC, 2015), 7, 394–5; Dixon, 'Luther's Ninety-Five Theses'; Helmar Junghans, *Wittenberg als Lutherstadt* (Berlin, 1979), 173–4; Steffens, *Luthergedenkstätten*, 250–60.

39 James Boswell, *The Journal of his German and Swiss Travels, 1764* (New Haven and London, 2008), 132.

40 Francis Atterbury, *An answer to some considerations on the spirit of Martin Luther* (London, 1687), 39; Pierre Bayle, *Historical and Critical Dictionary* (London, 1710), 3: 2065–7.

41 Voltaire, *Letters Concerning the English Nation* (London, 1733), 49–50; Zeeden, *Legacy of Luther*, 151–2.

42 Zeeden, *Legacy of Luther*, 162–83; Heinrich Bornkamm, *Luther im Spiegel der Deutschen Geistesgeschichte* (Heidelberg, 1955), 117–37; Hans J. Hillerbrand, 'The Legacy of Martin Luther', in Donald K. McKim (ed.), *The Cambridge Companion to Martin Luther* (Cambridge, 2003), 234.

43 Joseph Priestley, *A General History of the Christian Church from the Fall of the Western Empire to the Present Time* (4 vols, Northumberland, PA, 1802–3), 3: 147–50.

44 J. G. Burckhardt, *A System of Divinity, for the Use of Schools, and for instructing Youth in the essential Principles and Duties of Religion* (London, 1797), 31–2. See Susanne Steinmetz, 'The German Churches in London, 1669–1914', in Panikos Panayi (ed.), *Germans in Britain Since 1500* (London, 1996), 53.

Chapter 4

1 Joachim Kruse (ed.), *Luthers Leben in Illustrationen des 18. Und 19. Jahrhunderts* (Coburg, 1980), 57–61.

2 Nicholas Matthew, *Political Beethoven* (Cambridge, 2013), 18–19.

3 Hans A. Pohlsander, *National Monuments and Nationalism in 19th Century Germany* (Bern, 2008), 121; Ernst Walter Zeeden, *The Legacy of Luther: Martin Luther and the Reformation in the Estimation of the German Lutherans from Luther's Death to the Beginning of the Age of Goethe*, tr. Ruth Mary Bethell (London, 1954), 184–6.

4 Dieter Hensing, 'Der Bilder Eigner Geist: Das schwierige Verhältnis der Lutherbilder zu ihrem Gegenstand', in Ferdinand Van Ingen and Gerd Labroisse (eds), *Luther-Bilder im 20. Jahrhundert* (Amsterdam, 1984), 6; Friedrich Ludwig Zacharias Werner, *Martin Luther, oder Die Weihe der Kraft: eine Tragödie* (Berlin, 1807), 78, 96; 'Werner, Friedrich Ludwig Zacharias', *Encyclopædia Britannica* (11th ed., 29 vols, Cambridge, 1910–11), 28: 523–4.

5 Helmar Junghans, *Wittenberg als Lutherstadt* (Berlin, 1979), 174–5.

6 Martin Steffens, *Luthergedenkstätten im 19. Jahrhundert: Memoria-Repräsentation-Denkmalpflege* (Regensburg, 2008), 260–5; Jukka Jokilehto, *A History of Architectural Conservation* (Abingdon, 1999), 115–16; UNESCO World Heritage Site Evaluation (whc.unesco.org/archive/advisory_body_evaluation/783.pdf) (accessed January 2017).

7 Silvio Reichelt, *Der Erlebnisraum Lutherstadt Wittenberg: Genese, Entwicklung und Bestand eines protestantischen Errinerungsortes* (Göttingen, 2013), 30–1; Friederike

Lübke, 'Placing Luther on a Pedestal', in Thomas Schiller et al. (eds), *Perspectives 2017*, tr. David Dichelle (Hannover, 2013), 16.

8 Thomas Albert Howard, *Remembering the Reformation: An Inquiry into the Meanings of Protestantism* (Oxford, 2016), 37, 42–3; Stan M. Landry, *Ecumenism, Memory, and German Nationalism, 1817–1917* (Syracuse, NY, 2014), 9–10; John Tonkin, 'Reformation Studies', in Hans J. Hillebrand (ed.), *The Oxford Encyclopedia of the Reformation* (4 vols, Oxford, 1992), 3: 403–4.

9 Landry, *Ecumenism*, 14–16; Thomas Albert Howard, *Protestant Theology and the Making of the Modern German University* (Oxford, 2006), 192–3.

10 Howard, *Remembering the Reformation*, 39–42; Landry, *Ecumenism*, 3–4; Robert and Richard Keil (eds), *Die burschenschaftlichen Wartburgfeste von 1817 und 1867* (Jena, 1868), 14–15; Stephen Michael Press, 'False Fire: The Wartburg Book-Burning of 1817', *Central European History*, 42 (2009), 621–46.

11 Heinrich Bornkamm, *Luther im Spiegel der Deutschen Geistesgeschichte* (Heidelberg, 1955), 169; Leopold von Ranke, *History of the Reformation in Germany*, tr. Sarah Austin (London, 1905) 153.

12 Rainer Fuhrmann, *Das Reformationsjubiläum 1817: Martin Luther und die Reformation im Urteil der protestantischen Festpredigt des Jahres 1817* (Bonn, 1973), 19; Howard, *Remembering the Reformation*, 46.

13 Dorothea Wendebourg, 'Vergangene Reformationsjubiläen. Ein Rückblick im Vorfeld von 2017', in Heinz Schilling (ed.), *Der Reformator Martin Luther 2017: Eine wissenschaftliche und gedenkpolitische Bestandsaufnahme* (Berlin, 2014), 270–1; Howard, *Remembering the Reformation*, 43–4.

14 Claus Harms, *Das sind die 95 theses oder Streitsätze Dr. Luthers, theuren Andenkens* (Kiel, 1817), 3, 20, 23, 32; Fuhrmann, *Reformationsjubiläum 1817*, 34–7.

15 Landry, *Ecumenism*, 17–26; Scott Berg, '"The Lord Has Done Great Things for Us": The 1817 Reformation Celebrations and the End of the Counter-Reformation in the Habsburg Lands', *Central European History*, 49 (2016), 69–92; Hartmut Lehmann, 'Vom Helden zur Null', *Frankfurte Allgemeine Zeitung*, 26 Oct., 2016 (online at http://www.faz.net/aktuell/politik/die-gegenwart/reformationsjubilaeum-2017-vom-helden-zur-null-13230882.html, accessed January 2017).

16 Herman Paul and Bart Wallet, 'A Sun that Lost its Shine: The Reformation in Dutch Protestant Memory Culture, 1817–1917', *Church History and Religious Culture*, 88 (2008), 38–42; James Coleman, *Remembering the Past in Nineteenth-Century Scotland: Commemoration, Nationality and Memory* (Edinburgh, 2014), 123; *The British Critic and Quarterly Review*, 9 (1818), 220; Henry Forster Burder, *The Reformation Commemorated; A Discourse Delivered at the Meeting-House, St Thomas's Square Hackney, December 28th, 1817* (London, 1818).

17 William Ward, *The Reformation from Popery Commemorated: A Discourse Delivered in the Independent Meeting House, Stowmarket, November 9, 1817* (Stowmarket, 1817), 5, 21.

18 Hartmut Lehmann, *Martin Luther in the American Imagination* (Munich, 1988), 77–82; Frederick H. Quitman, *Three Sermons: The First preached before The*

Evangelical Lutheran Synod... *And the Second and Third on the Reformation by Doctor Martin Luther, Commenced October Thirty-First, AD 1517* (2nd ed. Philadelphia, 1818), 17, 20.

19 Quitman, *Three Sermons*, 19; Lehmann, *American Imagination*, 78; *Documentary History of the Evangelical Lutheran Ministerium of Pennsylvania and Adjacent States* (Philadelphia, 1898), 490; Howard, *Remembering the Reformation*, 57.

20 Lehmann, *American Imagination*, 78; John Frederick William Tischer, *The Life, Deeds and Opinions of Dr Martin Luther*, tr. John Korz (Hudson, NY, 1818), 16–17; Thomas J. Davis, 'Images of Intolerance: John Calvin in Nineteenth-Century History Textbooks', *Church History*, 65 (1996), 244.

21 F. C. Schaeffer, *An Address Pronounced at the Laying of the Corner Stone of St Matthew's Church* (New York, 1821), 19–21.

22 Hannah Farnham Sawyer-Lee, *The Life and Times of Martin Luther* (Boston, 1839), 5, 26–7.

23 Thomas Hodgskin, *Travels in the North of Germany* (2 vols, Edinburgh, 1820), 1: 65–6; David Eastwood, 'Hodgskin, Thomas (1787–1869)', *Oxford Dictionary of National Biography*, online edition; John Strang, *Germany in MDCCCXXXI* (2 vols, London, 1836), 2: 23–4.

24 Henry E. Dwight, *Travels in the North of Germany in the Years 1825–6* (New York, 1829), 259–62; Henry Hiestand, *Travels in Germany, Prussia and Switzerland* (New York, 1837), 131–3.

25 M. Reichard, *An Itinerary of Germany or Traveller's Guide through that Country* (London, 1819), 448–9.

26 John Aiton, *Eight Weeks in Germany; Comprising Narratives, Descriptions and Directions for Economical Tourists* (Edinburgh, 1842), 340; Karl Baedeker, *Handbuch für Reisende durch Deutschland und den Oesterreichischen Kaiserstaat* (Coblenz, 1842), 413. The first English edition of Baedeker's *Northern Germany* guide appeared in 1873: see <http://www.bdkr.com/index.php> (accessed January 2017).

27 Theodore Parker, *Life and Correspondence* (2 vols, New York, 1864), 1: 216.

28 Harriet Beecher Stow, *Sunny Memories of Foreign Lands* (2 vols, Boston, 1854), 2: 362–3; Hartmut Lehmann, *Luthergedächtnis 1817 bis 2017* (Göttingen, 2012), 52–3; Roy Morris, 'Introduction' in David B. Sachsman, S. Kittrell Rushing, and Roy Morris Jr (eds), *Memory and Myth: The Civil War in Fiction and Myth from Uncle Tom's Cabin to Cold Mountain* (West Lafayette, IN, 2007), 2.

29 Mary S. Griffin, *Impressions of Germany by an American Lady* (Dresden, 1866), 418; John Howard Hinton, *Letters written during a tour in Holland and North Germany* (London, 1851), 198–215 (quotations at 199, 201, 206–7, 211, 215).

30 Barry Stephenson, *Performing the Reformation: Public Ritual in the City of Luther* (Oxford, 2010), 91.

31 Helmar Junghans, *Wittenberg als Lutherstadt* (Berlin, 1979), 184–5; Steffens, *Luthergedenkstätten*, 271–4.

32 Richard Allen Lamb, *Last Letters of R. L. Allen. With a Memoir of the Author* (New York, 1871), 413. See also Henry M. Harman, *A Journey to Egypt and*

the Holy Land, in 1869–1870 (Philadelphia, 1873), 316; Samuel Gosnell Green, *Pictures from the German Fatherland* (London, 1880), 86 (who believed the original doors were destroyed by the French).

33 Henry W. Bellows, *The Old World in its New Face: Impressions of Europe in 1867–8* (2 vols, New York, 1868), 1: 372–3; E. Guers, *How French Soldiers fared in German Prisons*, tr. Henry Hayward (London, 1891), 319–20.

34 George Cubitt, *The Life of Martin Luther: to which is prefixed an Expository Essay on the Lutheran Reformation* (New York, 1853), 63–5.

35 W. Pembroke Fetridge, *Harper's Hand-Book for Travellers in Europe and the East* (18th edn, 3 vols, New York, 1879), 2: 616; John Stoughton, *Homes and Haunts of Luther* (London, 1875), 262–5.

36 Jean-Henri Merle d'Aubigné, *History of the Reformation of the Sixteenth Century, Vols I–IV*, tr. H. White (New York, 1851), 100; Milton Spenser Terry, *Rambles in the Old World* (Cincinnati, 1894), 50–2.

37 *The Great Reformation: An Address by Rev. Prof. W. J. Mann DD* (Philadelphia, 1873), 3–5, 7, 30.

38 Lehmann, *American Imagination*, 176–93; J. M. R. Bennett, 'The British Luther Commemoration of 1883–1884 in European Context', *Historical Journal*, 58 (2015), 543–64; Lehmann, *Luthergedächtnis*, 59–77.

39 Karl Wirth, *Das christliche Kirchenjahr* (Nuremberg, 1845), 74; Karl Bernhard Hundershagen, *Das Luthermonument zu Worms in Lichte der Wahrheit* (Mainz, 1868), 76–7. Cf. the remarks of Frederic H. Hedge, in *Commemoration of the Four hundredth Anniversary of the Birth of Martin Luther by the Massachusetts Historical Society, November 10, 1883* (Boston, 1883), 27.

40 Thomas Welter, *Lehrbuch der Weltgeschichte für Schulen* (Munster, 1861), 246; Ernst Zimmermann et al, *Allgemeine Kirchen-Zeitung, zugleich ein Archiv für die neueste Geschichte* (Darmstadt, 1866), 762; Ernst T. Jäkel, *Dr. Martin Luther: Geschichte seines Lebens* (Elberfeld, 1871), 123. See also Ernst Julius Saupe, *Bilder aus Luthers Leben* (Zwickau, 1861), 27; Ferdinand L. Fischer, *Kurzgefaßte Geschichte der christlichen Kirche* (Langensalza, 1862), 153; August Emil Frey, *Geschichte der Reformation* (New York, 1880), 43.

41 Thomas Austin Bullock, *The History of Modern Europe* (London, 1871), 31; Edwin David Sanborn, *History of New Hampshire, from its first discovery to the year 1830* (Manchester, N.H, 1875), 12.

42 James Bowling Mozley, *Essays, Historical and Theological* (London, 1878), 356; William Aubrey, *The Rise and Growth of the English Nation* (3 vols, London, 1895), 2: 82.

43 Charles A. Dickey, *Martin Luther: A Sketch of his Character and Work* (Philadelphia, 1884), 16. See Howard, *Remembering the Reformation*, 79.

44 Thomas Archer, *Decisive Events in History . . . Illustrated* (London, 1878), 126.

45 Thurman L. Smith, 'Luther and the Iserloh Thesis from a Numismatic Perspective', *Sixteenth Century Journal*, 20 (1989), 195–6.

46 Kruse, *Luthers Leben*, 78–9, 81–3; Heinrich Gottlieb Kreussler, *Denkmäler der Reformation der Christlichen Kirche* (Leipzig, 1817), 6–7.

47 Kruse, *Luthers Leben*, 90, 95, 102–3; Max Jordan, *Das Werk Adolf Menzels, 1815–1905* (Munich, 1905), 4; Heinrich Eduard Maukisch, *Germania: Deutschlands wichtigste Ereignisse und das Leben seiner berühmtesten Männer in leicht fasslichen Erzählungen für die Jugend dargestellt* (4th edn Berlin, 1850), reproduced at <http://www.akg-images.co.uk> (accessed January 2017); <http://www.lutherdekade-jueterbog.de/archiv-2010.html> (accessed January 2017); Friedrich Bülau, *Die deutsche Geschichte in Bildern* (2 vols, Dresden, 1862), 2: 100–1.

48 Kruse, *Luthers Leben*, 180–3; Victor L. Conrad (ed.), *Scenes from the life of Martin Luther: in fifty pictures of the most memorable events in his remarkable career* (Philadelphia, 1883). On Hare, see Peter Marshall, 'Luther among the Catholics, 1520–2015', in Declan Marmion, Salvador Ryan, and Gesa E. Thiessen (eds), *Remembering the Reformation: Martin Luther and Catholic Theology* (Minneapolis, 2017), 26–7.

49 Kruse, *Luthers Leben*, 192–4, 207, 222–5.

50 Lehmann, *American Imagination*, 185–6; Otto Kammer, *Reformationsdenkmäler des 19. und 20. Jahrhunderts* (Leipzig, 2004); Henrike Holsing, 'Luthers Thesenanschlag im Bild', in Joachim Ott and Martin Treu (eds), *Luthers Thesenanschlag—Faktum oder Fiktion* (Leipzig, 2008), 151–3.

51 Gustav König/Heinrich Gelzer, *Dr Martin Luther der deutsche Reformator* (Hamburg, 1851), 51.

52 *The life of Martin Luther: the German Reformer, in Fifty Pictures* (London, 1853), v; *The Life of Luther in Forty-Eight Historical Engravings by Gustav König, with Explanations by Archdeacon Hare* (New York, 1857), 57–8; Julius Charles Hare, *The Mission of the Comforter* (2 vols, London, 1846), 2: 827; N. Merrill Distad, 'Hare, Julius Charles (1795–1855)', *Oxford Dictionary of National Biography*, online edition; Victor L. Conrad (ed.), *Scenes from the life of Martin Luther: in fifty pictures of the most memorable events in his remarkable career* (Philadelphia, 1883), 3, 6.

53 The most detailed study is Henrike Holsing, 'Luther – Gottesmann und Nationalheld. Sein Image in der deutschen Historienmalerei des 19. Jahrhunderts', University of Cologne PhD thesis (2004).

54 The work can be viewed at <https://commons.wikimedia.org/wiki/File:Der_Anschlag_von_Luthers_95_Thesen.jpg> (accessed January 2017).

55 Illustration no. 141 in Holsing, 'Luther', viewable online at <kups.ub.uni-koeln.de/2132/1/diss_holsing_abbildungen.pdf> (accessed January 2017).

56 Thomas Carlyle, *On Heroes, Hero-Worship, and the Heroic in History* (London, 1841), 107–31, quotation at 123.

57 Holsing, 'Thesenanschlag im Bild', 158–9.

58 Holsing, 'Thesenanschlag im Bild', 167–8.

59 *Deutsche Zeitschrift: unabhängige Monatshefte für die politische und geistige Gestaltung der Gegenwart*, 16 (1903), 143; Holsing, 'Thesenanschlag im Bild', 168–9.

60 Otto May, *Martin Luther: Sein Leben und seine Wirkung im Postkartenbild, 1883–1945* (Hildesheim, 2014), 26–8.

61 A helpful website, with enlargeable photos of the multiple elements is <http://www.vanderkrogt.net/statues/object.php?webpage=ST&record=derp073 (accessed July 2016).
62 August Ebrard, *Gustav König: Sein Leben und seine Kunst* (Erlangen, 1871), 289–90 ('was auch eine todte Geschichte für die bildende Kunst ist').
63 Johann Wolfgang von Goethe, *Sämtliche Werke* (30 vols, Stuttgart, 1850–51), 2: 315: 'Auch ich soll gottgegebene Kraft / Nicht ungenützt verlieren, / Und will in Kunst und Wissenschaft / Wie immer protestieren.'
64 Mary Anne Cursham, *Martin Luther, a Poem* (London, 1825).
65 Robert Montgomery, *Poetical Works* (New edition, London, 1853), 201; Robert Dingley, 'Montgomery, Robert (1807–1855)', *Oxford Dictionary of National Biography*, online edn.
66 Rolf King, 'The Figure of Luther in German Dramas and Novels of the Nineteenth Century', University of Wisconsin PhD thesis (1933), chs. 3–4; Ferdinand Gustav Kühne, *Wittenberg und Rom: Klosternovellen aus Luther's Zeit* (3 vols, Berlin, 1877), 3: 314.
67 John G. Morris, *Blind Girl of Wittenberg: A Life-Picture of the Times of Luther and the Reformation* (Philadelphia, 1856), 118. The original title is *Martin Luther: kirchengeschichtliches Lebensbild aus der Zeit der Reformation* (Leipzig, 1851).
68 Joseph Sortain, *Count Arensberg; or, The days of Martin Luther* (2 vols, London, 1853), 1: 105–13.
69 *Luther and the Cardinal: A Historical-Biographical Tale* (London, 1883), 60, 66–7, tr. by Julie Sutter from Armin Stein (Herman Nietschmann), *Cardinal Albrecht* (Halle, 1882).
70 Frank Wakeley Gunsaulus, *Monk and Knight: A Tale* (Edinburgh, 1893), 11, 24, 287.
71 William Stearns Davis, *The Friar of Wittenberg* (New York, 1912), 113–18.
72 Otto Devrient, *Luther, historisches Charakterbild in sieben Abtheilungen, ein Festspiel* (Leipzig, 1884), 25–31.
73 Alexander Scharbach, 'German Militarism in Strindberg's "Die Nachtigall von Wittenberg"', *Scandinavian Studies*, 29 (1957), 1–11.
74 Franklin Johnson, Review of Thomas S. Lindsay, 'Luther and the German Reformation', *The American Journal of Theology*, 5 (1901), 375; J. W. Richard, 'The Beginnings of Protestant Worship in Germany and Switzerland', *The American Journal of Theology*, 5 (1901), 247.
75 François Pierre Guillaume Guizot, *General History of Civilization in Europe*, ed. G. W. Knight (New York, 1896), 316–17.
76 George Cross, 'The Doctrine of the Future Life: The Protestant Recoil', *The Biblical World*, 39 (1912), 255. For a more positive early-twentieth-century assessment of the Theses' theological cogency: Preserved Smith, *The Life and Letters of Martin Luther* (Boston, 1911), 40.
77 Lehmann, *Luthergedächtnis*, 293.
78 H. L. Pohlman, *Political Thought and the American Judiciary* (Amherst, 1993), 13.
79 William Croswell Doane and Willard F. Mallalieu, 'Politics and the Pulpit', *The North American Review*, 155 (1892), 46.

80 Stephenson, *Performing the Reformation*, 92–3; *The County Gentleman: Sporting Gazette, Agricultural Journal, and 'The Man about Town'*, 5 Nov. 1892, 1506; *Los Angeles Herald*, 1 Nov. 1892, 2.

Chapter 5

1 Ernest G. Schwiebert, 'The Theses and Wittenberg', in Carl S. Meyer (ed.), *Luther for an Ecumenical Age* (St Louis, 1967), 120–1; Barry Stephenson, *Performing the Reformation: Public Ritual in the City of Luther* (Oxford, 2010), 93–4.

2 Silvio Reichelt, *Der Erlebnisraum Lutherstadt Wittenberg: Genese, Entwicklung und Bestand eines protestantischen Errinerungsortes* (Göttingen, 2013), 117–18; Anthony McElligott, *Rethinking the Weimar Republic: Authority and Authoritarianism, 1916–1936* (London, 2014), 85; Adolph Schalk, *The Germans in America* (Chicago, 1973), 23.

3 Gottfried Maron, 'Luther 1917: Beobachtungen zur literature des 400. Reformationsjubiläums', *Zeitschrift für Kirchengeschichte*, 93 (1982), 177–221; Dorothea Wendebourg, 'Vergangene Reformationsjubiläen. Ein Rückblick im Vorfeld von 2017', in Heinz Schilling (ed.), *Der Reformator Martin Luther 2017: Eine wissenschaftliche und gedenkpolitische Bestandsaufnahme* (Berlin, 2014), 271–2.

4 Hartmut Lehmann, *Luthergedächtnis 1817 bis 2017* (Göttingen, 2012), 152; Gerhard Besier, 'Human Images, Myth Creation and Projections: From the Luther Myth to the Luther Campaign', *Kirchliche Zeitgeschichte*, 26 (2013), 428.

5 Lehmann, *Luthergedächtnis*, 29; Martin Treu, 'Urkunde und Reflexion: Wiederentdeckung eines Belegs von Luthers Thesenanschlag', in Joachim Ott and Martin Treu (eds), *Luthers Thesenanschlag—Faktum oder Fiktion* (Leipzig, 2008), 67; Emil, Zeissig, 'Luther, der treue Diener seines Volkes', in *Deutsche Blätter für erziehenden Unterricht* (Langensalza, 1917), 339.

6 Stefanie Hein, *Richard Wagners Kunstprogramm im nationalkulturellen Kontext: ein Beitrag zur Kulturgeschichte des 19. Jahrhunderts* (Würzburg, 2006), 74; Lehmann, *Luthergedächtnis*, 30; Maron, 'Luther 1917', 36–7; Hermann Mosapp (ed.), *Luther als deutscher Volksmann: ein Volksabend* (Gotha, 1917), 6, 10. 'Du stehst am Amboß, Lutherheld, / Umkeucht von Wutgebelfer, / Und wir, Alldeutschland, dir gesellt, Sind deine Schmiedehelfer.'

7 Stan M. Landry, *Ecumenism, Memory, and German Nationalism, 1817–1917* (Syracuse, NY, 2014), 102–10; John Howard Morrow, *The Great War: An Imperial History* (Abingdon, 2004), 216–17.

8 Erich Marcks, *Luther und Deutschland: eine Reformationsrede im Kriegsjahr 1917* (Leipzig, 1917), 1–2, 11.

9 Patrick O'Hare, *The Facts About Luther* (New York, 1916); Hartmut Lehmann, *Martin Luther in the American Imagination* (Munich, 1988), 279–80; *The Spectator* (6 July, 1917), 24.

10 Lehmann, *American Imagination*, 282–3.

11 Keith Robbins, 'The "Reformation Jubilee 1917": Mixed Messages from the United Kingdom', *Kirchliche Zeitgeschichte*, 26, (2013), 213–4; C. H. K. Marten, 'Fletcher, Charles Robert Leslie (1857–1934)', rev. Richard Symonds, *Oxford Dictionary of National Biography*, online edn; *The Horrors of Wittenberg: Official Report to the British Government* (London, 1916); Preserved Smith, 'English Opinion of Luther', *The Harvard Theological Review*, 10 (1917), 157; *The Manchester Guardian* (5 Nov. 1917), 6.

12 James Stalker, *The Luther Celebrations of 1917* (New York, 1917), 3, 5–7, 14–15, 17.

13 Thomas A. Brady Jr, 'Luther Renaissance' in Hans J. Hillebrand (ed.), *The Oxford Encyclopedia of the Reformation* (4 vols, Oxford, 1992), 2: 473–6. For a detailed assessment, see James M. Stayer, *Martin Luther, German Saviour: German Evangelical Theological Factions and the Interpretation of Luther, 1917–1933* (Montreal, 2000).

14 Karl Holl, *Gesammelte Aufsätze zur Kirchengeschichte* (3 vols, Tübingen, 1921), 1: 265.

15 Heinrich Boehmer, *Der junge Luther* (1925; 2nd edn, Leipzig, 1939), 170.

16 Gerhard Ritter, *Luther: Gestalt und Symbol* (Munich, 1925), 9.

17 Esther P. Wipfler, 'Luthers 95 Thesen in bewegten Bild', in Ott and Treu (eds), *Thesenanschlag*, 179–84; Wipfler, *Martin Luther in Motion Pictures* (Göttingen, 2011), 20–8, 81–104 (quotation at 104), 131–2. The print of an earlier film, from 1911, is now lost (Wipfler, *Motion Pictures*, 81).

18 Susannah Heschel, *The Aryan Jesus: Christian Theologians and the Bible in Nazi Germany* (Princeton, 2008), 44–5; Alexander Gerstner, Gregor Hufenreuter, and Uwe Puschner, 'Völkischer Protestantismus. Die Deutschkirche und der Bund für deutsche Kirche', in Michel Grunewald and Uwe Puschner (eds), *Das evangelische Intellektuellenmilieu in Deutschland, seine Presse und Netzwerke (1871–1963)* (Bern, 2008), 412–13; Richard Steigmann-Gall, *The Holy Reich: Nazi Conceptions of Christianity, 1919–1945* (Cambridge, 2003), 58.

19 See Kyle Jantzen, 'Church-Building in Hitler's Germany: Berlin's Martin-Luther-Gedächtniskirche as a Reflection of Church-State Relations', *Kirchliche Zeitgeschichte*, 27, (2014), 324–48.

20 Dietrich Kuessner, 'Luther – Hitler: Ein Blick in die Schreckenskammern der Luther-Jubiläen 1933 bis 1946' (http://bs.cyty.com/kirche-von-unten/archiv/kvu103/luthit.htm, accessed January 2017); Lehmann, *Luthergedächtnis*, 153–5; Dean G. Stroud (ed.), *Preaching in Hitler's Shadow: Sermons of Resistance in the Third Reich* (Grand Rapids, MI, 2013), 23–4.

21 Hansjörg Buss, 'Der Deutsche Luthertag 1933 und die Deutschen Christen', *Kirchliche Zeitgeschichte*, 26 (2013), 272–88; Siegfried Bräuer, 'Der "Deutsche Luthertag 1933" und sein Schicksal', in Horst Bartel (ed.), *Martin Luther: Leistung und Erbe* (Berlin, 1986), 423–34; Thomas Albert Howard, *Remembering the Reformation: An Inquiry into the Meanings of Protestantism* (Oxford, 2016), 104–5; Steigmann-Gall, *Holy Reich*, 137–8; Josef Pilvousek, 'Katholische Reaktionen auf das Luthergedenken im Jahr der Machtergreifung', *Kirchliche Zeitgeschichte*, 26 (2013), 340.

22 Robert Kriechbaumer, *Die grossen Erzählungen der Politik: politische Kultur und Parteien in Österreich von der Jahrhundertwende bus 1945* (Vienna, 2001), 766–7; Tanja Hetze, *'Deutsche Stunde': Volksgemeinschaft und Antisemitismus in der politischen Theologie bei Paul Althaus* (Munich, 2009), 166; Volkmar Joestel, *1517: Luthers 95 Thesen, Der Beginn der Reformation* (Berlin, 1995), 131; Dietrich Kuessner, *Ansichten einer versunkenen Stadt: Die Braunschweiger Stadtkirchen, 1933–1950* (Wendeburg, 2012), 91.

23 Text (in English translation) online at <http://w2.vatican.va/content/pius-xi/en/encyclicals/documents/hf_p-xi_enc_14031937_mit-brennender-sorge.html> (accessed January 2017); George O. Kent, 'Pope Pius XII and Germany: Some Aspects of German-Vatican Relations, 1933–1943', *American Historical Review*, 70 (1964), 63.

24 *Life* (24 October 1938), 21.

25 Stroud, *Hitler's Shadow*, 25; Victoria Barnett, *For the Soul of the People: Protestant Protest Against Hitler* (Oxford, 1992), 34; Ralf Lange and Peter Noss, 'Bekennende Kirche in Berlin', in Olaf Kühl-Freudenstein, Peter Noss, and Claus Wagener (eds), *Kirchenkampf in Berlin 1932–1945: 42 Stadtgeschichten* (Berlin, 1999), 130–1; Jan Bank with Lieve Gevers, *Churches and Religion in the Second World War*, tr. Brian Doyle (London, 2016), 68.

26 James Carrol, *Constantine's Sword: The Church and the Jews* (New York, 2001), 428; Hans Buchheim, 'Bonhoeffer, Dietrich', in *Neue Deutsche Biographie* (25 vols, Berlin, 1953–), 2: 443–4.

27 Dietrich Bonhoeffer, *Letters and Papers from Prison*, ed. Eberhard Bethge (new abridged edn, London, 2001), 21.

28 Howard, *Remembering the Reformation*, 107–9; *Trial of the Major War Criminals Before the International Military Tribunal, Nuremberg, 14 November 1945–1 October 1946* (42 vols, Nuremberg, 1947–9), 12: 318.

29 Thomas Mann, *Germany and the Germans* (Washington, 1945), 3–4, 6–8, 10.

30 Lehmann, *Luthergedächtnis*, 189–212 (quotations at pp. 194–5, 210).

31 James Arne Nestingen, 'Approaching Luther', in Donald K. McKim (ed.), *The Cambridge Companion to Martin Luther* (Cambridge, 2003), 246–7.

32 Roland H. Bainton, *Here I Stand: A Life of Martin Luther* (paperback edn, New York, 1955), 60, 141, 301.

33 Dan Chyutin, '"A Remarkable Adventure": *Martin Luther* and the 1950s Religious Marketplace', *Cinema Journal*, 52 (2013), 25–48 (quote at p. 30); <http://www.imdb.com/title/tt0046051/fullcredits?ref_=tt_ov_wr#writers> (accessed January 2017); *The Observer* (4 Sep., 1955), 8; James Broderick, *'Martin Luther': The Film and the Facts* (London, 1954); Albert Hyma, *Martin Luther and the Luther Film of 1953* (Ann Arbor, 1957), 1–2. Quebec finally allowed public screening in 1962: *The Montreal Gazette* (26 July, 1962), 1.

34 The film is free to view at <https://archive.org/details/MartinLuther> (accessed January 2017).

35 Frank L. Baer, 'The Stained-Glass Windows of The Washington Cathedral', *Historical Magazine of the Protestant Episcopal Church*, 25 (1956), 277–85.

For reproduction and description, see <https://commons.wikimedia.org/wiki/File:Clerestory_window_12_-_War_Memorial_Chapel_-_National_Cathedral_-_DC.JPG> (accessed January 2017).

36 Erik H. Erikson, *Young Man Luther: A Study in Psychoanalysis and History* (paperback edn, New York, 1962), 227–8.

37 John Osborne, *Luther* (New York, 1963), 57–60, 74–6. See David Graver, '*Luther*: The Morbid Grandeur of Corporeal History', in Patricia D. Denison (ed.), *John Osborne: A Casebook* (New York, 1997), 115–26.

38 *The Times* (7 July, 1961), 15; (6 September, 1961), 15; (8 November, 1961), 2.

39 Barara Hallensleben, 'Vorwort', in Uwe Wolff, *Iserloh: Der Thesenanschlag fand nicht statt* (Basel, 2013), i–ii.

40 Daniel Jütte, 'Schwang Luther 1517 tatsächlich den Hammer?', *Frankfurther Allgemeine Zeitung*, 16 June 2014, online at <http://www.faz.net/aktuell/feuilleton/geisteswissenschaften/thesenanschlag-schwang-luther-1517-tatsaechlich-den-hammer-12994372.html> (accessed January 2017). For a judicious summary of the debate up to the end of the 1960s, see Hans-Christoph Rublack, 'Neuere Forschungen zum Thesenanschlag Luthers', *Historisches Jahrbuch*, 90 (1970), 329–42.

41 Konrad Repgen, 'Ein profangeschichtlicher Rückblick auf die Iserloh-Debatte', in Ott and Treu (eds), *Thesenanschlag*, 100–1.

42 See bibliography of Iserloh's works in Wolff, *Iserloh*, 253–7.

43 Repgen, 'Rückblick', 103. In fact, the precise date in June of the sealing of Magna Carta, though not the ratification itself, is a matter of debate: see <http://www.historyextra.com/article/medieval/15-june-1215-true-date-magna-carta> (accessed January 2017).

44 Wolff, *Iserloh*, 7; E. Gordon Rupp, review of Iserloh, *Luther zwischen Reform und Reformation: Der Thesenanschlag fand nicht statt*, in *The Journal of Theological Studies*, new ser. 19 (1968), 360–9.

45 Heinrich Denifle, *Luther und Luthertum in der ersten Entwickelung* (2 vols, Mainz, 1904–9); Hartmann Grisar, *Luther* (3 vols, Freiburg im Breisgau, 1911–12); *Die Literatur des Lutherjubiläums 1917, ein Bild des heutigen Protestantismus* (Innsbruck, 1918); *Luther*, tr. E. M. Lamond (6 vols, London, 1913), 1: 330.

46 Richard Stauffer, *Luther as Seen by Catholics*, tr. Mary Parker and T. H. L. Parker (London, 1967), 37–54; Joseph Lortz, *The Reformation in Germany*, tr. Ronald Walls (2 vols, London, 1968), 1: 228.

47 *The Tablet* (14 January, 1967), 17, 23; (11 December, 1965), 24; Erwin Iserloh, 'Aufhebung des Lutherbannes?', in Remigius Bäumer (ed.), *Lutherprozess und Lutherbann: Vorgeschichte, Ergebnis, Nachwirkung* (Münster, 1972), 69–80.

48 Wolff, *Iserloh*, 5, 149–50; Vinzenz Pfnür, 'Die Bestreitung des Thesenanschlags durch Erwin Iserloh', in Ott and Treu (eds), *Thesenanschlag*, 116–17.

49 Heinrich Bornkamm, *Thesen und Thesenanschlag Luthers* (Berlin, 1967), 1; Wolff, *Iserloh*, 7.

50 Repgen, 'Rückblick', 106–10; Volker Leppin, '"Nicht seine Person, sondern die Wahrheit zu verteidigen": Die Legende vom Thesenanschlag in lutherischer Historiographie und Memoria', in Heinz Schilling (ed.), *Der Reformator Martin Luther 2017: Eine wissenschaftliche und gedenkpolitische Bestandsaufnahme* (Berlin, 2014), 104–6. For the wider debates, see C. Scott Dixon, *Contesting the Reformation* (Oxford, 2012), especially ch. 2.

51 Reinhard Brandt, '"Reformator ohne Hammer": Zur öffentlichen Aufmerksamkeit für die Bestreitung des Thesenanschlags', in Ott and Treu (eds), *Thesenanschalg*, 131–3; 'Reformator ohne Hammer', *Der Spiegel* (3 January, 1966), 32–4.

52 Howard, *Remembering the Reformation*, 112–16; Gerhard Ringshausen, 'Das 450. Reformationsjubiläum 1967 in West und Ost', *Kirchliche Zeitgeschichte*, 26 (2013), 373–5, 384.

53 *New York Times* (6 March, 1966). There are no references to Iserloh in the digital archives of the British national newspapers, *The Times*, *The Guardian*, and *The Observer*.

54 *The Tablet* (28 September, 1968), 964; Robert E. McNally, *Catholic Historical Review*, 53 (1969), 465–6; Gordon Rupp, *Journal of Theological Studies*, 23 (1972), 327.

55 *The Guardian* (27 May, 1970), 14; (22 October, 1983), 17; (15 November, 1983), 14.

56 Sabrina Ramet, 'Politics and Religion in Eastern Europe and the Soviet Union', in George Moyser (ed.), *Politics and Religion in the Modern World* (London, 1991), 84–5; Howard, *Remembering the Reformation*, 117–18.

57 Patrick Major, *Behind the Berlin Wall: East Germany and the Frontiers of Power* (Oxford, 2010), 244.

58 Reichelt, *Erlebnisraum Lutherstadt Wittenberg*, 354; Joestel, *1517*, 148–50.

59 Luther Blissett, *Q*, tr. Shaun Whiteside (London, 2003), 4.

60 Brandt, '"Reformator ohne Hammer"', 136; Wipfler, 'Luthers 95 Thesen', 186–96; Luke Harding, 'Luther biopic has slim chance with the critics', *The Observer* (2 November, 2003), 22; Susan R. Boettcher, 'Luther Year 2003? Thoughts on an Off-Season Comeback', *Sixteenth Century Journal*, 35 (2004), 795–801.

61 <http://www.officeholidays.com/religious/christian/reformation_day.php> (accessed January 2017). See the range of contributions in Ott and Treu, *Thesenanschlag*. A recent major biography, Heinz Schilling, *Martin Luther: Rebell in einer Zeit des Umbruchs* (Munich, 2012), 164–5 thinks that 'recent source discoveries' do make it likely the Theses were actually nailed to the door, while insisting that 'the context was very different than that of the hammer-swinging monk constructed by Protestant rhetoric'.

62 Denis Staunton, 'Martin Luther was father of the Reformation, now buy the T-shirt', *The Observer* (11 February, 1996), 20; Stephenson, *Performing the Reformation*, 2–3.

63 *Baedecker Reiseführer Deutschland* (12th edn, Ostfildern, 2015), 687; *DK Eyewitness Travel Guide: Germany* (10th revised reprinting, London and New York,

2014), 121; *Fodor's Germany* (27th edn, New York, 2014), 763, 798, 801, 824; *Lonely Planet Germany* (7th edn, Footscray, Vic., 2013) seemingly accepts the historicity in its front matter, but at p. 549 inserts a note of intrigued scepticism.

64 <http://www.germany.travel/en/specials/luther/luther.html#!/event/search/category/luther> (accessed January 2017).

Epilogue

1 Reported in *The Tablet* (20 August, 2016), 33.

2 Quoted in Hartmut Lehmann, 'Fragen zur Halbzeit der Lutherdekade', *Kirchliche Zeitgeschichte*, 26 (2013), 451. Lehmann's exasperation with unreflexive complacency about the anniversary is shared by other German historians: see e.g. Wolfgang Reinhard, 'Reformation 1517/2017: Geschichtswissenschaft und Geschichtspolitik Schlussdanken', in Heinz Schilling (ed.), *Der Reformator Martin Luther 2017: Eine wissenschaftliche und gedenkpolitische Bestandsaufnahme* (Berlin, 2014), 298–305. The film is viewable at <https://www.luther2017.de/de/2017/reformationsjubilaeum/film/film-auf-dem-weg-zum-reformationsjubilaeum> (accessed January 2017).

3 Nikolaus Schneider, 'Hosting sisters and brothers from around the world', in Thomas Schiller et al (eds), *Perspectives 2017*, tr. David Dichelle (Hannover, 2013), 3; <http://kleinerundbold.com/aktuelles/meldungen/der-hammer-die-visuelle-klammer-der-nationalen-sonderausstellungen-2017> (accessed January 2017).

4 *The Deseret Weekly*, 45 (1892), 666.

5 Victoria Barnett, *For the Soul of the People: Protestant Protest Against Hitler* (Oxford, 1992), 4. See also Ronny Kabus, *Juden der Lutherstadt Wittenberg im Dritten Reich* (Norderstedt, 2015).

6 William Chapman, *The Life of Martin Luther: The Hero of the Reformation* (London, 1882), 50–1. The much-used phrase originates with Van Wyck Brooks, 'On Creating a Usable Past', *The Dial*, 64 (April 1918), 337–41.

Photographic Acknowledgements

De Agostini Picture Library/age fotostock: **3.1**; © akg-images: **2.2**, **4.6**, **4.7**; Wartburg Castle Museum/© akg-images: **4.9**; © epa european pressphoto agency b.v./Alamy Stock Photo: **5.5**; © Granger Historical Picture Archive/ Alamy Stock Photo: **1.1**; © INTERFOTO/Alamy Stock Photo: **5.3**; © Moviestore Collection Ltd/Alamy Stock Photo: **5.4**; © British Library/ Bridgeman Images: **4.5**; Staatliche Museen zu Berlin/© Mary Evans/ Süddeutsche Zeitung Photo: **4.8**; © Imagno/Getty Images: **1.2**; Heidelberg University Library (CC-BY-SA 3.0): **3.2**; The Internet Archive: **4.3**; Archiv der Lippischen Landeskirche (Archive of Church of Lippe), Bestand 01.01 Nr. 1587: **5.1**; Luther Memorial Foundation in Saxony-Anhalt: **4.1**, **5.2**; The Metropolitan Museum of Art, New York, Gift of Felix M. Warburg, 1920/www.metmuseum.org: **2.1**; © 2016 Scala, Florence/bpk: **4.1**; © Barry Stephenson: **4.2**; Universitäts- und Landesbibliothek Sachsen-Anhalt: **3.3**; Kunstsammlungen der Veste Coburg, Germany/www.kunstsammlungen-coburg.de: **4.4**

Index